Happiness and Education

Happiness
and
Education

NEL NODDINGS
Stanford University

CAMBRIDGE
UNIVERSITY PRESS

PUBLISHED BY THE PRESS SYNDICATE OF THE UNIVERSITY OF CAMBRIDGE
The Pitt Building, Trumpington Street, Cambridge, United Kingdom

CAMBRIDGE UNIVERSITY PRESS
The Edinburgh Building, Cambridge CB2 2RU, UK
40 West 20th Street, New York, NY 10011-4211, USA
477 Williamstown Road, Port Melbourne, VIC 3207, Australia
Ruiz de Alarcón 13, 28014 Madrid, Spain
Dock House, The Waterfront, Cape Town 8001, South Africa

http://www.cambridge.org

First published 2003
First paperback edition 2005

Printed in the United States of America

Typeface New Aster 9.5/13 pt. *System* LaTeX 2$_\varepsilon$ [TB]

A catalog record for this book is available from the British Library.

Library of Congress Cataloging in Publication Data
Noddings, Nel.
Happiness and education / Nel Noddings.
    p. cm.
Includes bibliographical references and index.
ISBN 0-521-80763-8
1. Education – Aims and objectives. 2. Happiness. 3. Moral
education. I. Title.
LB41.N55 2003
370′.1 – dc21
                                                    2002041547

ISBN 0 521 80763 8 hardback
ISBN 0 521 61472 4 paperback

Contents

Acknowledgments

Parts of this book and many of its central ideas have been tried out in lectures and seminars over the past three years. For helpful questions and encouraging comments, I thank faculty, students, and other listeners at Calvin College, Colgate University, the University of Southern Maine, Long Island University (Brooklyn), Eastern Michigan University, Teachers College Columbia, and the Bank Street College of Education. The project received an important boost when I was invited to give a lecture in the inaugural series of Seamus Heaney Lectures at St. Patrick's College in Dublin, Ireland (2000). Chapter 10 was stimulated and improved by interactions at the Conference on the Future of Education: Work, Education, and Occupation in Zurich (2002).

Special thanks are offered to Julia Hough, who sponsored the project with Cambridge University Press and contributed valuable suggestions. Thanks also go to Helen Greenberg for copyediting and Helen Wheeler for overseeing production.

I owe a considerable debt to the great educational critics of the 1960s. Although I hope I've added something worthwhile through my analysis of happiness – its manifestations, domains, and sources – schooling today would have been happier and more effective if policymakers had listened to those earlier critics.

Finally, thanks go to my students, children, grandchildren, and husband, from whom I have learned so much about both happiness and education.

Introduction

In the past few months, when I have told people that I'm writing a book on happiness and education, more than one has responded with some puzzlement, "But they don't go together!" Indeed, the fact that the two seem increasingly opposed these days is one motive for tackling the topic. Happiness and education are, properly, intimately related: Happiness should be an aim of education, and a good education should contribute significantly to personal and collective happiness.

An interest in biography has increased my concern about the connections among happiness, misery, boredom, and schooling. Why is it that so many bright, creative people have hated school? Observing this well-documented misery, why do we continue to justify it with the old excuse, "Some day you'll thank me for this"? Parents and educators are sustained in this attitude, in part, because so many adult children *do* thank us for their perceived success – a success, sometimes questionable, that they credit to their earlier misery. And so, they are ready, even eager, to inflict a new round of misery on others. Indeed, many parents and teachers are afraid *not* to do this, fearing that children will be spoiled, unprepared, undisciplined, unsuccessful, and ultimately unhappy.

Another motivating factor has been disappointment with my Christian upbringing. I have developed an aversion to the glorification of suffering that pervades Christian doctrine, to the fear-based admonitions to be good, and to the habit of deferring happiness to some later date. Some readers will be quick to point out that formal religions – even Christianity – also bring happiness to many lives and that the concept of joy is central to religious life. In the

1

discussion of religion, I have tried to balance these very different tendencies.

Through more than five decades of teaching and mothering, I have noticed also that children (and adults, too) learn best when they are happy. This is not to say that harsh methods are never effective in producing rote learning, nor does it mean that intermittent vexation and occasional failure are absent from a happy student life. On the contrary, challenge and struggle are part of the quest for knowledge and competence. However, struggle is an inevitable aspect of learning; we educators do not have to invent struggles for our students, and students who are generally happy with their studies are better able to bring meaning to difficult periods and get through them with some satisfaction.

Closely related to the observation that happy students learn better than unhappy ones is something I judge to be even more important. Happy people are rarely mean, violent, or cruel. Having said that, and I believe it is largely true of individuals, I will immediately modify it by noting that groups and even whole societies can be happy, while others suffer under their exploitation and neglect. We shall have to ask in what sense such people are happy. I will, however, affirm the initial claim: Happy individuals are rarely violent or intentionally cruel, either to other human beings or to nonhuman animals. Our basic orientation to moral education, then, should be a commitment to building a world in which it is both possible and desirable for children to be good – a world in which children are happy.[1]

These are the major observations that have led me to a study of happiness and education. But there have been smaller things, too. Why do we so often defeat our own purposes by choosing means that are in clear contradiction to our aims? If, for example, we teach poetry in the hope that it will be a lifelong source of wisdom and delight, why do we bore students with endless analysis and an emphasis on technical vocabulary? Why do we tell children to do their best and then give them low grades when their best is not as good as that of others? Why, for that matter, do we give grades at all?

I have also wondered why so few educational theorists have written about happiness. A. S. Neill has spoken out boldly on the topic, but most school people find Neill too permissive, and even I prefer more direction than Neill recommends.[2] The Japanese educator

Introduction

Tsunesaburo Makiguchi also makes happiness a primary aim of education, and his identification of happiness with the creation of value is interesting, but its focus may seem a bit odd to Western readers.[3] Another approach is that taken by Robin Barrow, who presents an analysis of happiness and some implications of that analysis for schooling.[4] His book, like those of Neill and Makiguchi, is well worth reading, but some readers may find it too abstract. As my own investigation proceeds, we will see that a few others have also discussed happiness in connection with education, but we are unlikely to find any mention of happiness in current writing devoted to school reform and standards. (I hasten to add that we find some such mention in writing that opposes the present movement.)[5]

In the chapters that follow, I first discuss some important definitions and descriptions of happiness. Is happiness episodic or can a whole life be described as happy? Is pleasure the main feature of happiness? Can only good people be really happy, and what does it mean to be good? Is there such a thing as a happy personality? Educators need not agree on exactly what constitutes happiness in order to agree that students should be given an opportunity to learn about the variety of views. What could be more important than sorting through these views to find or modify one's own?

Teachers should not define happiness for their students and, although I clearly prefer a complex description of happiness, I have tried to leave the concept open to continued exploration. Similarly, I have not tried to separate questions about the description of happiness from questions about how to achieve it. Understanding the possibilities and reflecting on them should in itself make a major contribution to finding happiness.

As the discussion proceeds, we encounter closely related topics that require further analysis. For example, one feature of happiness seems to be the absence of pain or suffering. I will reject the glorification of suffering so often found in religious traditions, but I will contend that true happiness requires a capacity to share unhappiness; that is, to be truly happy, we must be moved to alleviate the misery around us. We must ask whether there are times when an otherwise happy person *should* be unhappy. The analysis offered will not, however, be a "hair shirt" perspective. With the philosopher David Hume, I have little admiration for the ascetic virtues unless they are necessary for the happiness of others, and they rarely are.

To be happy, human beings must have important needs satisfied and, in considering needs, several fascinating questions arise: How far should parents and teachers go in satisfying expressed needs (those that arise in the one who has them)? How far should we press in establishing and meeting inferred needs (those that arise externally and are imposed on the one said to have them)? How do we distinguish wants from needs? Do we know what makes us happy? Are there things that *should* make us happy?

Throughout these chapters, I will refer to two great domains in which we seek happiness – the private (or personal) and the public (primarily occupational) – as well as a number of sources of happiness. For example, positive relations with other people are certainly a source of happiness in both private and public life. Similarly, a good character seems to contribute substantially to both personal and occupational happiness. However, despite such overlaps, I have separated the two large domains to facilitate the analysis. Part 2 looks primarily at personal life, and Part 3 considers public life.

Before discussing the sources of happiness in personal life, I consider a fundamental question of education – that of aims. Not only do I suggest that happiness should be an aim of education but also I encourage the restoration of aims-talk. In the past, great educators have devoted much thought to the issue of aims, but today we hear little such debate. It is as though our society has simply decided that the purpose of schooling is economic – to improve the financial condition of individuals and to advance the prosperity of the nation. Hence students should do well on standardized tests, get into good colleges, obtain well-paying jobs, and buy lots of things. Surely there is more to education than this. But what? This question is at the heart of aims-talk. What are we trying to accomplish? For whom? Why? Closely related to basic aims-talk is discussion of the function of aims in evaluating all we do. Are our aims consistent with one another? Are the means we have chosen compatible with our aims? *Aims-talk* – the continual dialogue and reflection on aims – is essential to the thoughtful practice of education.

Armed with some sense of what happiness is, its relation to suffering and the satisfaction of needs, and the centrality of aims-talk in education, we are prepared to explore several important sources of happiness in personal life: making a home, love of place and nature, parenting, and the development of personal and interpersonal capacities. In this last category, we will consider the development of character, spirit, intellect, and personality. Throughout all of this discussion, I ask readers to imagine how rich and satisfying studies of these topics might be and to wonder with me why we give them so little attention in our schools. Why do we insist on teaching all children algebra and teach them almost nothing about what it means to make a home? If one's answer to this is that making a home is properly learned at home, how do we provide for those children who do not learn this at home? Moreover, all of us still have much to learn about this task that is so central to our lives and happiness.

In Part 3, I consider the sources of happiness in the public domain. It is wonderful to find happiness in one's work. How can schools help in this quest? The role of community in supporting happiness is also considered and, finally, I ask whether happiness is likely to be enhanced by life in a democratic society. If democratic life influences our happiness at all, the effects are probably indirect, but the possibility is worth exploring. Perhaps even more important is a question of the special requirements exerted on citizens by life in a liberal democracy. What does it take to be happy in such a society?

In the last chapter of the book, I ask about happiness *in* education. Education aimed at happiness cannot be satisfied by simply teaching students about happiness. Here, again, aims-talk is crucial. If our means are to be compatible with our ends, then the quality of life in schools must yield some happiness, and students must be encouraged to put what they have learned into practice. Moreover, the evaluative function of aims-talk becomes important. Happiness is not the only aim of either education or life, but it is a central aim, and it can be used as an evaluative screen through which to judge everything we do. That sort of evaluation can change the lives of teachers and students.

PART 1

Happiness as an Aim
of Life and Education

In these opening chapters, I explore various views on happiness, on the relation between suffering and happiness, and on the satisfaction of needs as a major aspect of happiness. I then call for a revival of the discussion on aims (aims-talk) in education and attempt to justify the establishment of happiness as an aim of education. These chapters provide a foundation for the discussion of educating for happiness in personal life (Part 2) and in public life (Part 3).

1

Happiness

Most human beings want happiness for themselves and their loved ones. It is reported that the Dalai Lama once said, "Whether one believes in religion or not, we are all seeking something better in life – the very motion of our life is toward happiness." And William James started one of the chapters in *The Varieties of Religious Experience* this way:

> If we were to ask the question: "What is human life's chief concern?" one of the answers we should receive would be: "It is happiness."[1]

As we will see, there are some gloomy souls who deny that happiness is our chief concern and claim something else as a greater good but, even among the vast majority who agree with the Dalai Lama and James, questions arise about what happiness is and where we might find it. These two questions supply the subject matter of this chapter. Our ultimate question: How might schooling contribute to the attainment of happiness? will only be hinted at in this chapter, but keeping it in mind will help us to evaluate the views under consideration. I do not attempt a chronological account of happiness here, but I will start with classical views because they have been and continue to be so powerful in educational thinking.

Classical Views

The Greeks in the age of Socrates, Plato, and Aristotle wanted to make happiness safe from contingency;[2] that is, they wanted to define happiness in a way that makes it independent of health, wealth, and the ups and downs of everyday life. Happiness, from this perspective, is not episodic; rather, it should apply to a whole life or to the tendency of that life. In this, many religious traditions have agreed. They have said that human beings cannot count on happiness in their mortal lives and cannot achieve it by pursuing it directly. But, whereas the Christian and Moslem traditions posit an afterlife in which some will attain an absolutely dependable happiness, the Greeks located happiness in the full exercise of rationality. Reason, they argued, is the essential characteristic of man, and the development and use of reason constitute his genuine happiness.[3] In insisting on the primacy of reason, Greek thinkers believed that the exercise of reason makes it possible for man to live his life in harmony with the universe, which itself is characterized by order.

Aristotle gave us two views of happiness, both of which affect our thinking today. Actually, Aristotle wrote of *eudaimonia*, which is perhaps better translated as "human flourishing," but I will follow the common practice of calling it "happiness." In the view that has been most widely adopted, Aristotle analyzed happiness to find its components. This "comprehensive" view allows contingencies such as health, wealth, reputation, and friendship to enter the picture, but the exercise of reason is the major component of happiness. In his attempt to order the components of happiness, Aristotle pointed out that when we are ill, health seems most important; when we are broke, wealth seems most important; and so on. But, obviously, healthy and wealthy people can be unhappy. Thus, none of these components (or others like them) can be the most important factor in happiness. Is there anything that is both necessary and sufficient for happiness? As we proceed, we will see that philosophers, social scientists, and ordinary people are still engaged with this question. We still ask: What exactly are the components of happiness?

In his second view, often labeled the *intellectualist* view, Aristotle held that theoretical or contemplative thought *is* happiness, and such thought is superior to practical wisdom and activity in the world. Both views claim that the fullest exercise of rationality marks the divine aspect of human life. We are closest to the divine image when we are engaged in contemplative thought. In this mental activity, we are satisfying our god-given function – to think.[4]

Few of us today accept the intellectualist position. At least, few of us admit to it or state it publicly, but our school curriculum continues to be heavily influenced by it. The heavily abstract and theoretical subjects are more highly respected than practical, less theoretical ones. Aristotle created a hierarchy of human activity that devalues the practical and those who do the world's practical work. Indeed, he claimed that it was the function of some to do this sort of work so that those with greater intellectual capacity could fulfill *their* function – to think. John Dewey pointed out again and again the pernicious effects that this Aristotelian doctrine has had on education.[5] It created a sharp separation of theory and practice, and it artificially branded some subject matters as superior to others. Dewey liked to point out that mathematics – thought by Aristotle to be more perfect (next to theology) than other subjects – can be engaged either intelligently or stupidly. The same can be said for more practical activities such as cooking. Therefore, it is not the label or ostensible content of a subject that matters but how it is engaged or conducted. We should note, too, that Dewey warned us against making an error opposite to the intellectualist one. Emphasizing the practical to the exclusion of the theoretical is just as bad. "We lose rather than gain in change from serfdom to free citizenship if the most prized result of the change is simply an increase in the mechanical efficiency of the human tools of production."[6]

It is hardly an exaggeration to say that the view placing intellectual activity over all other forms of activity is still alive today. We see it active in the elevation of mathematics and physics over politics and natural history. We see it in the insistence that all students study algebra and geometry but not parenting, even though most of us become parents and relatively few use algebra. Oddly, we also see its influence in the sort of opposite reaction that worried Dewey – in the worship of purely physical activity such as professional sports. And, of course, it has been active in recent intellectual life. The great mathematician G. H. Hardy claimed with pride, "I have never done anything 'useful,'"[7] and the claim (although demonstrably false) was made in deference to what he regarded as better – mathematics that is pure and beautiful. It would not be hard to find other such cases. Again, the mistake is not in loving the abstract and beautiful but in devaluing the concrete and supposing it "ugly," as Hardy claimed.

Equating happiness with the life of pure thought strikes most of us today as the height of intellectual snobbery, and yet there is something in it that is not easily brushed aside. Surely the development of our human capacities has something to do with happiness, and rationality is one of our most treasured attributes. When I discuss happiness as pleasure, I will take seriously pleasures of the mind,[8] but I will not evaluate these pleasures as necessarily superior to all others. Rather, I will note that creating a hierarchy of human attributes puts tremendous pressure on people to "measure up" and may, thus, create unhappiness in some who would not otherwise be greatly troubled by their deficiency in a given attribute. There are also ethical problems in elevating rationality/reasoning over all other human characteristics. If it is a special form of rationality that gives a being moral worth, questions immediately arise about the status of beings, human and nonhuman, who lack this quality. We need not denigrate the gift of mind, but we must be careful not to make it the single mark of moral worth.

From this very brief discussion of classical views on happiness, we extract several things that must be explored further: If happiness is construed as a comprehensive state, what are its components? In particular, what are pleasures of the mind, and how are they developed? What have been the effects on the school curriculum of favoring the abstract and theoretical over the concrete and practical? Is it desirable to espouse a view of happiness free of contingencies? Let's consider this last question next.

Religious Views

Another way of escaping the contingencies associated with happiness in everyday life is to accept misery as our mortal lot and put our hope for happiness into an afterlife. If we believe in an afterlife and live so as to merit it, we are assured of happiness; it is a certainty. For many people, however, religious faith has also had the salutary effect of relieving earthly misery, indeed transforming it into contentment, which (they suppose) is the nearest thing to happiness that people should expect in earthly life.

We enter here an enormously complex area of human life. Belief in an afterlife of eternal happiness has helped countless individuals to find purpose in life and to maintain courage and moral goodness in the face of hardship and disaster. An austere adherence to strict moral rules and religious rituals does not deny that humans seek happiness above all else; indeed, such obedience confirms the desire for happiness, and some people have sacrificed most earthly pleasures in order to win this eternal happiness. Goodness and obedience – which seem to be extolled as superior to happiness – are really instrumental for deferred happiness. In another approach, reminiscent of Greek thought, a life of "perfect action" is said to bring its own form of happiness, if only contentment, not pleasure.

For followers of the instrumental version, an enormous problem arises. There may be no afterlife. As Freud pointed out, unless people find some other compensating factor in religion, they may simply be victims of illusion,[9] and intensive immersion in religious activity often takes a form similar to intoxication. In extreme forms, emphasis on living so that heaven is assured may lead to willful ignorance and a refusal to consider any views that might shake one's dogmatically held beliefs. The possibility of self-deception is also great. People convinced of the truth of their unexamined beliefs often claim to be happy, even though an objective observer may assess their lives as anything but happy. This observation raises a question to which I will return in a later section of this chapter: Do people know when they are happy?

Another negative effect of deferring happiness to an afterlife may be quietism, which, in its informal sense, leads people to leave everything in the hands of God. In this way, people need make no effort to improve the physical and social conditions of humanity but simply be content that all will come right eventually under God's control.[10] A major practical difficulty with this attitude is that it encourages the control of unscrupulous human beings, not God. People quieted by religion may not be easily aroused to work toward the betterment of their own condition. Hence the Marxist claim that religion is the opiate of the people.

Despite its often negative effects, involvement in religion also has demonstrably positive effects. Without some form of religious belief, people are hard put to define the purpose of life. It is comforting to believe that the purpose of life is, first of all, to know and love God. On the one hand, this statement of purpose opens the road to happiness for all people, provided only that they are believers. It contrasts sharply with the Greek notion that only those with significant talent and adequate leisure can achieve the most divine characteristics of human life – reason and contemplation. But, on the other hand, it begs the question of whether there is an a priori purpose of life, and it discourages the idea that humans must construct their own purposes. Some have found happiness in accepting the purpose promulgated by religious faith; others have found the idea intolerable and have turned to other avenues of exploration. Whichever decision is made, it is clear that, although neither is a sure path to happiness, both have contributed to the happiness of some individuals.

Given the volumes that have been written on religion and its contributions to happiness, it is surprising that much of contemporary psychology almost ignores it. One prominent volume devotes fewer than 2 pages (out of 574) to the connection between religion and happiness, and in those pages it concentrates on the measures of happiness associated with subjective well-being (SWB).[11] SWB is a definition/description of happiness to which we will give attention in a later section, and it is fair to say that the information social scientists have collected under that label rings true in present-day life. Health, wealth, friendly associations, a sense of purpose, satisfying work, self-esteem, loving intimacies, leisure enjoyment... all contribute to SWB.

Psychological studies are more descriptive than explanatory, however, and they tend to avoid both normative accounts (what *should* make us happy) and reports of joy or ecstatic happiness. Both are important omissions. We not only learn from accounts of joy and religious ecstasy (to be explored in a later section), but many of us achieve a form of happiness from hearing these accounts – even if we know that we would not be so moved by the reported experiences. On reading C. S. Lewis's account of his reluctant conversion to Christianity,[12] many of us experience a "pleasure of the mind" while remaining unmoved by any temptation to accept Christianity. We also learn something important about deep forms of religious happiness. They are not instrumental; that is, the convert does not pursue a religion in order to achieve happiness. In many cases, happiness comes as a surprising side effect. In Lewis's case, his conversion provided an explanation for joy he had already experienced.

Stories of this sort lead us to ask questions that are rarely raised by psychological/empirical studies: Have I experienced such joy? Under what circumstances? What is its source? As we consider the contributions that schooling might make to happiness, we should remember these stories and ask what might be gained by sharing them.

Psychologists have not always neglected religious experience. William James frankly studied and reported on the rapturous experiences associated with religious life. For people who undergo such experiences, it is usually not true that they have been pursuing happiness directly. Like the classical Greeks, they are seeking "the good." When the connection is made, everything changes:

> In this state of mind, what we most dreaded has become the habitation of our safety, and the hour of our moral death has turned into our spiritual birthday. The time for tension in our soul is over, and that of happy relaxation, of calm deep breathing, of an eternal present, with no discordant future to be anxious about, has arrived. Fear is not held in abeyance as it is by mere morality, it is positively expunged and washed away.[13]

James's fascinating study is chock-full of vivid personal reports of religious joy and ecstasy, but it also contains equally vivid accounts of suffering, melancholy, and the awareness of suffering. These I will discuss in the next chapter. Why talk about suffering in a book on happiness? The simplest answer is that happiness is often equated to an absence of pain and suffering. Therefore, if we seek happiness, we must find ways to avoid suffering. To a degree, this is clearly right, but there is another, somewhat paradoxical, connection between happiness and suffering. Sharing the suffering of others contributes to our own fulfillment as human beings. As Lewis pointed out, grief can sometimes bring joy in its wake. Unless we are sadists, we do not get pleasure from someone else's pain, so we are not talking here about happiness as pleasure but, rather, as a longer-lasting sense that we would not be fully human without the griefs and emotional pains we share.

So far in this discussion, we have seen that religion sometimes produces, allows, or encourages misery in the hope of achieving eventual happiness (in heaven). Few thoughtful religious thinkers today take this view, recognizing the negative features already discussed, but there clearly is a normative aspect in all the views under exploration. There is a sense that, if we want happiness, we should live or think in a certain way. Usually, what is prescribed is pursuit of the good. Happiness follows. It remains to explore the question What is the good? We have already met one answer from the Greeks – the contemplative life and/or the life of perfect action.

Augustine, in his dialogue with Evodius, makes the connection between happiness and the good explicit:

> Those who are happy, who also ought to be good, are not happy because they desire to live happily, which even evil men desire, but rather because they will to live rightly – which evil men do not.[14]

For Augustine, happiness cannot be attained, nor is it merited, by evildoers. In a corrupt form, this view has led to a variety of abuses. It has been used to justify the eternal punishment of hell. In its Calvinist interpretation, it has been used to blame people for their own misery. For example, good health and prosperity were often taken as signs that their bearers must be people who "live rightly." This, of course, is a logical error, for neither Augustine nor Socrates before him denied that evil people sometimes prosper, at least for a time. (That's why Augustine needs hell to balance the accounts.) Construing happiness as a state *merited* lands us back in the instrumental view. It is not one that I will embrace, but versions of it will arise later in our discussion of education.

That some ways of life are accompanied by happiness, that acts of goodness often confer a sense of fulfillment on their agents, seems indisputable, but even this view holds a possibility for corruption. Self-righteous smugness can masquerade as happiness. We can think of any number of insufferable characters from fiction (for example, Dickens's Mrs. Jellyby and Mrs. Pardiggle) who regarded themselves as deservedly happy. But what justifies my labeling such an attitude as a "masquerade" of happiness? Some normative inclination must nag at me – must say, "*This* can't be happiness. Real happiness is . . ." We are still searching.

Lewis and James have provided us with accounts of ecstatic religious experience, but such experiences also occur without specifically religious content. Abraham Maslow documented events he called *peak experiences*,[15] moments of transcendent ecstasy triggered by a great variety of occurrences. A beautiful sunset, a musical passage, the sight of a baby, the sound of the ocean, light coming through stained-glass windows – any of these and many more can induce a sense of transcendence, of great joy.

Martin Gardner also discusses a sense of the *numinous*, an appreciation of mystery manifested in awe and wonder, and he notes that great theologians almost invariably "have a profound sense of the numinous."[16] But the sense is not confined to theologians and believers. Albert Einstein expressed his awe of mystery in the universe, and so did atheists such as Bertrand Russell and H. G. Wells. Indeed, on reading such accounts and reminiscing on one's own experiences, it is hard to understand how some people seem to escape experiences of the transcendent. Those who have had these experiences treasure them. The questions then arise, What triggers them? How can I live so that these experiences are likely to occur? Is there anything that schooling can do to encourage their appearance?

If we are wary of particular strategies and modes of behavior that are chosen as instruments to effect happiness, we need not deny that human beings seek happiness. The difficult question is, in essence, how to ask the question. I can ask, How should I live in order to be happy? Or I can ask, How should I live? and hope that a committed answer will be accompanied by happiness, even though happiness is not the direct object of my quest. If we follow the second path, we need something like an *ultimate concern*, as described by Paul Tillich. An ultimate concern is "a meaning which gives meaning to all meanings."[17] This meaning is found for some in religious life, for others in intellectual, artistic, civic, or relational life of another sort. It is well documented, for example, that people can find rich spiritual experiences in connection with nature, in physical labor, in personal intimacy, in all sorts of sensory experience when a relation is established.

In one sense, some religious views broaden our view of happiness. Because happiness is not confined to the godlike functions of intellect, it is open to everyone. In another sense, however, the door is narrower, for in some religions, it is now open only to believers. Perhaps, instead of trying to define happiness, we should ask what *gives* people happiness and, thus, include much of what has been so far discussed – theoretical/contemplative thought, religious ecstasy, peak experiences triggered by a variety of events, and a set of fortunate contingencies such as health, wealth, and reputation (so long as these are accompanied by virtue).

Readers may suspect, at this stage, that I am making the whole enterprise too difficult. Why not go straight for pleasure? Isn't that the way most of us think of happiness?

Pleasure

Pleasure was a fundamental concept in nineteenth-century utilitarian thought. In describing the Greatest Happiness Principle, John Stuart Mill wrote: "By happiness is intended pleasure, and the absence of pain."[18] Ethical life was to be founded on the idea that a morally acceptable act would maximize the amount of pleasure over pain for those affected by the act. The principle is sometimes made into a slogan: The greatest good for the greatest number. The "good" here is happiness, and happiness is pleasure and the absence of pain.

It would take us too far afield to discuss the strengths and weaknesses of utilitarianism as an ethical theory, but it is easy to see that utilitarian thinking heavily influences social policy today. Why do we not insist that the legally established minimum wage be a living wage? Because, it is argued through economic utilitarian theory, such a wage would have the effect of eliminating many jobs and creating misery for a greater number. This may well be false, but the thinking is clear – act so as to create the greatest good for the greatest number. Misery for a few is to be preferred over misery for many.

If we follow Mill in the frank acceptance of happiness (pleasure) as the greatest good, we do not entirely escape Aristotle's emphasis on happiness and intellectual life, for Mill carefully describes the pleasures characteristic of well-developed human beings. In this, Mill echoes other Greeks, the Epicureans, in extolling pleasure but evaluating some pleasures as superior to others. Human pleasures, Mill says, are different from those of swine:

> For if the sources of pleasure were precisely the same to human beings and to swine, the rule of life which is good enough for the one would be good enough for the other. . . . Human beings have faculties more elevated than the animal appetites, and when once made conscious of them, do not regard anything as happiness which does not include their gratification.[19]

Thus Mill, quite as surely as Aristotle, evaluates the pleasures of the intellect above those of mere sensation, and he points out that no one who has experienced them would forgo them for the pleasures of a fool. But at least Mill adds to the austere contemplation of the Greeks feelings, imagination, and moral sentiments. Thus, we are invited to think more broadly about the special human capacities that contribute to happiness.

Even before Mill, David Hume insisted on the importance of pleasure in both social and ethical life. "The very aspect of happiness, joy, prosperity, gives pleasure; that of pain, suffering, sorrow communicates uneasiness...."[20] Hume urged us to consider the influence of pleasing personalities, social amenities, enjoyable gatherings, and attractive manners on our moral life. It is far easier to behave morally when we interact with friendly people in pleasant conditions than it is when we are faced with nasty people and miserable conditions. This is an argument I, too, have made for giving careful attention to the conditions in which we live and educate.[21]

But Hume also reminded us that wise people are able to "resist the temptation of present ease or pleasure" if, by giving way to that temptation, future happiness is sacrificed. Hume noted a wide variety of virtues required by those who would be wise, but the reasons he gave for acquiring these virtues are not those given by more austere or supernaturally oriented philosophies. The virtues are to be acquired because they are useful or pleasant or both. They are not obligatory because they satisfy the divine function of human being, or because God has decreed them, or because they will earn us a place in paradise. They give utility or pleasure, and both are affected to some degree by the needs and customs of a particular society.

Hume's analysis praised some self-regarding virtues – cultivation of talent, physical grace, modesty, wit – because they are pleasing both to their holders and to onlookers. Other qualities, praised as virtues in some traditions, left Hume cold:

Celibacy, fasting, penance, mortification, self-denial, humility, silence, solitude, and the whole train of monkish virtues; for what reason are they every where rejected by men of sense, but because they serve to no manner of purpose; neither advance a man's fortune in the world, nor render him a more valuable member of society; neither qualify him for the entertainment of company, nor increase his power of self-enjoyment?[22]

Hume makes us comfortable in including humor, recreation, enjoyment, and fun in our definition of happiness. Pleasure was paramount for Hume, but it is not a selfish or self-indulgent pleasure that he praised. Every act, every virtue was to be judged on the basis of whether it yields pleasure or utility to the self or to the community. Again, we cannot explore fully the ethical implications of Hume's position, and there is rightly some concern that Hume may have been too optimistic in supposing that the interaction of individual pleasure/utility and that of society can be counted on to work for the best. He said little about personal and cultural evil. But his view of pleasure is attractive to many of us today and, if we are unwilling to equate happiness and pleasure, few of us would deny that pleasure plays an important part in happiness.

Subjective Well-Being

Recognizing all the complications we've discussed so far, social scientists today often use SWB (Subjective Well-Being) as a definition of happiness.[23] Armed with this definition, they ask people questions ranging from How much fun are you having? to Does the future seem hopeful?[24] Answers to questions of this sort can then be correlated with answers to the straightforward question: Taken all together, how would you say things are these days – would you say that you are very happy, pretty happy, or not too happy?[25] Now, of course, we can spot difficulties with this approach immediately. Doesn't one's mood matter? Perhaps that issue can be addressed by repeating the questions at various intervals or taking large samples so that we can drop the predictable percentage of people in a bad mood. But can we use this approach with children? Do people (not only children) really know what makes them happy? This is a deeper, very difficult question.

To complicate matters further, Robert Lane notes that, in Western societies, "income, education, health, and intelligence (!) have all increased since World War II, but they have not made us happier."[26] It is true that an increase in wealth that lifts people out of poverty makes them happier and, clearly, relief of pain and chronic illness increases happiness (or, at least, decreases unhappiness), but beyond poverty, increased wealth does not often bring increased happiness, and a lot of physically healthy people are unhappy. Well, what does bring happiness? Here we should be careful about settling on just one contributor, but Lane provides empirical evidence for companionship as the main source of happiness.[27] If he is right, what does this mean for education? I'll return to this question.

20

Perhaps we are on the wrong track entirely in identifying happiness with SWB. We all know people who, like Mill's fool or pig, seem perfectly happy living in a way that we deplore. How can the sloppy, beer-guzzling couch potato be happy? Aristotle and Mill would be aghast at the thought. Yet Mill, at least, would be equally aghast at telling adults what should make them happy, and this illustrates a paradox for liberal democracies. The emphasis on choice in such societies means that we do not interfere in the lives of adults unless they are harming others. Yet we cannot bring ourselves to have genuine respect for the ways of life that proliferate under a system of choice. Our only choice seems to be intelligent and sensitive education.

There is, as we have seen, a normative aspect to definitions of happiness. SWB cannot be the whole story because, among other complications, a society just does not approve of many forms of pleasure-seeking that some people might choose. Moreover, societal disapproval affects an individual's SWB. I cannot feel very happy if I feel the disapproval of those around me and, of course, societal pressures work for both good and ill. They press people into behaviors and attitudes that may, in the long run, produce greater happiness; for example, as educators, we believe that good character has something to do with happiness, and so we continually try to find effective methods of character education. But social pressures also cause both temporary and permanent unhappiness by inducing envy, guilt, self-denial, self-indulgence, greed, and a host of other ills. As a result of internal and external conflicts, many people are not sure what would make them happy or why they are unhappy. And a few, nagged by an overzealous conscience, religion, or family, come to believe that they have no right to happiness.

Still another complication is that we can be happy in one part (domain) of our lives and unhappy in another. One may be happy in working life and unhappy in family life or vice versa. To have a substantial effect on overall happiness, the domains assessed must be considered important in one's life. For example, John might be somewhat unhappy with his athletic performance but not regard the domain of athletics as important in his life. He can shrug off his lack of physical prowess and, while he recognizes it, the deficiency does not affect his overall happiness. However, consider the effects that enormous family pressure might have on John. If, in John's intimate

21

circle, rewards go to those who are athletically competent (and he is labeled a clutz), John may experience increased unhappiness.

Consider, then, what it means to children when they discover that intellectual (academic) prowess is valued above all. It must hurt to learn early on that one is not quite "up to" the best human beings. Loving families help to cushion this blow. Sensitive teachers help. But it is small wonder that many young people turn to other domains, say athletics, where they can achieve some acclaim. Some turn to gangs, and some escape into alcohol and drugs. Reasonable people deplore these alternatives (even the athletic one if the student neglects academics), but we do not ask serious questions about bringing balance to our evaluations. We don't do much to help students understand how societal values affect their SWB.

Subjective, Objective, and Normative Influences

It seems obvious that a judgment of happiness is best made by the person who claims or disavows happiness. As outsiders, we can say, "Well, she should be happy!" but we cannot credibly say that someone *is* happy if that person says that she is not. Thus, SWB or something like it is essential for those studying happiness.

However, there are objective features of happiness, and these have long been recognized. Even Aristotle acknowledged that health, wealth, reputation, friends, freedom from worry and fear, and certain sensual pleasures play a role in happiness. It is unlikely that people who are desperately poor or miserably ill would claim to be happy. But surveys have shown repeatedly that increased wealth, beyond the relief of poverty, does not often bring with it greater happiness. Sometimes policymakers use the results of such surveys to decide that not much needs to be done about poverty because "money isn't everything." But enough money to buy necessities and a few luxuries, enough to achieve relief from financial anxiety, does seem important. A living wage, medical insurance, safe housing, and sufficient resources to hold up one's head in society are all very nearly essential for happiness. Only a callous society would ask its poor to rise above their misery through an effort of will.

The opposite mistake is made in today's schools. Often we equate happiness with financial success, and then we suppose that our chief duty as educators is to give all children the tools needed to get "good" jobs. However, many essential jobs, now very poorly paid, will have to be done even if the entire citizenry were to become well educated. Thus the answer to poverty cannot be completely formulated in educational terms. Poverty is a *social* problem, not merely an educational one.

Moreover, we do our students (and our society) a significant disservice when we define happiness entirely in terms of financial success. A good society will make sure that its people do not suffer from a lack of those resources that constitute objective happiness, but its educational system will encourage them to explore and appreciate a full range of possibilities for promoting happiness. Education, by its very nature, should help people to develop their best selves – to become people with pleasing talents, useful and satisfying occupations, self-understanding, sound character, a host of appreciations, and a commitment to continuous learning. A large part of our obligation as educators is to help students understand the wonders and complexities of happiness, to raise questions about it, and to explore promising possibilities responsibly. The greater part of this book will be devoted to exploration of the connection between education and happiness. At this point, based on the analysis so far, I reject the notion that the connection is adequately described in terms of economic opportunity.

Some positive sense of well-being is clearly necessary for happiness. It is contradictory to say, "Alice is happy, but she doesn't know it," although people often make retrospective comments along these lines: "I didn't know how happy I was then." This suggests that we do not well understand happiness in general or even our own happy/unhappy states. Studies of SWB are thus essential to our knowledge about happiness. But a positive response on SWB is not the last word on happiness, nor does it tell us how happiness is achieved or under what circumstances it is likely to be long-lasting. Should we pursue happiness or just hope that it appears? George Orwell once commented, "Men can only be happy when they do not assume that the object of life is happiness."[28] If Orwell was right, something like Tillich's ultimate concern is a more reliable foundation for happiness than its direct pursuit.

Are some people just naturally happy? The stereotype is Eleanor Porter's excessively optimistic Pollyanna. Not many actual people come close to Pollyanna in perpetual happiness, but social scientists have documented a personality type that inclines toward the happy side.[29] As so often happens in psychology, several competing schools of thought have been advanced to explain why it is that, in roughly similar situations, some people will see the good or happy side and others the bad or unhappy side. William James described the tendency toward happiness as *healthy-mindedness* and identified two ways of being healthy minded. In one, the *involuntary* way, a person just *is* happy; he or she naturally looks on the bright side. If we were to examine the lives of such people, we would probably find some objective factors contributing to their overall sense of well-being, but many of these people retain their optimism even through difficult times. They are what social scientists call *happy personalities*. James's label for them, *healthy-minded*, is a bit odd because, as his account goes on, it seems that he has greater regard for the "sick soul" than for the healthy-minded one.

James gave considerable space to his analysis of voluntary healthy-mindedness. This cast of mind becomes systematic, James said, and requires believers to shut out or hush up any signs of evil:

> But more than this: the hushing of it up may, in a perfectly candid and honest mind, grow into a deliberate religious policy, or *parti pris*.[30]

It then becomes a philosophy of optimism, and it is clear that James did not admire it, although, with characteristic honesty, he admitted that "we all do cultivate it more or less" because the realities are simply unbearable. When happiness becomes a philosophy, it becomes a duty. Unhappiness, then, is "not only painful, it is mean and ugly."[31] It is a sign of ingratitude; it is inconsiderate of others, because it makes bad situations worse. We must discipline ourselves toward the happy outlook.

> But it is impossible to carry on this discipline in the subjective sphere without zealously emphasizing the brighter and minimizing the darker aspects of the objective sphere of things at the same time. And thus our resolution not to indulge in misery, beginning at a comparatively small point within ourselves, may not stop until it has brought the entire frame of reality under a systematic conception optimistic enough to be congenial with its needs.[32]

When the subjective thus overwhelms the objective, we may go about talking of "best possible worlds" and the unimportance of mere bodies. We may, as Dewey feared, lapse into quietism and "let God run the world," as though the misery around us were invisible and we have no obligation to relieve it.

There are difficulties, then – sources of dissatisfaction – with both subjective and objective descriptions of happiness. We cannot be entirely satisfied with an objective description because it seems soulless; it misses something vital at the heart of the concept. The subjective is indeed built into the concept. If it is carried to extremes, however, the subjective loses touch with reality as it appears in everyday life.

To complicate matters further, it is apparent that human beings do not have complete control over either objective or subjective factors. People have always recognized their relative incapacity to control objective factors. We do not choose the conditions into which we are born, and all sorts of contingencies plague human life. Indeed, it is our recognition and abhorrence of contingency that have led us to seek certainty in religion, reason, and magic. As we have seen, there are also regrettable effects from moving in the direction of subjective certainty, and few of us want to submit ourselves to the discipline required for religious ecstasy, a possibility to be discussed in the next section. Even if we were so inclined, many of us would reject such a path as inadequately sensitive to the realities of human suffering. There is something insufferably smug and decidedly uncomforting in responding to someone's tragedy, "Doubtless it is God's will."

We lack control over the subjective not only because of weakness of will and sympathy for the suffering of others but also because normative factors in our society affect the way we look at things. As I pointed out earlier, it is hard not to be affected by the values our society places on certain capacities. When we express our feelings, teachers and parents may add to our confusion by telling us, "You shouldn't feel that way." When we are unaccountably unhappy, we are told, "Count your blessings." We are assured that the wicked will not prosper forever and that they do not deserve happiness. A natural question then arises: Do *I* deserve to be happy? Young people may be understandably torn between feeling that they do not deserve happiness and feeling that, paradoxically, they have an obligation to be happy.

Today, when we (in prosperous societies) have more control over objective factors than ever before in history, we are inclined to put all our eggs into the objective basket. Schooling reinforces this temptation by emphasizing education's role in producing economic success. Yet social scientists report that we are not happier as a re-sult of our increasing prosperity and control.[33] Perhaps the appro-priate response to this phenomenon is, You shouldn't feel that way! or Count your blessings! or Pull up your socks! Alternatively, our response might be more sympathetic and intelligent. We might probe more deeply into what it means to be happy.

Ecstatic Happiness

As we probe more deeply, should we discuss ecstatic happiness? I said at the start that I would only treat those views that have had an effect (or *should* have an effect) on education. We would be hard put to find a significant form of education that has directed itself at ecstatic happiness. Well, then, do I believe education *should* so direct itself? Not exactly. I believe that children should know about the various views on ecstatic happiness, especially the so-called peak experience, and such knowledge may increase the possibility that they will themselves have such experiences. They should hear about these experiences and learn how to evaluate them.

Consider, first, a form that may appear in their own lives. Falling in love. Niall Williams captures the feeling in his fictional description of what happens to a young man, Stephen, who is not at all inclined toward ecstatic happiness. Essentially, he is more like one of James's sick souls. But he falls in love with Gabriella:

> It was a micro-season of happiness, a blissed-out moment of aban-doned delight and Stephen Griffin could sit at the table in the brief pleasure of knowing: this is joy, this is the richness of things, the brimming sense of the impossible becoming real, when the Hollywood version of himself might have danced about the table and taken Mary White [his innkeeper/hostess] in his arms, spinning her in loops of gaiety, fox trotting and cha-cha-cha-ing out through the french doors and into the garden....
> She had spoken to him. Gabriella Castoldi had spoken to him....[34]

Do such things happen to real people? Of course. Are they mere infatuations? Often. But sometimes they are the beginning of lifelong devotions. Young people should hear about both possibilities. What could be more wonderful than to have the impossible become real? How does one maintain the reality?

Another form of ecstatic happiness is well documented in religious history. In his chapter on mysticism, James described mystical experiences from both Catholic and Protestant Christianity, Hinduism, and Sufism. Whatever the source, these experiences are characterized by ineffability, a noetic quality, transience, and passivity. The experience often calls forth a torrent of poetic language, but the writer/speaker insists that words are inadequate; the experience is ineffable yet marked by certainty. It is not a mere feeling; the one undergoing it is filled with a knowledge that seems eternal. But, although the certainty remains, the experience and its affective accompaniments are transient. The ecstatic moment passes. Finally, it is something that happens to a receptive mind; there is no sense of active creation on the part of the one experiencing it.

Although mystical experience is described as passive, it seems that rigorous discipline usually paves the way. Meditation, orison, music, and ritual ceremony can set the stage, but the experience itself cannot be forced. Now and then it even occurs without warning and, seemingly, without preparation. However, the enlightenment characteristic of mystical experience is very like the "illumination" that follows active preparation in the intellectual field, followed by a passive period of "incubation."[35] When illumination (or enlightenment) occurs, it has the appearance of spontaneity. My guess is that the moment of religious ecstasy is well prepared whether or not the receiver acknowledges the preparation.

Students should certainly hear about some of these experiences. The ones described by James are deeply moving. Years ago, when I taught high school mathematics, I made it a point to give students accounts of preparation, incubation, and illumination. Predictably, many hoped to skip the preparation stage and achieve illumination straight out of a period of neglect they prayed would serve as incubation. We laughed about this. The preparation stage cannot be skipped, but what exactly does it involve? When should one quit "for a while" and turn things over to God or to mathematical grace?

Another way of avoiding rigorous preparation is to use some substance that will produce the desired effect. It is common in schools today to do something along the lines of drug education/prevention. Unfortunately, the message is always one filled with admonitions – one designed to induce fear and a resultant commitment to abstinence. I am not advocating an endorsement of drug use, but I think a reasonable program would let today's kids know that they are not the first people in the world to seek altered states of consciousness. Human beings have long sought substances that would prolong life, increase sexual pleasure, induce a superconsciousness that connects to the eternal, enhance creativity, or bring peace to troubled minds. Moreover, history reveals cycles of societal enthusiasm, tolerance, and condemnation for various drugs. Freud, for example, was an early cocaine enthusiast. In our worst moments as a society, we have attached racial or ethnic stereotypes to drug use – the Chinese to opium, blacks to cocaine, Mexicans to marijuana.[36] This is a history of which students should be aware.

What do we seek when we submit ourselves to the intoxication of drugs, alcohol, or religious superconsciousness? The list varies. In addition to the states named previously, many simply want to be part of the group – everyone's doing it. Some want desperately to escape reality, if only for a short time. Men who work hard for poverty wages and see no possibility of improvement, kids who can't measure up in school, women who are dissatisfied with their lives and the selves they have become – all may turn to a chemical form of escape. Not everyone who drinks, smokes, or otherwise gets high is a good-for-nothing, and the stories of those who indulge are not always accounts of failed willpower. In one of Paulo Freire's studies, a group of impoverished workers responded to a picture of several men by picking out a drunkard as the most responsible. They said:

> "The only one there who is productive and useful to his country is the souse who is returning home after working all day for low wages and who is worried about his family because he can't take care of their needs. He is the only worker. He is a decent worker and a souse like us."[37]

Comments such as these should turn us away from self-righteous calls to willpower and admonitions to "just say no." The objective factors in happiness take on a fresh importance. Students need to understand not only the awful consequences of addiction but also why people seek escape through chemical means. It is not just a personal message that should be given (don't get hooked!) but a social message. One should help to build a society in which it is less likely that people will feel the need to escape.

Finally, by way of setting the stage for later chapters, education should offer many, many opportunities for students to hear about and participate in activities that may yield minor ecstasies – gardening, hiking in the wilderness, holding an infant, watching a sunrise or sunset, cooking a terrific meal, coming home to the companionship of family, listening to favorite music, surfing an ocean wave, coaxing a houseplant into bloom, reading poetry, having tea and cookies with an elderly grandma. . . .

Domains of Happiness

Before discussing domains in which happiness may be found or lost, I should say just a little about happiness with respect to stages of life. In education, we are particularly interested in childhood and, certainly, childhood has figured prominently in accounts of happiness. Childhood is often identified, too romantically I think, as a period of innocent and undiluted happiness. Romantic poetry has encouraged this view. But even those who think it is a mistake to romanticize childhood feel that there is something especially poignant and morally suspect about an unhappy childhood. We want childhood to be happy, but we do not want to secure that happiness at the expense of future happiness. This too we must keep in mind for later discussion. Here I will concentrate on the domains of activity in which we seek happiness.

The first task is to choose a set of categories that do not prejudice the analysis at the outset. I want to avoid one that separates the intellectual and manual, cognitive and noncognitive, spiritual and mundane, and so on. How are our ordinary lives organized? Most of us recognize a separation (at least in hours) between paid work and personal life, so let's name these as two important categories. A third domain might be labeled *civic* or *community* life. In a child's life, these three domains might be labeled *home*, *school*, and *street* or *play yard*. We know from a multitude of studies that children experience these domains as sharply separate. As we think about happiness and education, we need to ask where children find happiness in present experience and also how best to prepare them for future happiness.

Notice right at the start that public schools in liberal democracies pay very little attention to preparation for personal life. Most of our attention goes to preparation for higher forms of education, and thus for the world of paid work. We do give some lip service to preparation for civic life, but most of our attention in this area goes to national histories, voting rights, and the like. It is preparation for civic life writ large, not for, say, neighborhood life. Civic life, as interpreted in school, is not a domain in which many of us seek happiness. Happiness lies closer to home. The domain of community comparable to the child's street or play yard is absorbed almost entirely into the category of personal life. For most of us, this is the domain of greatest possibility, anyway, so let's start there.

Consider one major task faced by every adult – that of making a home. The historian Theodore Zeldin remarks:

> If it [making a home] is one of the great personal and collective works of art that all human beings spend their lives attempting to raise up and to keep from falling down, then the art of creating homes, as distinct from building houses, still has a long way to go, and still remains within the province of magic. Instinct or imitation are not enough to make a home.[38]

One reason that the making of homes is still dependent on "instinct or imitation" is that we simply do not take preparation for that great art seriously. It was for a time taken seriously, but for women only. If women were educated at all in the eighteenth and nineteenth centuries, most were educated to be homemakers. But, of course, this form of education was considered intellectually inferior to that offered men. To count as important, any course or program of education had to prepare one for the public world, not the private world. This legacy exerts its influence today. Courses (few and far between) in homemaking or child-rearing are rarely accepted for college entrance credits, and they are widely regarded as courses for those who do not quite measure up academically.

I am not advocating a semester of sewing and another of cooking. I am asking a deep philosophical question: What does it take to make a home? And I am asking it in connection with the question of happiness. If the domain of personal life – in particular, home life – is one of the great arenas in which happiness may be found, why do we not give it more attention in schools? One reason, already suggested, is that homemaking has been considered "women's sphere," one requiring no special preparation – just the apprentice-ship of daughters to mothers. Today, when daughters rightly expect to claim a place in the public world, they need (or, at least, will be required to undergo) an education exactly like that of their brothers. Then, it would seem, if homemaking is to grow beyond instinct and imitation, both sons and daughters may need special preparation for this great art, since they will be expected to share in its practice.

Another reason – a complex one – for its neglect is the very division under discussion and how it has been interpreted in liberal demo-cratic theory. Adults in a liberal democracy are supposed to be free to pursue their private lives in any way they choose, provided that their choices do not preclude similar choices by others. The fierce protection of privacy in home and family life is part of this legacy of separation. Schools are to concern themselves with preparation for public life; homes (and religious institutions, if a head of family chooses to belong) should control and direct preparation for private life. Of course, this was hypocritical right from the start, because all-female schools did prepare girls for home life, but the work of these schools did not threaten the privacy and autonomy treasured by male heads of households.

However, once we are convinced that the topic is one of the first importance for human flourishing, we can begin to explore its intel-lectual depths. Then the enterprise loses its innocence. It promises genuine equality. It might well threaten the status and organiza-tion of the entire school curriculum. Here I confess to being of two minds. On the one hand, I want to argue that questions of home-making are profoundly philosophical and worthy of rigorous intel-lectual study. On the other, I would hate to see the topic subjected to the tedious and pompous rigmarole characteristic of academic life. I don't think schools kill curiosity and creativity in everything they do, but it is a near thing. Guarding against that result is a topic for another chapter, but I'll touch on it toward the end of this one. Let's suppose for now that homemaking could be well taught if we chose to do so.

Gaston Bachelard provides an intriguing start for the phenomeno-logical study of home and homemaking. He writes of the house:

> For our house is our corner of the world. As has often been said, it is our first universe, a real cosmos in every sense of the word.[39]

As Bachelard analyzes the house, it becomes clear that he is talking about a home and not just a shelter from the elements. He says:

> If I were asked to name the chief benefit of the house, I should say: the house shelters daydreaming, the house protects the dreamer, the house allows one to dream in peace. Thought and experience are not the only things that sanction human values. The values that belong to daydreaming mark humanity in its depths. . . . It derives direct pleasure in its own being.[40]

Thus, a home shelters not just the body, but the imagination. One's first home is "physically inscribed in us," writes Bachelard. "It is a group of organic habits."[41] It is colored by reality, imagination, longing, actual and created memories. Literature, art, and song are filled with descriptions of it and longing for it. And what metaphors it has invited! Bachelard discusses doors, windows, corners, creaking stairs, cellars, attics, chests, drawers, polished tables, and locks in all their real and metaphorical meanings. He invites us to think about our own "Blue Beard" rooms and our fear of cellars.

He speaks of reading a house or room, and this wording leads us to other similar ideas. John Elder, for example, talks of "reading the mountains of home" and of "hiking a poem."[42] Edward Casey asks us to think of rooms (and houses) as extensions of our bodies.[43] We are reminded in all these readings of just how important *place* is in our lives. Think for a moment about how we might "read a room." How is it read by a detective? By an artist? By a child? By a dog? By a burglar? By a vampire?

From the utterly practical, through daydreaming, arises the image, and the image (unanalyzed, warns Bachelard) begets a new being: "This new being is happy man."[44] He does not mean that one has to be a poet to be happy or that poets are always happy; often they are not. But there is something in the image that contributes immeasurably to human flourishing, and it does not stand in need of scholarship. "It is the property of a naive consciousness," writes Bachelard; "in its expression, it is youthful language."[45] All the more reason to treat what is close to home with both reverence and wonder. And here we have uncovered something that adds to our conception of happiness. It is neither raw pleasure nor philosophical contemplation; it is something with roots in the earth and branches in the heavens. It includes the "minor ecstasies" mentioned earlier.

When we read the poems of Hardy, Frost, Dickinson, Whitman, or Heaney, we find them filled with ordinary things (oh, there are classical references, to be sure) – apples, calves, wild roses, gates, fodder, a spoon bait, beggars, polished linoleum – and everyday activities – peeling potatoes, mending wall, playing ball, hiking a trail; and ordinary jobs – clerking, fishing, farming, laying brick, draining pasture, driving trucks, selling hardware, teaching children . . . Who could despise his own work when he sees it celebrated by Walt Whitman? Here is another preview of what must be considered in educating. While we give all children opportunities to learn so that they can be happy in Aristotle's image (or yours and mine?), we should take care not to cause them to think less of the lives their parents have led and of those many of them will also lead. As Whitman put it, we must say to children: "Why what have you thought of yourself?/Is it you then that thought less of yourself?"[46]

Beyond the house and its everyday objects and activities is a region, and again we find it odd that the love of place so celebrated in art and so often a factor in both child and adult happiness is neglected in schools. In the United States, our emphasis is on educating for a global economy; it is an education proudly (and stupidly) designed to transcend place. I visited a classroom recently in which a teacher told visiting parents, "This is a biology class; in here we study living things." Except for the captive human beings, there was not a living thing (visible) in that room. There wasn't even a picture of a living thing! One would never know from its appearance or its subject matter that this school sits within walking distance of the Atlantic Ocean and not far from a fascinating natural region called the *pine barrens* – an area so interesting that the essayist John McPhee addressed a whole book to it.[47] Today's schools ignore it, but place figures prominently in the happiness of individuals, and it is also central to creative work. The great Irish poet William Butler Yeats said, "Creative work must have a fatherland." I would prefer "homeland," but I share the sentiment.

The house and what lies beyond it are clearly places in which happiness is often found. But a home contains people and, if today's social scientists are right, companionship is the single greatest factor in producing the subjective sense of well-being. How well do we prepare children for companionship? If we can believe the figures given to us by Lane and other social scientists, the answer has to be "not very well," since years of education do not correlate highly with happiness and, thus, presumably not with the satisfactions gained through companionship.

In today's school, we insist that all children study algebra and geometry but, in fact, relatively few will use what they learn there in later life. Indeed, some years ago, the comedian Fran Leibowitz urged high school students "to remain unconscious in algebra class. I assure you," she said, "in real life, there is no such thing as algebra." Of course, she exaggerated some. Algebra and other forms of mathematics are enormously important for some purposes and for some people. But the majority could get by well with knowledge of only a few topics in academic mathematics. In contrast, all of us face the tasks of making a home and finding companionship, and most of us become parents. When these great tasks are treated at all in school, they are "add-ons," designed to address a social emergency such as teenage pregnancy, and they never achieve the status of respectability granted to the traditional disciplines.

When we think of preparation for personal life, we think also of development of the *person* who will find (or fail to find) happiness in personal life. Here, again, we move beyond a simple conception of SWB. Consideration of the person suggests some attention to the spiritual, ethical, and personality features of life. Schools usually do something in the line of moral education, but often character education (the approach most often used today) concentrates on socialization and control. Current programs in the United States, for example, emphasize the inculcation of traditional moral virtues, but they often neglect the kinds of social virtues identified by David Hume. Hume reminded us of "a manner, a grace, an ease, a genteelness...which catches our affection,"[48] and he insisted that these qualities have something to do with ethics precisely because they contribute to human happiness.

Today's care theorists (ethicists who make the caring relation basic in moral theory) agree with Hume, and they give some moral credit to the second member – the cared-for – in caring relations. How good we can be depends at least in part on how others treat us. It is easier to parent a sunny, responsive child than a sullen, withdrawn one, easier to teach agreeable, eager students than resistant ones, easier to treat hopeful, cooperative patients than those who have given up and fail to follow directions.

A thoroughly relational view puts less emphasis on moral heroism and more on moral interdependence. Recognizing the domain of human interaction as the principal arena of happiness, it concentrates on creating the conditions under which people are likely to interact with others in mutually supportive ways. Insofar as certain agreeable qualities contribute to these conditions, we value them: politeness, wit, cultivated taste, unhurried serenity, a talent for listening, hospitality. And we are led to redefine responsibility as response-ability, the ability to respond positively to others and not just to fulfill assigned duties. When we think seriously about happiness and education, we extend the range of qualities we seek to develop.

The themes suggested so far will be expanded when we consider what might be done in schools. But, as a preview, I should say a bit about the other great domain in which some of us find happiness – occupational life. In today's education, occupational (economic) life is the focus of our attention. We want every child to succeed, and this has come to mean that every child should be prepared for college and the sort of work that requires a college education. What of all the children who will become bus and truck drivers, retail sales clerks, appliance repair people, construction workers, material handlers, heavy equipment operators, railway engineers and conductors, house painters, plumbers, bakers, farm workers, beauticians, postal workers, cooks, waiters, hotel clerks, house and office cleaners, auto mechanics and salespeople, dog and horse groomers, telephone/electric line workers, prison guards, hospital attendants, grounds keepers, maintenance workers, managers of laundromats and dry cleaning shops, installers of burglar alarms, carpet layers, window washers, steel workers, fishermen, sailors, caterers, cashiers, chimney sweeps, roofers, makers of china and glassware, decorators, musicians, florists, entertainers, moving men... and what would happen to our society if no one were willing to do this work? Do these people represent failures of schooling, or do we fail them when we lead them to believe that only economic success *is* success?

Perhaps every child should hear Walt Whitman's lovely "Song for Occupations" and be invited to create a new song for the present day in his or her own place. It is commendable, of course, to give every child an opportunity to choose college-related study if he or she is so inclined, but no child should be made to feel that other forms of work are only for those who aren't up to the work that really counts. This is a delicate and difficult issue, but teachers who think it through carefully may begin to stretch the standard curriculum so that it includes the interests and talents of all children and not just the few.

Deeper Than SWB

Education, of all enterprises, cannot neglect what I earlier called the normative aspect of happiness. In the better of his two conceptions of human flourishing, Aristotle (like most thoughtful teachers before and after him) put great emphasis on that component of happiness that arises from the practice of virtue. According to this view, people cannot really be happy unless they have a sound character and exercise the virtues characteristic of such a character. If we take the view of those who use SWB as the definition of happiness, Aristotle's claim is doubtful. Yet most of us in education believe something like it. We hope that children will learn to derive some happiness from doing the right thing, from satisfying the demands of their souls. We shrink from people who are happily untroubled by the misery of those around them. There is a kind of happiness that creeps through, even in the presence of pain and misery, when we know that we have done what we can to improve things. Thus, education for happiness must include education for *un*happiness as well, and that will be the focus of Chapter 2. Children should learn (something many seem to know almost instinctively) that sharing the unhappiness of others, paradoxically, brings with it a form of happiness. This is a major conclusion reached by care theorists, who argue that those things we do to improve the relations of which we are part will work for our benefit as well as that of others.

Finally, I want to say something about the oft-vaunted pleasures of the mind that we as educators are supposed to promote. These are of two kinds. The first, familiar to all teachers, is the body of intellectual work thought to stimulate minds. Our hope is that children will seek out this material because it promises a form of pleasure. The second (referred to in note 8) might be called the *psychological view*. From this perspective, pleasures of the mind are those memories, anticipations, associations, and imaginative colorings that add pleasure to ordinary events. Both types require further discussion, but here I want merely to introduce some thoughts on the first (or schoolteacher) type. For me, these pleasures are real but, like Whitman, I do not despise what gives pleasure to others, nor do I insist that others must get pleasure from what pleases me. However, because I have always loved learning, reading, thinking, teaching, and discussing, I would like children to have opportunities to share these pleasures. How can we provide such opportunities?

For example, should we introduce children to poetry in school? Poetry can help us to connect the various domains of life. It gives delight. It helps us to find a bit of happiness in unhappiness and a core of unhappiness in momentary happiness. It can contribute through that powerful thing – the image – to happiness now and in the future. I have never encountered a child under, say, seven who doesn't love poetry. But I almost never encounter a teenager who likes it. What have we done in our schools? We've wrecked the experience of poetry. We have poisoned something that we say we teach because of the lifelong delight it offers. Whereas the best poetry connects us to everyday life, school-taught poetry separates us even further from it. Do kids really have to know the difference between dactylic hexameter and iambic pentameter? (We might like them to hear the difference.) Do they have to take apart every phrase and metaphor? Do we have to give tests on poetry? When we say that we are offering something to children that should increase their lifelong happiness, we should take care not to destroy the possibility. Some things, even in schools, should be offered as gifts – no strings, no tests attached.

In my own mathematics teaching, and even today in introducing graduate students to elementary logic, I have often used *Alice in Wonderland* for its wonderful examples of logic and illogic. But I don't give tests on it! It is a free gift, offered to increase pleasure and the possibility of incidental learning. G. K. Chesterton, in comments on *Alice*, remarked on the proclivity of teachers to wreck that which should be shared with delight. He wrote:

> Poor, poor, little Alice! She has not only been caught and made to do lessons, she has been forced to inflict lessons on others. Alice is now not only a school girl but a school mistress. The holiday is over and Dodgson is again a don. There will be lots and lots of examination papers, with questions like: (1) What do you know about the following: mimsy, gimble, haddocks' eyes, treacle-wells, beautiful soup? (2) Record all the moves in the chess game in *Through the Looking Glass*, and give diagrams. (3) Outline the practical policy of the

White Knight for dealing with the social problem of green whiskers. (4) Distinguish between Tweedledum and Tweedledee.[49]

Not everything can be learned incidentally, but many things can be. Much of value sticks to us, as Robert Frost said, "like burrs" when we walk in the fields. There should be lots of free gifts in education, lots of aimless but delight-filled walks in the fields of learning. Although we agree that there is more to happiness than SWB, it doesn't hurt to pause now and then and ask children and ourselves: How much fun are you having?

In this chapter, we have discussed several views of happiness and its pursuit. It seems to occur in different domains of everyday life; I can be happy in one and unhappy in another. It has a normative aspect and a spiritual one; I am affected by what my community expects of me, and I can be deeply affected by spiritual connections or lack of them. It is influenced by personality. Although it seems to occur episodically, we seek happiness for our lives as a whole. It involves pleasure, but there are many forms of pleasure, and some seem less conducive to long-term happiness than others. Still, pleasure or fun, if it is not harmful, should be freely enjoyed. Happiness, we saw, is often identified with the satisfaction of needs and wants and, especially, with the desire to be free of suffering. If we cannot be sure of achieving happiness, can we work effectively to avoid suffering and unhappiness? We turn to that question next.

2

Suffering and Unhappiness

M ill spoke of happiness as pleasure and the absence of pain. If we believe that the "motion of our lives is toward happiness," then we have to consider ways in which to reduce pain. In a naive approach, this seems right, and it may seem not only right in a simple sense but right in a fully justified sense after we have examined and criticized arguments that give pain and suffering a privileged place in human life. There are those who argue that pain and suffering do play a positive role in human flourishing, and those arguments carry into education and child-rearing. The slogan "no pain, no gain" is heard in every realm of human endeavor. Should we endorse it?

Throughout this chapter (and the entire book), I will use a pragmatic test to decide whether or not to adopt a particular position: What will be the effects of adopting X? Analysis of effects will be guided by care theory; that is, among the effects considered, I will be concerned with the effects on caring relations and, especially, on those we care for.

Suffering and Meaning

Is there meaning in suffering? In some religious traditions, an affirmative answer is assumed. Perhaps the most influential school of thought on the link between suffering and meaning involves the notion of soul-making. I will explore this very important idea in a later section of this chapter. For now, notice that the question itself may mislead us. We hesitate to reply straight-out no, but many of us would like to avoid the suggestion that meaning *inheres* in suffering – that meaning has been implanted there to be found. As we will see, such an assumption implies that suffering is inflicted on us so that we will learn something valuable embedded in the suffering. If this is what is meant by the initial question, I will respond with a firm no. The effects of accepting the idea that suffering contains meaning somehow necessary for human flourishing are likely to be harmful to both those we care for and our caring relationships.

We can hardly deny, however, that people do often find meaning in suffering. Rejecting the idea that meaning is inherent in suffering, one can still consider the question Can we create some meaning out of suffering? The history of humanity forces us to answer yes. But is the task of creating meaning from suffering somehow obligatory? Is it something we should do and can do if we just make up our minds to it? Some existentialists, for example, suggest that, whatever happens to us, we – as essentially free beings – can always choose our attitude toward it, even if we cannot escape the suffering itself. This suggestion is reminiscent of Greek thought, especially that of the Stoics.

Viktor Frankl, an eminent existentialist psychiatrist, argued this line. He used as evidence the remarkable variety of behaviors displayed by concentration camp inmates. Some gave up and died, some became meanly self-protective, and still others became almost saintly in their altruism. This suggested to Frankl that human beings are free to choose their attitude toward situations of great suffering. I will argue that the undeniable variety of responses to suffering proves no such thing. Because we are uniquely different beings, with different pasts and different fears, our situations are never identical, no matter how alike they seem from the outside. The choices we make in situations of great stress are never completely free; they are always at least partly conditioned by our past experiences.

Frankl went so far as to say that

> existential analysis recognizes the meaning of suffering, installs suffering in a place of honor in life. Suffering and trouble belong to life as much as fate and death. None of these can be subtracted from life without destroying its meaning. . . . Only under the white heat of suffering, does life gain shape and form.[1]

Frankl does caution us that a passive acceptance of suffering must not be chosen too readily. The suffering must be genuinely unavoidable. Then the suffering may be endured and "noble." Suffering unnecessarily, giving up without a fight, is "ignoble" suffering. But who is to say when a person has objectively reached the end of his tether? One person may suffer nobly under treatment X, while another exhibits multiple signs of human weakness. Change the treatment to Y, however, and the responses may be reversed.

I think here of Winston Smith in Orwell's *Nineteen Eighty-Four*.[2] Faced with his greatest fear, deliberately inflicted on him by the evil O'Brien, Winston betrays both Julia, his beloved, and what he takes to be his most basic human capacity – to choose. As a result, he is a thoroughly broken man. In another situation, one that might seem even more horrendous to others of us, Winston might have suffered nobly. Frankl asks too much.

The root of conceptual difficulty lies in Frankl's basic assumption. He says, "Three factors characterize human existence as such: man's spirituality, his freedom, his responsibility."[3] Where do these characteristics come from? Frankl draws on a long tradition of supposing that truly "human" characteristics must differentiate the human animal from all others. But why? Even if we can identify characteristics that belong either in kind or degree exclusively to human beings, why are not those we share with others in the animal kingdom just as fundamental? Why not list susceptibility to suffering, mother love, the instinct for self-defense, our need for social interaction, and all the physical needs with which we are so familiar? Further, it seems reasonable to question the concept of essential freedom (behaviorists have denied it entirely),[4] and today's care theorists define responsibility as response-ability, a capacity neither essential nor innate but learned and developed in actual life with other beings. From this latter perspective, there is limited freedom, and response-ability is largely (but not entirely) dependent on how one has been treated by others.[5]

Can we imagine human life without suffering? Pointing to the reality of loss and death, Frankl is certainly right to say that suffering is part of natural life. But should it be given a "place of honor" or should we dedicate ourselves to eliminating as much suffering as we can? The worry here is that, in glorifying suffering, we will inflict it too easily on one another and fail to help in time of trouble. Some suppose their misery is merited (we'll discuss this next) and others that they must seek meaning in it. Among the latter, some construct an answer that lifts them out of suffering; others sink into it as though no happiness were ever theirs.

What are we to make of the contradictory stories we hear from some great thinkers? Frankl cites Goethe approvingly. Said Goethe: "There is no predicament that we cannot ennoble either by doing or enduring."[6] But that same Goethe – often considered an optimist – also said:

> I will say nothing against the course of my existence. But at bottom it has been nothing but pain and burden, and I can affirm that during the whole of my 75 years, I have not had four weeks of genuine well-being. It is but the perpetual rolling of a rock that must be raised up again forever.[7]

This statement is so completely at odds with Goethe's work and other comments made even in his old age that one wonders again how greatly people are affected in their assessments by moods, recent disappointments, minor failures, and the like. Juxtapose his own gloomy description of his life as "pain and burden" with this description by an admiring critic:

> The restoration of peace, the hope for a new era of national greatness bring back to the septuagenarian all the joyfulness and vigour of his youth.... His whole being seems illumined, and he seems to illumine whatever comes within his ken....[This is] a man who to the very end of his life drinks in the joys of existence, in whom the sunset, the clouds, the winds, the glance of a beautiful eye, the sound of a gentle voice, call forth melodies of the deepest power.[8]

Goethe obviously cultivated pleasures of the mind, not only the pleasures of learning, thinking, expressing, but also the pleasures added to bodily sensations by attitudes of appreciation, memories, and pleasing associations. However, we can now discern something sinister in pleasures of the mind construed in the latter way. If appreciation and pleasant associations can add significantly to the pleasure of an event, so may dislikes, fears, and unpleasant associations change an otherwise pleasant experience into an unhappy one. Thus we are faced with what might be called *pains of the mind*. And just as pleasures of the mind are not *all* in the mind, neither are such pains. Both are rooted in disposition as well as past experience. Goethe, a prototypically joyous artist, suffered pains of the mind. If he did, what can we demand of ordinary people? How much control do we have over our personalities and casts of mind?

As James points out, one cannot bring someone struck with gloom out of it by saying, "Stuff and nonsense, get out in the open air!" or "Cheer up, old fellow, you'll be all right ere-long."[9] James says, "Our troubles lie too deep for *that* cure.... We need a life not correlated with death, a health not liable to illness, a kind of good that will not perish, a good in fact that flies beyond the Goods of nature."[10] This, we have already seen, is what the Greeks sought; it is also the Good sought by the great religions. I have rejected this approach (as James did), and I agree with James that the melancholy soul is not entirely unrealistic but merely more deeply affected by that which inevitably occurs in "the normal process of life."[11]

Escape from melancholy seems to involve a deliberate effort to re-member the joys that are also part of most lives. Is Frankl right, then, after all? Is it up to us to choose a noble attitude? It does seem right to look fairly on the world and one's own life, remembering joys as well as pains. But Frankl goes too far. It is not always possible to choose our attitude; circumstances or evil-doers may foreclose what free-dom we might have had, physical or emotional illness may prevent us from feeling joy, our constitution may not be a happy one, or we may simply need time to recover from a disappointment. Finally, if we give suffering a "place of honor," we may contribute to its occurrence and continuance.

Young people should learn about the ways in which others have looked at suffering. They should hear heroic tales of noble responses to suffering, but they should also hear about unrelieved suffering and make a commitment to compassion. They should hear about ways to capture small joys, to escape melancholy without damaging the possibility of future happiness, to avoid the extremes of seeking perfect happiness on the one hand and of glorifying suffering on the other. Perhaps most important of all, they should learn to feel some social responsibility to reduce suffering.

Frankl glorified suffering because he believed that, without it, life would lose meaning. Religionists have glorified it because they believe that it will somehow be turned about – that greater happiness will be the eventual reward of those who undergo unmerited suffering. The philosopher Nietzsche glorified it as a way to become stronger and more powerful. Consider what he wished for his disciples:

> To those human beings who are of any concern to me I wish suf-
> fering, desolation, sickness, ill-treatment, indignities – I wish that
> they should not remain unfamiliar with profound self-contempt, the
> torture of self-mistrust, the wretchedness of the vanquished: I have
> no pity for them, because I wish them the only thing that can prove
> today whether one is worth anything or not – that one endures.[12]

Nietzsche follows this dreadful passage with two sections on education. He advocates a *hard* school and *hard* discipline, a school so
designed that

> much is demanded; and sternly demanded; that the good, even the
> exceptional, is demanded as the norm; that praise is rare, that indul-
> gence is non-existent; that blame is apportioned sharply, objectively,
> without regard for talent or antecedents.[13]

He goes on to insist that both soldier and scholar are best shaped
by this hard discipline. He is wrong, and we have access to many
life stories to show that he is wrong. Moreover, the soldier is shaped
mainly by external discipline, the true scholar by internal discipline
that is often engendered by love and gentleness.

Oddly, if we make small changes in Nietzsche's statement on the
hard school, we can find similar statements pervading today's recommendations on education. Both Nietzsche and some present-day
policymakers overlook the obvious fact that making the exceptional
the norm simply changes the definition of what is exceptional and
leaves even more students feeling inferior. Those who were inferior
before are still inferior. A beneficial change would require abandoning any personal use of words like *exceptional* in favor of occasional
use for specific acts and in special domains – domains chosen by the
students. Moreover, it is not the purpose of schooling to make all children into either soldiers or scholars. And it is certainly not our hope
that all children will learn "obeying and commanding."[14]

Nietzsche extolled suffering because he believed that the meaning of life is best described in the will to power. Frankl often quoted
Nietzsche favorably because he believed that the purpose of life is to
exercise an essential freedom – a form of power over ourselves. But
Frankl did not recommend, as Nietzsche did, the deliberate infliction of suffering. Having himself suffered so horribly at the hands of

others, he sought meaning in that suffering. He supposed, mistakenly, that the inevitability of some suffering in human life implies a loss of meaning if we somehow escape most of it. If we reject the views of both Nietzsche and Frankl, we must find some other approach to meaning. I have already suggested serious consideration of Tillich's ultimate concern, but I have not yet explored fully what might be meant by this. As we continue the search, we will see that an ultimate concern takes many forms and that it may even take a sort of comprehensive form – that is, it may be described as a set of smaller concerns that, taken together, constitute an ultimate concern. This possibility will help us to put the idea of an ultimate concern into the hands and minds of all children, not only those with a deep religious commitment or an existential-heroic cast of personality.

I have not rejected entirely the notion that we can construct some meaning from suffering. If the construction of new meanings contributes to a happier life, it is certainly worth trying to do. When we are able to do this, however, it is because some meaning already exists for us and makes it possible to use the suffering in its service. I want to insist that suffering is a bad thing – something to be avoided, relieved, and never deliberately inflicted on another. I will argue in the next section that there is a form of suffering, healthy guilt, that should be accepted and even cultivated in ourselves, but we will still prefer to avoid it by behaving in ways that do not bring it on. Suffering is not essential to meaning, and we do not risk losing our essential humanity if we reduce it to a minimum.

Merited Suffering

Here I will take, and try to defend, a bold position: No one deserves the deliberate infliction of pain or suffering by another. I am not the first to make such an assertion, of course, but today we seem to hear it even less often than fifty years ago.[15] Self-infliction of the suffering of guilt should be encouraged under appropriate conditions, and I will say more about this later, but the deliberate infliction of pain on those who do wrong simply does not pass the pragmatic test. Its effects seem to be harmful overall, and it certainly does not help in establishing relations of care and trust.

There is no convincing evidence, for example, that capital punishment deters murder, and it inflicts considerable suffering on both those who undergo it and those who must inflict it.[16] Similarly, there is little evidence that corporal punishment helps to keep order either in a community or in an individual soul. Many, if not most, American schools maintain order without it, and professional opinion is strongly against its use by parents. When people are a clear danger to others, they must be imprisoned or otherwise restrained but, even then, there is no reason beyond vengeance to deprive them for long periods of sunshine, fresh air, and companionship. The suffering of imprisonment should not be deliberately inflicted *as suffering*, but it may well be an unavoidable side effect of society's need to protect itself. If we reject the notion that suffering is deserved, we may find more enlightened ways than we now employ to protect society and restore its deviants to useful citizenship.[17]

In addition to physical suffering, some communities deliberately inflict psychic suffering on wrongdoers in the form of shame. Indeed, there are those today who would like to see an increase in the use of shame to socialize young people. However, experienced psychiatrists often argue against shaming those who commit infractions. James Gilligan, for example, provides persuasive evidence that shame diminishes the self and generates violence.[18] Similarly, the philosopher Bernard Williams argues that shame tends to be narcissistic; it turns the attention of one shamed to her own condition and away from that of her victim.[19] Guilt, in contrast, keeps the focus on those who have been harmed and begs for restitution.

It is useful to distinguish between healthy guilt and unhealthy guilt. Healthy guilt is earned in the sense that we really have done something to harm or wrong another, and we sincerely want to make whatever restitution is possible. Further, there *is* something we can do; we are not helpless. Unhealthy guilt is guilt that persists even when objective outsiders see no reason for it or when either no attempt at restitution is made or none can be made. In the latter cases, unhealthy guilt is similar in its effects to shame – it focuses on the wrong party and nurses its own unhappiness without helping the one wronged. If we give up the idea that the deliberate infliction of pain on others is sometimes justified, it will be necessary to encourage the cultivation of healthy guilt. We should want to live so as to merit as little guilt as possible and, when we deserve it, to make restitution.

I said earlier that the idea of merited suffering (inflicted from the outside) does not pass the pragmatic test. How does it fail? First, the threat of pain as punishment does not seem to be effective, and those who suffer such punishment often become more angry and dangerous as a result. When the threat is directed at young people, it is dramatically ineffective, in part because the young mistakenly see themselves as invulnerable and, even more important, because many have not developed a reflective cast of mind that would use the threat of punishment as a deterrent. The possibility of being tried as an adult or even caught and tried at all just does not enter their thinking.

Second, the idea of merited suffering has led to widespread anxiety. Many sufferers who deserve comfort and support (from themselves and others) go about asking themselves: What did I do to deserve this? When the suffering is clearly unconnected to any act of the sufferer, this question and its accompanying mental agony are less than helpful; they are harmful. When there is a connection, reflection can help to prevent future occurrences. We *do* sometimes bring unpleasant things on ourselves by carelessness, refusal to take advice, or some other lapse of prudence or virtue. Even then, we do not *deserve* whatever actual pain results, but we do have to recognize our role in incurring it. We should emerge wiser from such experience. Injuries to ourselves induce feelings of regret and resolutions to exercise greater prudence, but they do not usually create guilt. However, when our lapses hurt others, we do feel guilt and recognize the attendant suffering as merited. Then it makes sense to accept the pain of guilt and work toward a concrete form of restitution. There is no absolution, and forms of promised absolution that excuse us from restitution only make it more likely that we will lapse again. A good part of virtue is self-protective. We do not welcome the merited suffering of guilt.

The challenge is to get the cause–effect relation in proper order. When we have done something that harms or wrongs another, we deserve the pain of guilt. When we have done something careless or stupid, we may bring unwelcome consequences on ourselves, but we do not deserve the resulting pain. However, when we experience an episode of suffering, it is not necessarily (or even usually) the case that we have done something to deserve the suffering or to bring it on ourselves.[20] Other good people should not increase that suffering by suggesting that it is somehow merited (remember here Job's "friends" who self-righteously suggested that possibility to him), or that it contains a meaningful message, or that the experience will make the sufferer stronger. What the sufferer needs is comfort, consolation.

47

The religious traditions – I refer here to the three great monotheisms – are not innocent in the perpetuation of suffering. True, they also offer consolation and urge charity and compassion, but both the Jewish penitential tradition and the Christian doctrine of original sin lay a heavy burden of guilt on humankind. Paul Ricoeur comments:

> The harm that has been done to souls, during the centuries of Christianity, first by the literal interpretation of the story of Adam, and then by the confusion of this myth, treated as history, with later speculations, principally Augustinian, about original sin, will never be adequately told.[21]

This legacy provides another powerful reason for rejecting the notion that we deserve our suffering. Believing that we are sinful by nature and that every episode of suffering has somehow been earned is debilitating. It also makes us feel godlike when we inflict suffering on others. We feel both powerful and justified.

The distinction drawn between healthy and unhealthy guilt seems basically right but, as we delve a bit deeper, we see a more complex picture. Sometimes unhealthy guilt is unavoidable. It is our guilt (we have done something we regard as bad), but it is inflicted nonetheless by external forces. Anthony Cunningham discusses the case of Sethe in Toni Morrison's *Beloved*.[22] Sethe decided in desperation to kill her children rather than have them subjected to the pain and humiliation of slavery, and she succeeded in killing the baby, "Beloved." Ever after, she suffered guilt, and the suffering did not diminish with the years. It didn't help for others to tell her to shake it off, to get on with her life. As Cunningham so effectively analyzes the situation, Sethe would have suffered guilt no matter what decision she had made. Contrary to the Kantian insistence that a moral agent can always choose according to the moral law and shrug off as "nothing to me" those consequences beyond her moral control, human beings – good human beings – are just not built that way.[23] Sethe, like all good parents, accepted the responsibility for protecting her children and, when she was unable to do so, she suffered inconsolable grief and guilt.

Was the guilt unhealthy? Of course. It accomplished nothing and made many things worse. But notice that it was Sethe's essential goodness that made her vulnerable to such guilt.[24] A parent who cared less might have justified her act and moved on.

Consider another suffering mother, Sophie, in William Styron's *Sophie's Choice*.[25] In this story, a cruel Nazi officer forces Sophie to choose one of her children to accompany her to freedom and leave the other to die in a concentration camp. A Kantian might say that Sophie should have refused the choice. Both children would have died, but Sophie would not be at all culpable morally. The only thing under her control as a moral agent was to make the moral choice, refusing to comply with the Nazi's order. Could she have escaped guilt this way? Trapped in such a horrible situation, Sophie was not thinking of guilt but of love and loss. Guilt was an inevitable side effect. In tragedies of this sort, the victim is not trying to preserve herself as a moral agent. She is trying to protect her loved ones. There may be no greater evil ever committed than to destroy at one blow both a loved one and the moral agency of one who loves.

That observation leaves us with a challenge to my original bold assertion. Do I really believe that no one deserves to have pain deliberately inflicted on him? Doesn't basic justice cry out for the perpetrator of cruelty to suffer as he has made others suffer? I will reaffirm my assertion. To begin with, if we are decent people, we cannot possibly inflict suffering that comes even close to what these moral monsters inflict. We could not bear the "weight of filthy images" that accompanies the deliberate infliction of such suffering.[26] The practice still does not pass the pragmatic test. It does not make things better. Indeed, psychopaths sometimes welcome cruel punishment, not because they feel guilty but because it somehow proves that others (the decent folks) are not so very different from themselves.

What we have to do instead is to help all children develop the dual capacity for caring and for healthy guilt when they violate their responsibility as carers. Beyond that – beneath it, perhaps, as a foundation – we must provide the conditions under which children can be truly happy. Happy people are not cruel and violent and, because they do suffer with others, they will act to prevent or alleviate that suffering.

Soul-Making

We must return briefly to the idea rejected earlier – that meaning is somehow inherent in suffering. The difficulty in denying this is that one must deny a central premise of almost every form of religion – namely, that there is purpose in the universe and that this purpose must somehow be pointed at the good. One could, of course, accept the possibility of purpose in the universe and still reject the notion that the purpose (whatever it is) has anything at all to do with the well-being of human beings, or one could even argue that the purpose is not directed at human good but, rather, at human misery. Logically, we can neither deny nor affirm that there is purpose in the universe. Its order suggests that there may be purpose. But what can this purpose (if there is one) have to do with human beings? This is the question that the great religions have tried to answer and that skeptics have answered by saying, Nothing! And we had better band together to help ourselves![27]

In Hinduism and Buddhism, suffering is sometimes considered illusionary; that is, there would be no suffering if we perceived things rightly. This can be a cruel attitude, suggesting that sufferers can overcome their pain – just "cheer up" – if they take the trouble to acquire the appropriate knowledge. But there is a compassionate side, too. Even if suffering is, at bottom, illusionary, it is acknowledged that the suffering is real for individual sufferers. Good people will try to relieve that suffering. Still, there is a lingering stigma attached to suffering. Sufferers either deserve their pain (for past transgressions) or bring it on themselves through lack of knowledge and discipline. Those who suffer are guilty, at least, of ignorance.

Suffering is a major topic for every religion. In Christianity, theodicies have been developed to explain the problem of evil. The basic question is, How can there be an all-good, all-knowing, and all-powerful God when evil and suffering surround us? It would take us too far afield to explore this question fully,[28] but one solution is so embedded in questions of happiness and suffering that we must consider it. This is the idea that the purpose of human life is soul-making and that suffering is somehow necessary to this purpose.

Its simplest expression is found in C. S. Lewis's response to his wife's dreadful pain in dying of cancer:

> But is it credible that such extremities of torture should be necessary for us? Well, take your choice. The tortures occur. If they are unnecessary, then there is no God or a bad one. If there is a good God, then these tortures are necessary. For no even moderately good Being could possibly inflict or permit them if they weren't.[29]

Lewis overlooks several possibilities. There may be a creator-God (as discussed by Spinoza and Einstein) who has no relation to us as individuals. There may be strong competing evil forces in the universe responsible for suffering (the Manichaean solution); that is, God may be powerful but not omnipotent. Alternatively, God may be fallible or still struggling toward a better self;[30] he (she, or it) may be sorry for the harms inflicted. There may be many gods, only some of whom are benevolent. In any case, Lewis has not answered the question of why such extremes of suffering are necessary for some of us and not others. When the question Why me? is asked, the answer seems to be You need it more than others, and we are left with the awful feeling that, after all, we do somehow deserve the suffering.

Lewis's simple answer is inadequate in other ways. It does not consider the problem of animal pain. In what way is *this* necessary? Lewis does treat the problem in another volume.[31] Like so many other apologists for innocent suffering, he first questions whether and to what degree animals suffer. He points out that their lives are not wholly characterized by the terror of being killed and devoured. Finally, realizing that he has begged the question – why an all-good God would create a world in which its creatures must eat one another to stay alive – he suggests that Satan or some other fallen angel introduced this evil feature into the world and that "man's" fall helped to perpetuate pain in the animal kingdom.

John Hick, in struggling with the same problem, has suggested that the better question is, Why were the lower animals created at all?[32] In this line of thinking, all of creation points toward human life, and suffering in the animal kingdom serves an instrumental purpose in teaching humans about their special place and obligations.

None of these answers is satisfactory. When we add to the question of animal pain the suffering of little children, the problem is insurmountable. In Dostoevsky's *The Brothers Karamazov*, Ivan gives a devastating (and irrefutable) argument against the notion that an all-good God created or watches over the world.[33] Recounting stories of horrible childhood pain, Ivan asks his brother under what conditions he might, if he had the power, accept or establish such a world of pain. Alyosha cannot answer but insists that somehow (through Christ) all will eventually come right. Alyosha lives by faith, Ivan by logic and evidence.

The only weak spot in Ivan's argument is that the examples he offers involve cruelties inflicted on children by human beings. These are acts of moral evil, and one could argue that human beings are entirely responsible for them. To make the argument stronger, we need to consider natural evil – all the illnesses, accidents, birth defects, starvation, and pains of deprivation that children suffer. One cannot argue that a three-year-old dying of some painful disease is gaining a more worthy soul. One can at best say that the child will go directly to heaven without having to earn anything through soul-building. But what of the nine-year-old who supposedly has attained the age of reason? Is she supposed to struggle for the meaning of her suffering? To endure and earn stars in her crown?

We see also a connection between the suffering of natural evil and that inflicted by moral evil. If the suffering inflicted by natural evil can be justified, then perhaps that which is deliberately inflicted by human beings can also be justified. Perhaps such pain, fully justified by the behavior of its victims, is not a moral evil. Perhaps it is a moral obligation to inflict such pain. This is the position I have rejected.

The point of this discussion on religion and suffering is not to teach agnosticism or atheism, although it is important that young people come to understand that many good people have rejected religion not only for logical reasons but, perhaps more important, for ethical reasons.[34] The point, in a discussion of happiness, is to find ways of alleviating suffering. When we believe that suffering is necessary for the purpose of soul-making, we may become too accepting of suffering in both ourselves and others. When we believe, instead, that there is neither purpose nor meaning in the suffering that arises in the natural world, we move toward the freedom to seek happiness. Moreover, we should be even less tolerant of the moral evils by which human beings inflict suffering on others. We reject *entirely* the idea that the deliberate infliction of suffering can be justified.

I should make it clear that my rejection does not imply a lack of admiration for those who endure unavoidable suffering with courage and optimism. Such people set noble examples for all of us, but it is their vital capacity to find what happiness they can that should move us, not their ability to stand more and more pain.

I have not, either, rejected the obvious truth that some people find or, better, "construct" meaning out of their suffering. There are countless examples of wonderful people who turn their own pain and

suffering into channels of service to others. It can be argued, however, that these people already had meaning in their lives – meaning
usually derived from caring relations – and now that meaning has become more focused as a result of their suffering. It is not the suffering
itself that held meaning.

Unhappiness and the Loss of Meaning

We saw in Chapter 1 that, despite growing prosperity and better
health care, people in market democracies are less happy than they
were some years ago. What accounts for this? We could argue, as Paul
Tillich did in the mid-twentieth century, that we are living in an age
characterized by the fear of meaninglessness and that such fear can
be traced to loss of connection to God.[35] But the loss documented
by Lane and others is still more recent. If the problem is spiritual
longing,[36] it has been aggravated in the past two decades. It would be
a mistake to brush this possibility aside, and I will devote some space
in a later chapter to the possibility of spiritual renewal.

Let's consider here another set of possibilities. Perhaps the information age is just wearing us out. In Alan Lightman's novel *The Diagnosis*,
we are reminded forcefully of what we experience daily:[37] technical
medicine without human touch, constant pressure to pile up material acquisitions, e-mail, voice mail, FedEx, message centers, phones
ringing (even on trains and boardwalks), constant checks on time,
traffic jams, road rage, machine failures, choking smog, airline de-
lays, artificial sounds mimicking nature, television drowning us in
drug ads while the nation fights a war on drugs, sex, and violence-
soaked entertainment, brief "quality time" for the children in our
lives, overscheduled children, acute body consciousness in an age of
increasing obesity, junk food. . . .

These things are bound to take a toll. Newspapers are filled with
bizarre stories in addition to international concerns and the usual
human tragedies: A man dressed like Elvis stalks Willie Brown, mayor
of San Francisco; an artist produces a photograph of herself as a nude
female Christ presiding with twelve black disciples at "Yo Mama's Last
Supper"; young workers in Clinton's administration remove all the *W*'s
from White House keyboards; a man surrenders to police after being
accused of deceiving women into removing their shoes (a spider!) so
that he can stroke their feet.

There is a general erosion of trust. We don't believe our political representatives or the stories we are told about national and international events. In schools, we demand "accountability" because we no longer know the teachers of our children and, too often, it is clear that the school does not know our children. We endorse (and then find embarrassingly foolish) zero-tolerance rules, we tolerate (even insist upon) metal detectors in our schools, random drug testing and locker searches, armed or unarmed police in the corridors, locked doors that present clear hazards in case of fire, high-stakes tests that terrify our kids and remove the joy from learning, ridiculously short (twenty-minute) lunch "hours" that sometimes start as early as 10:30 in the morning, lists of rules and penalties that have displaced near-universal acceptance of general civility, a pathological level of competition in our "best" schools, building designs (e.g., the panopticon) that make every nook and cranny visible for surveillance, video equipment donated with the agreement that ads will be displayed, an overemphasis on winning at sports and participation for the sake of having something on one's college application, closed campuses, and parking lot violence.

None of the things listed in the previous paragraph were common in schools fifty years ago. They can be listed among both the causes and effects of a widespread malaise attributable at least in part to technological changes. If we pause long enough to reflect on these changes, we realize that the sweeping recommendations of some scholars – for example, David Myers – may not address our problems at the appropriate level. To say, for example, that our culture should welcome children, reward initiative without encouraging exploitive greed, balance liberties, and take care of the soul gains easy assent but just doesn't accomplish much.[38] We need much more specific help in the form of options, and that is what I will explore in the chapters to come.

Jean Baudrillard, the French social/media critic and semiologist, has said that we live in an age dominated by the object and by spectacle.[39] He contends that the objects are now, in a significant sense, in charge; it is almost as if *they* had plans and purposes and we have become objects to be used and pushed around by these new subject-objects. We are no longer subjects. Certainly the unfortunate Bill Chalmers of *The Diagnosis* feels this way, and most of us feel this way from time to time. For example, I really do not care at all who reads my e-mail. Why would anyone want to read it? But I am now forced by my university to add password security to protect my e-mail. Forced. I will not be able to access my own e-mail unless I do this. I understand that, if hackers can get into my account, they can (somehow) more easily get into those of others, so I should comply willingly. Is this not exactly what Baudrillard is talking about? I, the once unique locus of existential valuation, am now an object directed by technology. *It* is the subject; I merely obey.

On his second claim, that we are spectators enthralled by spectacle, there can be scarcely any argument. Some of us resist, but the vast majority (in technologically developed nations) have given in. Baudrillard writes:

> The only real pleasure in the world is to watch things "turn" into catastrophe, to emerge finally from determinacy and indeterminacy, from chance and necessity, and enter the realm of vertiginous connections, for better or worse, where things reach their end without passing through their means, where events attain their effects without passing through causes. Like wit, like seduction – where things proceed not by the detours of sense but via the speedways of appearance.[40]

Can Baudrillard be right? I watch very little television – typically a half hour of news each night. Tonight I will almost certainly see violence between Israelis and Palestinians, the misery of refugees in Afghanistan and Guinea, the further misery of earthquake victims in El Salvador and India, and a political scandal or two. Am I looking forward to the show? Will I sip coffee or a cordial as I watch? Will you? Will we achieve a form of pleasure and, yet, become more unhappy? These are important questions.

Baudrillard points out, too, that even our vacations often deepen our unhappiness:

> A human being can find in a vacation a greater boredom than in everyday life – a redoubled boredom, because it is made up of all the elements of happiness and distraction. The important point is the predestination of vacations to boredom, the bitter and triumphal foreboding that there's no escaping this. How could we suppose that people were going to disavow their daily life and look for an alternative to it? On the contrary, they'll make a destiny out of it: intensify it while seeming to do the opposite, plunge into it to the point of ecstasy, seal the monotony of it with even greater monotony.[41]

What a gloomy picture. This does not always happen. Some people, at least sometimes, enjoy their vacations and come home refreshed, but Baudrillard's main point is well taken: How can we disavow our daily lives and hope to find happiness? As we continue our study of happiness, we will give much attention to everyday life as a source of joy and contentment.

I will end this chapter with a reminder. Suffering is not to be glorified, not to be installed in "a place of honor." It is to be eliminated, reduced, relieved. Sufferers should be helped and consoled, not regarded with suspicion. There is no purpose behind the suffering of natural evil, and there is no justification for the deliberate infliction of pain. Perhaps the well-documented recent reduction in happiness is more a result of technological changes than of an increase in real suffering. We have to consider both as we seek the freedom to move toward happiness.

Because the satisfaction of needs, including the need to be relieved of pain, is fundamental to well-being, and because I have acknowledged that well-being has something to do with happiness, we must discuss needs. What distinguishes needs from wants and desires? We turn to that discussion next.

3

Needs and Wants

We saw in Chapter 1 that happiness is often identified with the satisfaction of needs, wants, or desires. In this chapter, we will explore the nature of needs and how needs differ from wants. I will not try to distinguish between *wants* and *desires* but will use the terms synonymously.[1] Other related terms – *impulse* and *instinct* – will arise, and we will see how they fit into the web of needs and wants.

Needs, wants, desires, impulses, and instincts may all be thought of as expressions – verbal or bodily – of subjective longing. It is customary, however, to label some biological needs (and some instincts, if they are recognized at all) as objective because they appear in all human beings and survival depends on their satisfaction. It is reasonable to call the need for food, shelter, and protection from harm *objective*, but this label neglects the personal intensity of *my* hunger, cold, and fear. It may also cause us to draw an arbitrary line between needs that should receive public attention and those that can be left as mere wants to be satisfied in the private realm or not at all.

Needs are considered more fundamental than wants. We can at least imagine living a reasonably happy life in which our wants are few, our desires confined to pleasures of the mind, and our cravings rationally repressed. We cannot, however, imagine living a happy life if certain of our needs are not met. Among these are the basic needs common to all human beings. I'll start the analysis with these.

Basic Needs

All human beings have certain biological needs. David Braybrooke refers to these as *course of life* needs,[2] and they include food, shelter, and adequate clothing, protection from harm, affection (at least in infancy), and some form of affiliation or connection to other human beings. It is tempting to call these *objective* needs because they do not depend on anyone's feelings to identify them and no reasonable person can deny their reality. However, even these needs are open to interpretation, and priorities among them shift with circumstances. Moreover, these are needs so keenly felt – so subjective in their manifestations – that no outsider has to suggest such a need to one who obviously has it. I prefer, therefore, to classify them with *expressed* needs – those needs that arise within the one who needs. Such needs may be verbally expressed or, unarticulated, they may be expressed through forms of body language.

By classifying basic biological needs this way, we complicate the analysis, because other expressed needs may not be matters of life and death. There is a temptation to keep basic needs in a very special category and, perhaps, to limit a society's responsibilities to meeting just these needs. However, I will argue that, as a society, we can no longer be content with the identification and minimal satisfaction of these needs. Nancy Fraser has argued persuasively that there are several discourses on needs, each incorporating a different interpretation of the concept and its place in social thought.[3] Here we are interested in how the satisfaction of needs contributes to happiness and, because we have already acknowledged that a deep form of happiness involves a sympathetic response to the joys and sufferings of others, we cannot ignore a public consideration of needs. We face two complications that might be avoided by a simpler analysis. First, because our happiness is bound up with that of others, we must listen to others as they express needs. We can't decide a priori what others need. Second, for those who live in liberal economies, needs may go well beyond course of life needs. When a liberal democratic public considers needs, it must move beyond basic biological needs.

It is worrisome but useful to see that there is no longer a sharp line between basic needs and other expressed needs. Alison Jaggar acknowledges that people "want and need far more than physical survival,"[4] but she thinks that social philosophy must start with basic biological needs. She is certainly right that these needs cannot be ignored, but it might be better to start the discussion more holistically. In the best homes, for example, we do not usually start with separate, easily identified biological needs. We think of family members in this time and place, with these available resources. Children are immersed from the start in a set of practices and expectations that both generate and evaluate needs. No good parent would settle for having each of her child's biological needs satisfied in a different place by different people. There is some holistic need that would remain unsatisfied under such a plan.

We see this need dramatically in homeless adults. They may receive breakfast in one place, dinner in another, shelter for the night in still another. A home, in contrast to mere shelter, is not often listed as a basic biological need. Yet a home serves an integrating function; it gathers needs under one roof and gives its members an essential form of identity.[5] Under an adequate interpretive analysis, a home becomes a basic need.

When we evaluate the need for a home as basic, we begin to see other associated needs that may also be considered basic. A home provides part of a person's identity. What must it be like to have no answer to the questions Where do you live? What is your address? A home is also a place where we keep our belongings. We take so for granted having a place for our things that the idea of such a place as a basic need might never occur to us. Home is a place, too, that provides some privacy, a place where we bathe, take care of our bodily needs, and engage in socially approved sex.

It is useful, too, to consider other deprived adults as we conduct an analysis of needs. The conditions of those who are imprisoned suggest further needs that we may overlook because we take their satisfaction for granted. Is there, perhaps, a basic human need for sunshine and some connection to the natural world?[6] If it is true that such a need is basic, should a society's prison policies take it into account?

If we are sensitive to context from the start, we see that needs in contemporary liberal democracies are different from needs in earlier societies and from those in today's preindustrial cultures. When we include self-respect in a list of basic needs, we are immediately made sensitive to cultural contexts. In today's liberal democracies, people are hard pressed to maintain self-respect if they have no medical insurance or income security. Are these, then, basic needs? They are certainly expressed needs in such societies and, as such, their satisfaction plays a role in attaining happiness.

Resistance to this way of thinking has a long history. Social theorists have traditionally confined needs to the private realm. In public (in liberal democracies), we speak of rights, not needs, but it can be shown historically that rights have arisen from expressed needs. The concept of needs precedes and underlies that of rights. One great problem, a reason for resisting emphasis on needs, is that they are indeed sensitive to context. They proliferate in prosperous societies. What may start out as a privilege or mark of wealth may become a need expressed by many and, if the expression is backed by enough power and sympathy, it may even become a right. Some forms of discourse promote this kind of discussion, and others seek to stifle it.

Sometimes expressed needs develop from inferred needs. The latter are needs that arise externally and are then imposed on those said to have the need. Vaccinations, childhood discipline, and schooling are all examples of inferred needs. In many cases, the great hope of parents and educators is that inferred needs will become expressed needs. We hope, for example, that children will feel a need to read, to be polite, to help others, and so on.

As we will soon see, some inferred needs create internal conflicts between wants and needs. Children can internalize needs that are morally bad as well as some that are morally good. They can accept inferred needs, such as the pursuit of wealth and fame, that may wreck their chances of happiness instead of enhancing them.

Different people infer different needs for their children, for fellow citizens, and even for people in far-flung parts of the world, and we spend too little time in discussing and analyzing these needs. To make matters worse, needs are manipulated. If I believed everything I see and hear in advertisements, I might express needs that would otherwise not occur to me. Are these properly called *needs*, or should we refer to these as *wants*, and what's the difference? I will return to the analysis of needs because much more should be sorted out, but before we can do that, we must say something about wants.

Wants

It seems right to classify the host of urges aroused by advertising as wants. They are certainly not survival needs, and their satisfaction seems to contribute little to happiness. Moreover, if we are going to submit needs to public interpretation, we have to find a way to distinguish between wants and needs. We cannot put the society in a position where it feels compelled to respond positively to every expression of wants.

Life in the best homes may give us some help in making the needed distinction. When do good families acknowledge wants (or desires) as needs – that is, as wants that should be met by persons other than the one who wants? I have offered these criteria:

1. The want is fairly stable over a considerable period of time and/or it is intense.
2. The want is demonstrably connected to some desirable end or, at least, to one that is not harmful; further, the end is impossible or difficult to reach without the object wanted.
3. The want is in the power (within the means) of those addressed to grant it.
4. The person wanting is willing and able to contribute to the satisfaction of the want.[7]

Under these circumstances, we say, "Jack really needs a new violin" (to play in the school orchestra); "Patty needs new soccer shoes" (to join a team); "Mother needs a food processor" (to save time in preparing meals); and so on. When a need is acknowledged, a good family works toward its satisfaction. An acknowledged need places an obligation on those who have acknowledged it. That obligation might be one of direct responsibility to satisfy a family member's need or one of indirect responsibility, say, to vote in a way that will promote satisfaction of the need for all who express it.

Many of us use the criteria just listed in determining our own needs. We assess the stability and intensity of our want, its connection to something we deem worthwhile, the feasibility of satisfying it, and our own willingness to work for it. When we consider whether it is within our power to fulfill it, we are forced to consider competing wants that may, of course, include the needs of others.

Must a want rise to the level of need before it is satisfied? Warm, loving families respond generously to many wants that are not needs. Indeed, we might say that everyone has a need to have at least some wants (non-needs) satisfied. It would be a cold world if every one of our wants had to be approved as a need before it was met. In contemporary Western societies, it seems right to say that the satisfaction of some wants is itself a basic need. If we are in a position to satisfy our own wants, of course, we don't usually worry about a distinction between needs and wants.

Most of us agree that the satisfaction of some wants occurs regularly in good homes. Both givers and receivers are delighted by the occasional satisfaction of wants. Is there anything that can be said about such satisfaction at the public level? Should a society try to satisfy some wants that are not recognized as needs? If our answer is yes, a positive move would be to ensure every worker and family a living wage. With that basic resource, people should be free to make choices about the satisfaction of wants. However, there is more that a conscientious society might do. It might try to educate people so that they have a better understanding of their needs and wants. A major aim of this book is to discuss the possibilities of doing this.

Educating people to understand their wants and needs is surprisingly controversial. A market economy thrives on consumer spending, and capitalist governments have an economic reason, as well as a political one, to allow prolific advertising. Freedom of speech protects advertising, but so does good economic sense. Wants drive consumers to spend and thus support a growing economy. But if we are convinced that a dramatic increase in wants is partly responsible for the decline in happiness, should we do something to reduce these wants? No reasonable person wants the stock market to collapse, but many of us are uneasy about the constant barrage of ads that manipulate our wants. If we agree that censorship should not even be considered, is there anything else we can do? This question lies at the heart of much of our later discussion about education.

Liberal democracies today are also market economies, and we may find ourselves caught in a situation well described by Isaiah Berlin. Berlin pointed out that it is almost certainly impossible to attain all the goods we value at one time – as a package, so to speak. Indeed, any two great positive goods may come into conflict at a particular time. Berlin said, "To admit that the fulfillment of some of our ideas may in principle make the fulfillment of others impossible is to say that the notion of total human fulfillment is a formal contradiction, a metaphysical chimaera."[8]

Suppose, for example, that I decide to live a life of utter simplicity. I read Thoreau, the Nearings, Wendell Berry, and a host of books on living close to the land and farming for self-sufficiency.[9] I may become convinced that this is the life for me. But there is no escaping the fact of interdependence in the twenty-first century Western world. I still must buy some things, use public roads occasionally, seek medical advice, and probably use energy for fuel and light. Moreover, not everyone can live this way (or would want to), and so I certainly cannot suggest that the schools educate all children for a life of extreme simplicity. Yet there is no reason why a life of simplicity should not be presented as a possibility, and it would almost certainly be a good thing if students were encouraged to modify their wants and reduce their demands as consumers. Or *would* such moves be good? There remains that worry about supporting a thriving economy. Perhaps living a simple life and maintaining a thriving economy are two goods that cannot be realized simultaneously.

Let's consider another extreme approach to the management of wants and desires. One can try (spiritually) to overcome all desires and deny all wants. Berlin refers to this move as a *retreat to the inner citadel*. He writes:

> This is the traditional self-emancipation of ascetics and quietists, of stoics or Buddhist sages, men of various religions or of none, who have fled the world, and escaped the yoke of society or public opinion, by some process of deliberate self-transformation that enables them to care no longer for any of its values, to remain, isolated and independent, on its edges, no longer vulnerable to its weapons.[10]

It is obvious that most people are not attracted to the idea of giving up all wants and desires. It is too high a price to pay for the promised freedom from longing. Recall David Hume's attack on the cold, ascetic virtues (Chapter 1). Most of us would prefer the company of Hume to that of the ascetic in his hair shirt, and we might well find it annoying that some of those who have ostensibly given up the world still depend on others for food and other basic needs. A permanent and universal retreat to the inner citadel is impossible.

We may all occasionally feel the need for such retreat, however, and then it is hoped that an inner citadel exists. When the "world is too much with us," we seek escape into solitude and inner resources. Because that need arises, although it may not always be recognized, some attention should be given to building that inner self. What a horror it would be to retreat to an inner citadel and find it empty. This fear reflects what is widely believed to be a postmodern malady.

If we reject both the idea of a total personal (spiritual) retreat and an ordinary life of utter simplicity as described by Thoreau, can we come to some acceptable compromise? As citizens of a market democracy, we cannot brush aside the issues of consumerism. Consumption is necessary to economic growth, even to economic stability. In the early 1940s, Joseph Schumpeter wrote, "It remains to notice what to many economists is *the* postwar problem *par excellence*: how to secure adequate consumption."[11] Schumpeter went on to criticize the idea that saving is somehow incompatible with investment and that the main problem is to get people to spend more freely. In persuasive terms, he argued that people usually save with an investment (or a major expenditure) in mind. This suggests that intelligent saving and intelligent consumption go hand in hand. They are not antithetical.

Schumpeter acknowledged that people sometimes express a "desire to save unaccompanied by a desire to invest – a desire to hoard" – but he insisted that this desire has to be "explained by special reasons" and not by any general law of psychology.[12] When people have experienced the shock and uncertainty of severe economic depression, for example, they may react with a desire to hoard whatever resources they acquire. The fear is that even basic needs may be unmet in a time of continuing or growing deprivation. The more general tendency, Schumpeter argued, is for people to save and invest, not to hoard. Thus, Ms. Jones may not be running up credit-card debt with constant consumption, but she may nevertheless contribute significantly to the economy by a major expenditure funded by careful savings.

If, as we saw in Chapter 1, consumption does not in itself bring happiness, and if intelligent consumption does not necessarily imply doom for a market economy, it makes sense to ask how we might educate so that consumption does not work against individual happiness. Ordinary wants, well considered, should serve to maintain the economy. Instead of issuing a wholesale condemnation of the consumer culture, it makes better sense to ask what might be meant by intelligent participation in that culture.

How much of our wanting is rational? On this, we could side with Hobbes, who insisted that all wants are pre-rational and, in fact, stimulated by the environment, hence conditioned, or with Kant, who argued that our very freedom consists in submitting pre-rational desires to the examination of reason. Hobbesian persons, we might say, are free when they get what they want; Kantian persons are free when their wants are brought into line with moral reason.[13] There are problems with both positions at the extremes. Experience tells us quite clearly that many wants are nonrational (not necessarily irrational), but some do seem to arise from reason. The latter sort emerge when we have thought for a bit (sometimes reluctantly) about what we *should* do or about what it is reasonable to do given an assessment of our situation. In the next section, I will discuss inferred needs and, in that analysis, we will see that one of the great hopes of educators is that the young will eventually make the needs we infer for them their own; that is, inferred needs will become expressed needs. In the same vein, we hope that their pre-rational wants will be, when appropriate, subjected to rational analysis. The qualifier "when appropriate" will be very important, because there are wants that need no such analysis. Character, affection, generous inclinations, nonviolent exuberance, and many other habits, attributes, and moods can often be trusted to generate wants that need not be analyzed, that may indeed be diminished by such analysis.

The rational analysis of wants is basic to liberal thought. The freedom to do what one wants to do is the defining characteristic of what Berlin has called *negative* liberty.[14] On this view, no one should interfere with anyone else's free pursuit of wants so long as that pursuit does not hinder a comparable pursuit by others. *Positive* freedom, in contrast, is described as the freedom to do what one *ought* to do. Since Kant, these two views of freedom have been in considerable tension. For Kant, freedom consists in doing what reason instructs should be done. This is not the negative liberty described by later liberal philosophers, but neither is it the positive freedom that would allow the community to dictate what should be done.

Despite the great emphasis on choice and fulfillment of wants in liberalism, few liberal philosophers defend the notion that all wants that are not incompatible with the freedom of others are to be equally respected as signs of autonomy.[15] It is clear that almost no one believes this in connection with the young, and most of what we do in education denies any such assumption. Hobbes's *wanting thing* is thought to need, if not external control, at least education in order to want the right things.[16] The character traits described by John Stuart Mill – responsible exercise of reason, cultivation of noble feelings, a preference for "higher" pleasures – are not easily acquired and maintained.[17] Mill insisted that mature people – those in full possession of their rational faculties – should be entirely free to satisfy their legitimate wants, but that insistence does not mean that Mill did not distinguish among admirable, foolish, and deplorable wants.

We must, then, ask how we should promote admirable wants and discourage the foolish and deplorable. Answering that question will be the major work of the following chapters. My task in this section has been to make the education of wants both desirable and ethically appropriate. It seems reasonable at this stage to believe that, to be happy, we need to know when wants can be freely indulged and when they should be subjected to rational analysis. Intelligent wanting will almost certainly contribute to individual happiness. It should also contribute to the general social good, not only by sustaining a viable economy but also by promoting the satisfaction of wants in others. Recall that, in an earlier discussion, we recognized that our own happiness depends at least in part on the happiness of others. Therefore, as we seek an intelligent approach to the satisfaction of wants, we have to consider the wants of others.

Whatever we decide to do by way of education, it is clear that we (a we somehow to be defined) will have decided that others, perhaps all people, need to be so educated. The need to have one's wants educated is not likely to be expressed either verbally or in signs of severe bodily stress, although the latter can happen in extreme cases. It would seem, then, that the need we have now uncovered is an inferred need, one that is identified externally and imposed on those said to have it.

Inferred Needs

When we speak of children's needs for schooling, discipline, green vegetables, and more hours of sleep, we are referring to what I have called inferred needs. Children rarely express such needs, although adults may detect certain bodily signs that make it possible to classify the needs as either expressed or inferred. The important point for now is that an inferred need is not consciously recognized by the one who is supposed to have it. Indeed, inferred needs and wants often clash, and adults sometimes have to deny children's wants in order to satisfy what they (the adults) have inferred are real needs.

Children are not alone in experiencing conflicts between needs and wants. Adults often undergo such conflicts, but both the needs and wants are felt to be theirs. The needs are expressed needs in that important sense. Ms. Smith may feel a real need to attend a meeting that conflicts with something she wants to do even more. Her need might arise as part of a deeper need to be a moral person – to keep promises, fulfill obligations, and so on. Or it might be an instrumental need – to keep her job, get a raise, prevent an opponent from launching an ill-conceived project. Conflicts such as these abound in adult life, but adults are conscious of most of the conflicts, and often there is no other human being against whom they can direct an objection. In some cases, of course, the self becomes its own opponent.

In contrast, the conflict between inferred needs and the wants of children is marked by a difference in origin and locus of feeling. It is an adult who has identified the need and the child who has the want. The child can often shrug off the responsibility to analyze want and need by identifying the adult as the opponent. If the opponent can be defeated or sweet-talked out of her conviction that X is really a need, the child can escape coming to grips with X.

Pressing inferred needs on children (or on anyone) often involves coercion. Adults insist, for example, that children attend school, go to the dentist, and come at least close to a reasonable bedtime. Sometimes children see and accept the need easily, and sometimes they resist strongly. When and how should we use coercion?

From the perspective of an ethic of care, the use of coercion raises a question. It is not that care theorists believe coercion is always wrong. There are occasions in which coercion is necessary. But coercion damages the caring relation. As Martin Buber said in connection with the teacher's presentation of school studies, coercion "divides the soul in his care into an obedient part and a rebellious part."[18] If a need can be met without it, it is better to avoid coercion. If not, then the act of coercion must be followed by explanation, discussion, and perhaps consolation. The child should be allowed to express his unhappiness or fear, and the adult should respond with understanding and sympathy.

There are many situations in which coercion can be avoided. Sometimes the inferred need can just be discarded; it is not really a need after all. With older children, persuasion is sometimes effective. However, one should not attempt to use persuasion just to forestall using coercion. If Mother knows at the outset that she will not allow Jimmy to stay home from school, it is better to admit this at the start and then add an explanation. Persuasion suggests an openness on the part of

67

both participants in the dialogue. The adult hopes that the child will accept the inferred need, but she must be open to the possibility that the child will persuade her that the need is not crucial – perhaps even mistaken. When adults enter dialogue on inferred needs with children, the outcome should be genuinely in doubt. Otherwise, children will feel used and manipulated, and the caring relation will again be damaged. When that happens, an important source of happiness is weakened.

If coercion is thought to be necessary, it can be softened by explanation, negotiation, and sympathy. Suppose Mr. Jones insists that his teenage son, Dan, take a third year of college preparatory mathematics in preparation for possible admission to an elite college. Dan hates mathematics and, in fact, is not even sure that he wants to go to an elite school. But he is uncertain; he has not yet decided – even in broad terms – what he wants to do as an occupation. Mr. Jones might have been persuaded to let the math go if Dan had been ready to argue passionately for a future in trade or art but, detecting Dan's uncertainty, he gently presses the case for a third year of math. He promises help, too, and emotional support. "Your mom and I won't get on your case if you can't make A's. Just try." Then, seeing obvious signs of misery on his son's face, he adds, "Look, son, I'm sorry. I don't understand, either, why someone who will probably study literature or history needs a third year of algebra. You'll have my sympathy all the way."

Allowing a child to express his misery over a conflict between the needs inferred by adults and his own wants is important for emotional health. Alice Miller has written persuasively on the distortion of character that often results when children are coerced "for their own good" into doing things they hate or accepting punishment without expressing their pain.[19] When the coercion is followed by adult insistence that the hated act or punishment is indeed in the child's best interest, the damage is even greater. Instead of an external opponent, the child now faces an internal one. He is at war with himself and may come to believe that cruelty really can be justified by declaring that it is in the best interest of the victim. In her retrospective analysis of members of the Nazi high command, Miller found that all of them had suffered highly moralistic upbringings. As a result, they seemed unable to distinguish between needs foisted on them by authority and their own wants. Freud, too, pointed out the psychological upheaval caused by clashes between *civilization* (the demands of authoritative society) and *instinct* or wants.[20] Some such conflict is necessary to instill conscience, but much of it is an unnecessary source of unhappiness.

In his discussion of the conflict between civilization and instinct, Freud said that guilt is a product of this conflict. Freud's emphasis on guilt reflects his "intention to represent the sense of guilt as the most important problem in the development of civilization and to show that the price we pay for our advance in civilization is a loss of happiness through the heightening of the sense of guilt."[21]

In Chapter 2, however, I described a healthy form of guilt that contributes to the maintenance of caring relations. I said there that we *should* feel guilty if we have hurt another and have not yet made restitution. Unhealthy guilt is guilt that persists when there is nothing that we can do or that turns in upon oneself. The latter is the kind of guilt discussed by Freud. It arises from and maintains a battle between the ego (often in defense of the id) and the superego. Its object is not the harm done to another but some deprivation inflicted on the self. As seekers of happiness, we have to ask whether this sort of guilt can be minimized.

Parents and teachers can reduce this form of guilt considerably by respecting children's wants and sympathizing when these wants conflict with inferred needs. There is no reason for a boy to feel guilty because he doesn't want to study math, go to school on a given day, analyze poetry, or go to college. On the contrary, his expressed want should trigger reflection in the adult who has inferred the need. Perhaps the boy should be allowed to stay home today; perhaps he does not even need to go to college. But if the inferred need holds up under scrutiny, the adult's job is to offer help and consolation.

Discussion of the conflict between inferred needs and wants suggests another question for consideration: Do we know what we want? It is common for adults to say that children do not know what they need, and that is reason enough for adults to press inferred needs on them. Sometimes we even assert that another person does not know what he or she wants. Once in a while, in a fit of malaise, we even say this of ourselves. If we understand ourselves reasonably well, we may respond to the concerns of others, "I don't know what I want. I'm just grumpy. Leave me alone." Such moments occur as part of moods, and we need not worry about their occasional appearance. The deeper question is more general: Beyond a vague search for happiness, do we know what we want?

Understanding our Wants

It is understandable that people who have, from childhood, been deprived of their own feelings and opinions would also be unclear about what they want. Such people are unable to express their wants even to themselves. Often they take the attitude that "life is earnest, life is real" and seek only to do what they regard as their duty. Happiness is rejected as an impossible goal. Indeed, these people often condemn the pursuit of happiness in others as though all happiness is a selfish indulgence in pleasure.

In the contemporary United States, even those who escape the worst forms of moralistic upbringing usually suffer a bit from our puritanical heritage. We have been warned against too much laughter and gaiety – "Laugh before breakfast, cry before dinner" – and we may moderate our delight as though a jealous god might snatch it from us. In these cases, we know what we want, but we are afraid to show it.

Flitting unreflectively from one activity to another is also a sign that people do not know what they want. John Dewey counseled that adults make a mistake when they arbitrarily cut off the impulses of children, but they also err when they let impulses act without direction. "Impulse is a source," Dewey wrote, "an indispensable source, of liberation; but only as it is employed in giving habits pertinence and freshness does it liberate power."[22] In a note on the same page, Dewey says that he has intentionally used the "words instinct and impulse as practical equivalents." With this usage, he wants to show that instincts are neither fixed nor limited in number. Rather, they represent primitive wants that can be directed toward "serviceable" action. Properly directed, they can work to satisfy both needs and more stable wants.

Freud makes a similar point:

> Actually the substitution of the reality principle for the pleasure principle implies no deposing of the pleasure principle, but only a safeguarding of it. A momentary pleasure, uncertain in its results, is

given up, but only in order to gain along a new path an assured pleasure at a later time.[23]

Children must learn how to manage impulse (or instinct) and be convinced that deferred gratification may yield great satisfactions. This process involves guided experimentation, reflection, and generous support. What do you really want? A test is how much one is willing to work toward what one professes to want, but there is no disgrace in deciding that the thing initially wanted is no longer of interest. This, too, is important learning. How long the trial should be, how much encouragement should be given to persist, and whether extrinsic rewards should be offered are all difficult questions that have no formulaic answers. Agreeing with Emerson, Dewey says this is difficult work. As Emerson said, it involves "immense claims on the time, the thought, on the life of the teacher. It requires time, use, insight, event, all the great lessons and assistances of God; and only to think of using it implies character and profoundness."[24]

To use methods that both respect and direct the impulses of children requires skills that many adults have not developed. To help children assess their wants and develop the power that is potential in their impulses, we should be able to direct our own impulses, and we should understand our own wants.

Many of us – even those whose self-understanding has not been distorted by pathological parenting – are unsure of what we want or how to assess our wants. We make the mistake of supposing that happiness can be a sort of steady state of pleasure. Those who make this error are in constant pursuit of "highs." Freud advised us to remember that happiness construed as pleasure is necessarily episodic; there are no permanent highs. On the other hand, he said, unhappiness can be more or less permanent; it may be episodic, of course, but it may also be a state of mind. Indeed, Freud – like James's sick soul – seemed to think we would be reasonable to accept as a fact that life is basically unhappy. If we are fortunate and wise, we will aim for happiness as contentment. Contentment allows for some pleasure, but it also accepts the inevitability of unhappiness. Again, we may be suspicious of contentment because it may lead to quietism or to an easy avoidance of developing our own capacities.

Those who are unsure of what they want sometimes seek help in magic, astrology, or other forms of fortune telling. The main character in one of Steinbeck's books gazed at the stars as he thought about a recent tarot card reading:

> What is the saying – "The stars incline, they do not command"? . . . Do the cards incline but not command? Well, the cards . . . inclined me to give more thought than I wanted to, to a subject I detested. . . . Could I incline to want what I didn't want?[25]

Ethan Hawley, the speaker, wanted his family to be happy, and that led him to consider goals in which he was otherwise uninterested. Pushed into wants that were alien to him, he did things that he despised and later regretted. One might argue that, for all his musings, he did not really understand himself or his wants.

There are times, too, when whole groups of people suffer malaise, not knowing what they want or why they are unsatisfied with lives that society evaluates as happy. Betty Friedan shocked American society when she exposed the roots and the extent of women's unhappiness in traditional roles.[26] Since then, it has almost certainly become easier for women to choose professional lives, and many women may be happier at home, knowing that they have chosen this way of life. At least it is now recognized that individual women may want something for themselves that is different from the wants society has prescribed for them.

Although we can be mistaken or confused about what we want, most of us have some insight into how our wants fluctuate. We may want ice cream today, for example, but if we were offered it every day, we know our want would diminish. Similarly, we may hate salt pork and peas (the diet of seventeenth-century sailors), yet understand that we could get used to it and, perhaps, even look forward to such a meal. Social scientists have found that we are not very accurate in assessing the degree of these changes in wants, but at least we usually get the direction right.[27] Practice in assessing present wants and subjecting them to the criteria suggested earlier might lead us in the direction of moderation and even contentment.

We are ready now to move toward a discussion of how we might educate for happiness. I have suggested that happiness is found in various domains of contemporary life, and we must look at these. Happiness has a normative aspect; that is, it is connected to the norms by which we are guided. It is affected by the satisfaction of needs and wants, but we have some control over what we want, and understanding our wants may contribute to moderation and contentment. It also has something to do with our personalities and, although we may have little control in this area, understanding can help. Happiness depends greatly on being free of suffering, and I have argued that it is a mistake to glorify suffering or to suppose that we are ever justified in deliberately inflicting it. It depends, perhaps most importantly, on loving connections with others – intimate relations with a few and cordial, cooperative relations with most of those we meet regularly.

I have argued that the tension between expressed needs (and/or wants) and inferred needs must always be treated sensitively. Self-understanding helps, but parents and educators must reflect continually on the needs they infer for children. Coercion raises a question, and answering the question demands our best thinking.

Finally, our most fundamental and general question is how education may contribute to happiness. Can we aim at it directly? What aims might be associated with happiness? We consider next the role of aims in educational planning.

4

The Aims of Education

People want to be happy and, since this desire is well-nigh universal, we would expect to find happiness included as an aim of education. Its failure to appear among the aims usually stated might be a sign that Western society is still mired in a form of Puritanism or, more generously, it may be generally believed that, as Orwell said, happiness cannot be achieved by aiming at it directly. If the latter is so, what should we aim at that might promote happiness?

Until quite recently, aims-talk figured prominently in educational theory, and most education systems prefaced their curriculum documents with statements of their aims. What functions have been served by aims-talk, and what have we lost (if anything) by ceasing to engage in it? What has taken its place?

I will start this chapter by arguing that we need to talk about aims, and I will fill out that argument with a discussion of aims-talk and the purposes it served in earlier educational thought. Looking at contemporary educational policymaking, we'll see that talk of aims might be considered a missing dimension in the educational conversation. Finally, by discussing aims in some depth, I will set the stage for exploring ways in which education might actively support the pursuit of happiness.

Aims-Talk and Its Purposes

Suppose we visit an algebra class and watch a lesson on the factoring of trinomials. The learning objective is clear. The teacher has listed several familiar types of trinomials, and the students are occupied in identifying them and performing the factorizations. If we ask

Ms. A (the teacher) why she is teaching this topic, she will probably reply that the next topic is combining algebraic fractions, and one cannot easily find the appropriate common denominator without a knowledge of factoring. Now, of course, one could proceed by simply multiplying denominators, but the expressions quickly become unwieldy and, to get the required answer, one would eventually have to factor. Ms. A's response is entirely appropriate if (1) we have already found good reasons for teaching algebra to these students and (2) we have agreed that algebra consists of a certain sequence of topics. When a teacher is asked about a lesson objective, she or he almost always responds with an explanation of how this learning objective fits with others that come before and after it. Today most mathematics textbooks are organized in this way.

An observer might get a somewhat deeper response from Ms. A to the question Why are you spending so much time on this topic? To this, Ms. A might reply that her course of study (or textbook) emphasizes solving equations; many of these involve rational expressions that need simplification – factoring again – and so this topic requires much attention. This answer is unsatisfactory in its apparent circularity, but it does point at a larger goal and not just at the next skill to be mastered.

Without trying to draw a sharp line of demarcation, I will associate objectives with lessons and goals with courses or sequences of courses.[1] Most of our "why" questions are answered within the prescribed system; that is, we explain why we are doing something in terms of other objectives or, occasionally, in terms of goals.

Such answers assume, as noted previously, that we have good reasons for teaching algebra to these particular students and that the course of study we are presenting as algebra will be recognized and approved by mathematics educators. The second criterion is easily tested by submission to a group of experts who are in a position to say whether a given course of study is adequate as algebra. Experts may, of course, differ on whether the course is appropriate for gifted, average, or slow learners, but that analysis brings us back to the first question: Do we have a good reason for teaching algebra to *these* students?

Discussion of aims, in contrast to that of objectives and goals, centers on the deepest questions in education. What are we trying to accomplish by teaching algebra? Who benefits? Should our efforts be designed to enhance the society (or state) or should they be directed at benefits for the individual? If we are concerned with something like self-actualization, what does this mean? Do we have to say something about human nature? If we are concerned with the welfare of the state, must we describe the sort of state in, and for, which we will educate? Is there an inherent conflict between individuals and societies? This is just a sample of the questions that must be considered when we engage in aims-talk.

Some people object to wasting time on aims-talk. Wasn't all this settled long ago? People have been debating questions concerning the aims of education since the days of Plato and, in our times (within a century or so), talk of aims has not changed schooling dramatically. Why not avoid such useless talk and get on with the practical business of educating children? Even teachers talk this way and seem to have little patience for conversations that do not culminate with something useful for tomorrow's lessons.

In response, one might argue that aims-talk is to education what freedom is to democracy. Without freedom, democracy degenerates into a form quite different from liberal democracy. Similarly, without continual, reflective discussion of aims, education may become a poor substitute for its best vision. Moreover, just as freedom takes on newer and richer meanings as times change, so must the aims of education change. Even if they might be stated in fairly constant general terms, the meaning of those constant words will take on new coloring as conditions change. To be literate today, for example, is different from being literate in the days of Charlemagne (who could read but not write) or in colonial America, where people did not need the forms of visual literacy required by present-day media.

It has always been one function of philosophers of education to critique the aims of education in light of their contemporary cultures. It has been another of their functions to criticize the society with respect to a vision of education. In the next section, we will see that some philosophers have started with a description of ideal or actual states from which they have derived recommendations for education. Others have started with a vision for the education of individuals and asked what sort of state might support that vision. Simply accepting the state as it is and the system as it is (merely pushing it to perform its perceived function more vigorously) is a dangerous (and lazy) strategy. I will argue that this is the policy we have followed for the past two decades, and it is likely to prove ruinous.

Another objection to aims-talk is that it often culminates in asking too much of schools.[2] This was an objection raised against the aims suggested in 1918 by Clarence Kingsley in the famous Cardinal Principles Report.[3] Herbert Kliebard comments:

> By far the most prominent portion of the 32-page report was the statement of the seven aims that would guide the curriculum: "1. Health. 2. Command of fundamental processes. 3. Worthy home-membership. 4. Vocation. 5. Citizenship. 6. Worthy use of leisure. 7. Ethical character."[4]

Oddly, while more radical educators such as David Snedden thought the report was still far too academic, later critics blamed it for laying the foundation of *life adjustment* education, asking the impossible of schools, and making the academic task of the schools more difficult. People in the latter camp wanted to reduce the responsibility of the schools to academic learning. They insisted that no institution could take on such a broad array of responsibilities.

Whether the task is possible depends on how it is understood, and it is a function of aims-talk to deliberate and come to a useful understanding on this. I have always found the Cardinal Principles quite wonderful. Indeed, I do not see how schools can operate as *educational* institutions without attending to at least these aims, and obviously I want to add another – happiness. Everything depends on the next step: How shall we employ these aims in guiding what we do in constructing a curriculum, in classroom teaching, in establishing interpersonal relationships, in designing school buildings, in management and discipline, and in community relations?

If we were to proceed in the way advocated by scientific curriculum makers (for example, Franklin Bobbitt),[5] the task might indeed be impossible, because our next step would be to derive objectives from our aims. Imagine the work required to establish learning objectives for each of these large aims! Where would each objective be placed, and who would teach it? It is not necessary, however, to proceed in this fashion. We might even argue that it is a mistake to do so; specifying the entire curriculum as objectives before teachers and students begin to interact forecloses the freedom of students to participate in the construction of their own learning objectives.

As we engage in aims-talk, we have an opportunity to question the role of objectives in general. Do our aims suggest that every lesson should have a stated objective and, if so, what form should it take? Must each lesson have a specific learning objective, or is it sometimes appropriate to describe what the teacher will do and leave open what the students might learn?[6] In the midst of our aims-talk, we would pause also to note that some objectives might well be prespecified. When should this be done? By whom?

In earlier chapters, I suggested that Orwell and others might have been right when they said that happiness cannot be attained by pursuing it directly. The same can be said of several other aims in the Cardinal Principles. This does not mean, however, that they cannot function at all as aims. It means, rather, that we must continually reflect upon, discuss, and evaluate what we are doing to see if our objectives and procedures are compatible with our aims.

A little later, I will try to show that failure to engage in vigorous discussion of educational aims has marked the movement toward standardization and high-stakes testing. In that discussion, we will ask what the movement's advocates are trying to do and whether the systems and procedures they have recommended are likely to support or undermine their tacit aims. First, however, to get a better sense of how aims-talk might assist current thinking, let's look briefly at how it has functioned in the past.

Aims in Earlier Educational Thought

Plato's discussion of education is embedded in his analysis of the just state. As Socrates and his companions in dialogue try to create the design for a just state, they inevitably encounter issues concerning education. Plato does not start with the individual; that possibility with respect to the meaning of the term *just* is discarded early in the dialogue as too difficult. Talk shifts from the just man to the just state.[7] Thus, when education becomes the topic of analysis, the needs of the state are paramount. As the discussants consider the needs of the state and its collective people, they decide that the kinds of people needed fall into three categories: rulers, guardians (auxiliaries or warriors), and artisans (tradespeople and other workers).

Plato does not ignore individuals, but he treats them as representatives of classes organized according to their *natures*. Children are to be watched and tested to identify their talents and interests, and then they are to receive an education compatible with their demonstrated natures. Positions in the just state are not inherited; they are distributed through a procedure of diagnosis and education. Poor children from the artisan class may exhibit the "golden" attributes required of rulers, and children of rulers may show the "bronze" qualities typical of artisans.

Socrates brings the needs of the state and the individual together by noting that people will care for what they love. Thus, if the state needs people who will do their jobs well, it should be sure that they are trained effectively in occupations to which they are well suited. Those who love certain forms of work will care deeply about that work and become competent at it. Further, Socrates scorns the dilettante and the jack-of-all-trades. Everyone in the just state is to perform one essential job and do so expertly.

In his comments about the Platonic scheme of education, John Dewey commends the practice of providing different forms of education for children with different interests:

> We cannot better Plato's conviction that an individual is happy and society well organized when each individual engages in those activities for which he has a natural equipment, nor his conviction that it is the primary office of education to discover this equipment to its possessor and train him for its effective use.[8]

But Dewey draws back from Plato's organization of human beings into three classes. For Dewey, "each individual constitutes his own class,"[9] and the processes of education must be dynamic and flexible. Dewey's discussion of education is embedded in that of a democratic state/community, whereas Plato's aims at a perfect (some say totalitarian) state that is unchanging and hierarchically organized.

Plato had two great aims in mind for his system of education. First, for the benefit of the state, he wanted to educate the three large classes he identified, each group trained to the highest degree. Second, for the benefit of the individual, he insisted that education should be aimed at improvement of the soul, and by *soul* Plato meant the harmonious development of three parts: appetite (impulse or desire), reason, and spirit (energy).[10] The parallel to the three classes constituting the population of the just state is striking. In the individual, the three parts are also properly organized hierarchically, and a just soul places reason in the role of ruler, spirit in the role of guardian-auxiliary, and appetite in the role of artisan – one who is necessary to the whole but must be controlled by a wise ruler (reason).

We can draw a limited parallel between Plato's educational aims and those of today's reformers in the United States. First, the standards/testing movement is driven primarily by an aim that speaks to the welfare of the nation. Here the similarity is clear. If anything, the current goal in the United States is even narrower than Plato's because it concentrates almost entirely on the economic status of the country. Second, we see in Plato's plan the elements of what we now call a *meritocracy*. Offices and occupations are to be filled by those qualified, not by inheritance or political preference. This practice is also espoused (if not always enacted) by contemporary democracies.

With respect to individuals, however, the aims diverge. Plato was clear in the way he valued the three classes of individuals, and the high value he placed on rulers came directly from his underlying philosophy. The theory of forms made reason and theory superior to action and practice. Those who work with their minds were thought to be superior to those who work with their bodies. Our own society pretends to reject this ordering on the grounds that it is repugnant to a democratic society, but our actual social ordering suggests a considerable degree of hypocrisy, if not schizophrenia on the issue. The Platonic legacy is still strong, even if kept below the surface of discussion. We say we value all honest, necessary contributions equally, but we allow people who do essential manual work to live in poverty or near-poverty, and we embrace as an educational aim to prepare all children so that they will not have to do such work. We fail to ask an essential question: If we were to succeed in this effort, who would do the work so necessary and yet so despised today?

Not only do we fail to educate children along lines congruent with their *natural equipment*, but we insist that natural differences are so minimal that all children can profit from the education once reserved for a few. Unlike Plato, we do not even ask whether that education is appropriate for anyone, much less for everyone. The use of democratic language suggests that the same education for all is a generous and properly democratic measure when, in fact, it may well be both undemocratic and ineffective. It will be ineffective if Plato was right when he said that people will care for (and do well at) work they love.

Many will fail in schools because they are forced to do work they hate and are deprived of work they might love.

Plato's entire discussion of education in *The Republic* is pervaded by aims-talk. He and his companions eventually accept the broad components of a traditional curriculum – music (which then included all forms of literature) and gymnastic – but not without significant modification. They do not simply turn the details over to experts in music and gymnastic. Rather, they ask why these subjects should be taught; that is, they continually return to primary aims – improvement of the soul and benefit to the state. Socrates, Plato's spokesperson in the dialogues, does not want rulers and guardians to become muscle-bound athletes from single-minded concentration on gymnastic, nor does he want them to become *effeminate* (his unfortunate label) through over-concentration on music. Improvement of the soul requires harmony among the three aspects of self.

Referring to those aims directed at establishing and maintaining the just state, Socrates recommends certain constraints on the stories and poems to be heard by children. A discussion of Plato's plans for censorship would take us too far afield. For present purposes, what is important is his continuous attention to aims. The question What shall be taught? is never answered definitively without a thorough exploration of the companion question Why?

Plato also looked at elements of private life that contribute to happiness; he was concerned about how we should live – what virtues should be cultivated and what tastes developed. Today's reformers say little about forms of personal well-being that are aimed at neither the country's nor the individual's economic status. Plato at least argued for a form of happiness that arises in doing one's chosen work well, and Dewey also noted this aspect of happiness. But neither Plato nor Dewey said much about homemaking, parenting, or a host of other everyday occupations significant in personal life. I will argue that these must be included in our discussion of educational aims if we are concerned with the happiness of individuals.

Before leaving this brief account of aims in Plato, I want to emphasize again that I am not defending a hierarchical sorting of children according to specific academic criteria, but I will strongly defend different forms of education for children with different interests and talents. It seems entirely right for a democratic society to reject the elitist scheme offered by Plato, but the rejection must be honest and carefully argued. Have we really rejected Plato's ordering when we decide that all children will be prepared (in effect) for the category once classified as best? By our very designation of that curriculum as best, we may have aggravated the denigration of interests and capacities that do not require traditional academic preparation. At its most arrogant, this attitude says to others, "Now you will have a chance to be just like me, and then you will be worth something."

Another approach to educational aims is found in the work of Rousseau. I will limit the discussion of Rousseau's philosophy of education drastically because my main point is to contrast his approach to aims with that of Plato and to emphasize once again the centrality of aims-talk in any fully developed theory of education.

In contrast to Plato, Rousseau begins his *Emile* with the individual, not the state.[11] The aims of education are derived from the basic premise that the child is born good and will develop best (as nature intends) if education by people and education by things are well coordinated with the education provided by nature. With this basic aim – to produce the best possible (natural) "man" – Rousseau sets out to describe how education by people and things (the forms over which we have some control) should take place. Everything suggested for Emile's education is tested against this aim.

Rousseau does not ignore the needs of the state or society. Recognizing that Emile must live in association with others, he asks how best to prepare him as both a citizen and a man. The citizen Emile will become should be as little different from the natural man as possible. Making enormous assumptions about the natural man, Rousseau aims to produce men who will think for themselves, be models of civic virtue, understand and practice justice, and in general become whatever they are able and willing to become.

The concept on which Rousseau depends so heavily, Nature, is both ambiguous and notoriously problematic as he interprets it. Men and women are "naturally" different, Rousseau declares, and therefore their education should be different. Sophie, Emile's female counterpart, should be obedient, amiable, and useful. She should not think for herself but always seek the approval of proper men and society.[12] Book V of *Emile* is a feminist nightmare. But, although Rousseau's interpretations of nature are questionable and even inconsistent, he is consistent in referring to his stated aims involving nature. We can challenge him intelligently today precisely because we find his answers to the "why" questions unsatisfactory and objectionable. Even if Rousseau were to experience a sort of feminist epiphany and decide, as Socrates did, that there are no relevant intellectual differences between men and women so far as citizenship is concerned, we would still be able to criticize him with respect to the basic aim he has adopted – the natural man (or woman).

When John Dewey discussed aims in education, he said that his account of education "assumed that the aim of education is to enable individuals to continue their education – or that the object and reward of learning is continued capacity for growth."[13] He then went on to claim that such a view of education makes sense and can only be implemented in a democratic society. It takes a book-length discussion to support these claims and to show what they might look like in practice. But Dewey was careful later in the discussion to insist on a multiplicity of aims that change with the needs and beliefs of a society. Not only must these aims be considered together for coherence but each must be judged, we assume, in light of the overriding aim: Is the adoption of Aim X likely to further growth or impede it? Under what conditions?

At a similar level of abstraction, Alfred North Whitehead said that the aim of education should be to produce people "who possess both culture and expert knowledge in some special direction."[14] A bit later, he wrote, "There is only one subject-matter for education, and that is Life in all its manifestations."[15] Again, such statements demand full and lengthy discussion, but they give us a starting point to which we continually return.

As I try to promote happiness as an aim of education, I have to offer a convincing account of happiness, how it connects to human needs, what it means in the society we inhabit, how it might transform that society into a better one, and how it fits with a host of other legitimate aims. Like Dewey with growth and Whitehead with life, I have to show how happiness can be used as a criterion by which to judge other aims and the value of our aims-talk. Indeed, an important function of aims is to encourage the aims-talk that enriches both educational thinking and the wisdom of the race. We continually ask, If you are aiming at X, why are you doing Y? How does Y fit with X?

The Missing Dimension Today

At the beginning of the twenty-first century, educational discussion is dominated by talk of standards, and the reason given for this emphasis is almost always economic. The underlying aims seem to be (1) to keep the United States strong economically and (2) to give every child an opportunity to do well financially. There is something worrisome about both of these aims, if indeed they are the aims that drive the standards movement. First, the idea that schools play a role in making our economy competitive is cast in intemperate language that charges the schools with failure on this task. Why should the schools be accused of undermining the American economy during a time of unparalleled prosperity? The aim of keeping our economy strong seems reasonable, but the demands for accountability and standards at such a time seem oddly out of place. They make us suspect that something else is operating. Second, we should be deeply troubled by the suggestion that economic equity can be achieved by forcing the same curriculum and standards on all children. The question of what is meant by equity is answered hastily and with little justification. Finally, of course, the aims (with no debate) are far too narrow. There is more to individual life and the life of a nation than economic superiority.

The standards movement had its effective start in 1983 with the publication of *A Nation at Risk*.[16] Published toward the end of a significant recession, the report used alarmist language to rouse the American public to the great danger posed by a supposedly failing school system. It spoke of "a rising tide of mediocrity" and went so far as to say, "If an unfriendly foreign power had attempted to impose on America the mediocre educational performance that exists today, we might well have viewed it as an act of war."[17] Response to the alarm was nationwide, and by 2000 every state but one (Iowa) had established new (arguably higher) standards for the achievement of school children at all levels of K-12 education.

It is interesting to note that, without a discernible change in scores on most standardized tests of achievement, the United States moved quickly into a period of unprecedented prosperity – despite its supposedly abysmal schools. Indeed, several careful analysts have challenged the claims of *A Nation at Risk*,[18] but it is not my purpose here to argue the strength of their case. Rather, I want to show what has been missed by failing to engage in a discussion of aims.

One prominent claim of the alarmists was that achievement scores had fallen badly since the late 1960s. This might be something to worry about, and critics of the report set about finding explanations for the drop. For example, it was argued that many more students now take the SATs (one measure of academic achievement) and that, with a substantially different population, we should expect different scores and norms adjusted accordingly. This is entirely reasonable from a statistical perspective.

The debate could have been more thoughtful. Had our aims changed during the period of decline? Clearly, we were trying to prepare many more students for college. Why were we doing this? Did the society need more people with a college education? With a traditional college education? The reason most often offered was that everyone in a liberal democracy should have a chance to obtain the goods of that society. That seems right. But does such a commitment imply that access to those goods must come through successful competition in traditional schooling? What happens, then, to those who do not do well in the only form of schooling we now make available in the name of equity? Suppose instead that we created rich alternative curricula and provided guidance to those students who might welcome and succeed with them? Questions such as these go to the very roots of what we believe about democracy and democratic schooling.

When we neglect these questions, a narrow educational focus is encouraged, and we distract ourselves from the social problems that cannot be solved by schools. For example, all people need adequate medical insurance, livable and affordable housing, safe neighborhoods, and nonpoverty wages for honest work. It is shortsighted and even arrogant to suppose that all people can escape these problems through better education, particularly if that education favors those with specific academic talents or resources. The jobs that today pay only poverty wages will still have to be done and, so long as we measure success in schools competitively, there will be losers.

One can see the value of aims-talk vividly here. When advocates of uniform standards claim that everyone will benefit, we can raise reasonable doubts. As we have seen, it is one function of aims-talk to challenge the existing rules by which a society has organized itself.

85

Can poverty be traced to a lack of good education, or is the causal relation inverted? Why should anyone who works a full week at an honest job live in poverty? If everyone gets a college education, who will do today's poverty-level work? When we ask these questions, we begin to doubt the main argument offered by advocates of uniform standards. We may even be led to ask: What are these people really aiming at?

If the aim is justice – to provide all students with an education that will meet their needs – the solution is likely to involve the provision of considerable variety in school offerings and to include material that might contribute to personal as well as public life. Offering a variety of curricula does not mean putting together a set of courses labeled *easy*, *average*, and *hard* and then equating *hard* with *best*. It means cooperatively constructing rigorous and interesting courses centered on students' interests and talents. It means that the schools should show the society that a democracy honors all of its honest workers, not just those who finish college and make a lot of money.

John Dewey, in lines often misappropriated, said, "What the best and wisest parent wants for his own child, that must the community want for all its children. Any other ideal for our schools is narrow and unlovely; acted upon, it destroys our democracy."[19] Dewey did not mean, however, that the community should give all children exactly the same program of studies. Indeed, he argued so often and so insistently against sameness in the choice of content and curricula that it is hard to understand how anyone could read him this way. The best and wisest parent, Dewey believed, would want an education that is best for each individual child. In direct contradiction to Dewey's hopes, the standards movement keeps pressing for the same education for all.

At the same time, sensitive educators have attacked the tracking system that has been in place for so long in our schools. This system, in which children are placed in *tracks* according to their perceived academic capacities, has had pernicious effects. No reasonable observer could deny this.[20] However, the problem may not be tracking itself but rather the hierarchical values we put on the tracks. There is no obvious reason why students in a commercial or industrial track cannot develop "both culture and expert knowledge in some special direction," as Whitehead advised. The soul-destroying discrimination arises when we regard one track as better than another and place the

86

one loaded with academic information and skills at the top. A bad situation is made worse when we refer to the students in the top track as the "good kids," and teachers often do this. We add insult to injury when we assign the least competent teachers to work with students in the "lower" tracks.

So long as schools value only academic achievement (narrowly defined as success in standard school subjects), this problem will be intractable. I have considerable sympathy for those who, observing the suffering of lower-track students, recommend total abandonment of tracking, but surely this cannot be the answer if our aim is to educate each student to a standard compatible with his or her abilities and purposes. Students who seek careers that require knowledge and skills very different from the standard academic material are not given a fair chance by simply placing them in academic courses with those who actually want these courses. How fair is it to ignore students' own legitimate interests and coerce them into competing with students whose interests lie in the area of coercion? This issue goes to the very heart of democratic education, and I will devote considerable space to it in later chapters. The questions asked here are simply skipped over in the rush to standardized solutions.

Consider the way in which the National Council of Teachers of Mathematics (NCTM) begins its draft of *Standards 2000*.[21] No Socrates-like character asks "And shall we teach mathematics?" Even if the answer is a preordained "Of course, Socrates," asking the question raises a host of others: To whom shall we teach mathematics? For what ends? Mathematics of what sort? In what relation to students' expressed needs? In what relation to our primary aims? And what are these aims?

After a brief statement on "a time of extraordinary and accelerating change"[22] and the widespread use of technology, the document launches into "principles," the first of which is "The Equity Principle." It is worthwhile to examine this principle in some detail. It states as a basic assumption that "all students can learn to think mathematically."[23] It does not even try to make a convincing argument for this claim. It does not tell us what this means or why students should do so. Instead, it says:

An emphasis on "mathematics for all" is important because of the role that school mathematics has historically played in educational inequity. A student's mathematical proficiency is often used as a basis for decisions regarding further schooling and job opportunities. Furthermore, mathematics has been one of the subjects frequently associated with "tracking," a practice in which students are sorted into different instructional sequences that often results in inequitable opportunities and outcomes for students.[24]

Therefore, everyone must become proficient in mathematics. Without further argument, this is a non sequitur. Writers of the report do not pause to consider other, more generous ways of alleviating the inequity that has historically been associated with mathematics. For example, why not abandon the requirement that all college-bound students, regardless of their interests and abilities, present academic credits in mathematics? Why not consider ways to improve non-college courses so that the mathematics actually needed is taught sensitively and practically within those courses? Why decide that the road to equity is established by coercing everyone into becoming proficient in mathematics? A thorough discussion of aims might lead in a different direction.

We need a careful analysis of what is meant by equity, and we need a discussion of educational aims that moves in two directions – toward the aims we hold as a liberal democracy and into the actual activities we will provide in classrooms. Educational aims always reflect the aims – explicit or implicit – of the political society in which they are developed. A totalitarian state will engender educational aims that primarily benefit the state. A liberal democracy should generate aims more focused on the needs of individuals. Indeed, it must do this because it depends for its legitimacy on the capacity of its citizens to freely endorse and maintain it. And how is such a capacity developed? Surely, it grows, at least in part, out of guided practice in making well-informed choices. Thus we have an important argument against coercion right from the start.

Another argument against coercion is that coercion makes people resistant and unhappy. If we are serious about promoting happiness, we will recognize that every act of coercion raises a question. There are times when, after considering the question raised, we will still have to use coercion, but there are many times when, because we have paused to think, we will be able to use persuasion or even abandon the end toward which we planned to coerce. As we consider whether or not to coerce, our deliberation will almost always involve an analysis of needs and a commitment to negotiation.

Reviving Aims-Talk

I have argued that we need to talk about aims because aims provide criteria by which we judge our choices of goals, objectives, and subject content. Aims-talk can also be directed at the larger society and its policies. Both functions are important.

During the twentieth century, we made considerable progress in humanizing our schools. Corporal punishment has fallen into disfavor (and is illegal in many states), more students go to high school and more graduate, girls are encouraged to take courses in mathematics and science, programs are designed for children with disabilities, and meals are provided for poor children.

American education can be rightly proud of these attainments and aspirations. Still, we could do better in securing these goals and others by analyzing the aims that gave rise to them. Why, for example, have we decided to encourage young women to study math and science? Well, because it's the fair thing to do! Equity seems to require it. If equity is the aim, however, why are we not concerned that so few young men become nurses, elementary school teachers, social workers, early childhood teachers, and full-time parents? The response to this is that equity refers to equitable financial opportunities, and the occupations traditionally available to women do not pay well. But are they important? Well, of course. Why not pay appropriately for them, then, and strive for a balanced form of equity?

As we ask deeper questions about our aims – why are we doing X? – we uncover new problems and new possibilities for the solution of our original problem. In the case under consideration here, we are also led to use caution in encouraging young women to choose careers in math and science. If they want to study in these areas, our encouragement should be backed by generous support, but very bright young women are sometimes led to believe that any other choice is beneath them. Some girls interested in elementary school teaching, for example, have been told, "You're too good for that!" Their self-worth comes to depend on their rejecting traditional female roles. Inferred needs and internal wants are then in conflict, and the joy of doing something wholeheartedly may be lost.

89

Consider next the goal of providing a free, appropriate education to every child in the least restrictive environment compatible with that goal.[25] Trying to meet this goal has turned out to be enormously expensive, and it has also led to a proliferation of services and demands for services. Are too many children now labeled *learning disabled*? Why did we establish such a goal? Again, the answer seems to be equity. But what is meant by equity in this area?

Unless we ask this question, we are likely to engage in foolish and harmful practices. For instance, in some states, children labeled learning disabled (even those in special classes) must now take the standardized tests required of students in regular classes. It certainly makes sense to monitor the progress of these students and to ask continually whether we are doing the best possible job with them. Are we catching errors in labeling? Are we working hard enough to move capable students out of special education – to relieve them of any possible stigma attached to the label?[26] Are all the children learning something? Granted that these questions should be answered conscientiously, forcing all children to take these tests seems counterproductive. Some probably should be encouraged to take them, with only positive stakes attached. It is outrageous, however, to force these tests on all students in special education. From all over the country, we hear stories of sick stomachs, trembling hands, and wet pants. If by *equity* we mean providing an appropriate education for every child, it is dead wrong to expect the same performance from each child. Having forgotten our aim, we act as though all children are academically equal and can be held to the same standard.

We could analyze each of the goals I listed as admirable from the perspective of underlying aims, and it would be useful to do so. Sometimes the goals themselves require such analysis (as in the two cases just discussed). In other cases, we have to look at the outcomes associated with the goals and then go back to the original aim to see where we might have gone wrong. It seems entirely right, for example, to forbid corporal punishment and sexual harassment in schools, but does that mean that a teacher should never touch a student? Are appropriate hugs ruled out? Is a firm restraining hand on an angry arm ruled out? In the widespread use of zero-tolerance rules, good judgment is often sacrificed. The original aim is forgotten.

Even in the matter of feeding hungry children, we too often lose sight of our aim. Many people claim that we feed children because "hungry children can't learn." A better answer would be this: We feed hungry children because they are hungry! That answer helps us to direct attention to social problems beyond the classroom. Should we stop feeding hungry children if, after being well fed, they still do not learn as well as we think they should?

I want to turn now to an examination of practices that should raise questions about the aims of education. It is often helpful to see a familiar scene through the eyes of an intelligent and sympathetic stranger,[27] so let's pretend that a visitor from another world has visited our schools and wants to share his or her observations with us. The visitor talks with a representative educator, Ed.

Visitor: It struck me as odd that, although your people spend much of their time in homemaking, parenting, and recreation, these topics are rarely addressed in your schools.

Ed: That's because we regard the school as a somewhat specialized institution. Its job is to teach academics – the material that cannot easily be taught at home. Homemaking, parenting, and worthwhile forms of recreation are taught at home. Indeed, most of us believe that it would be an improper intrusion into family life for schools to teach such topics.

Visitor: Ah, yes. This is part of your liberal heritage, is it not? But what is done about the children who come from homes where these matters are not taught well? From what I've seen, there are many such children.

Ed: You're right, and this does worry us. However, we believe that people who have a thorough command of the fundamental processes will be able to learn these other matters on their own. They will have the skills to do so. And they will qualify for good jobs, so they will be able to provide the material resources characteristic of good homes.

Visitor: Hmm. Well, of course, there is something to that. But if children from poor homes (not necessarily poor in the financial sense, you understand) have great difficulty learning, it would seem that a society ought to attack the problem at all levels – do something to eliminate poverty, encourage adult interest in homemaking and parenting, and teach these things in school.

Ed: But parents don't want us to do this! They don't want the schools to prescribe methods of parenting or to pronounce one way of

91

homemaking better than another. We have a hard time teaching any sort of values in our schools.

Visitor: You would not want to indoctrinate, I understand. But these topics need not be presented dogmatically. In your English classes, high school students could read and discuss children's literature. In social studies, they could study the development of the home and forms of housing. In art, they might study the aesthetics of homemaking. In science, child development. In foreign language, patterns of hospitality might be studied. In mathematics, they might look at statistical studies that show the high correlation between socioeconomic status and school achievement. These are just examples, of course.

Ed: And very good examples! However, our schedules are already so full that I don't see how we could make room for all these things.

Visitor: Perhaps, if you will forgive my saying so, you haven't thought deeply enough about what you are trying to do.

Ed: We want to give all children the opportunity to learn what they need to succeed in our society. All children!

Visitor: That is commendable, very fine. But how do you define success? Have the schools failed a child if he wants to become an auto mechanic? Do they help a girl who wants to be a beautician?

Ed: We believe they should make those choices later. First, get a sound, basic education.

Visitor: In watching many classes and talking to many students, it seems that – because their interests and talents are ignored in school – many young people fall into these occupations instead of choosing them proudly. They feel they are not good enough for more desirable work. There is an injury inflicted on them.

Ed: We are getting off the subject. What has this to do with teaching homemaking and the like?

Visitor: It has to do with happiness, and that was my reason for bringing up those topics in the first place. If happiness is found in domains other than salaried work, shouldn't those other domains be treated in education? And since one's occupation also influences happiness, that too should be included in education. But I was just getting started. . . .

Ed: I hesitate to ask.

Visitor: It seems that your society, your government anyway, has been waging a losing war on drugs, –

92

Ed: Now I've got you! We *do* teach about the dangers of drug abuse.

Visitor: Yes, yes. But your television commercials are filled with ads for drugs, some of them quite dangerous. Do you help students to see how they are being manipulated?

Ed: Well, we worry most about illegal drugs.

Visitor: Have you noticed that many teenagers from low socio-economic status neighborhoods wear expensive name-brand clothing? They could clothe themselves for far less money and perhaps avoid taking part-time jobs that keep them from their studies.

Ed: So you want us to engage in consumer education as well as homemaking, parenting, and – you're not finished, are you?

Visitor: Perhaps we should let it be for now. It just seems so sad that, when everyone seeks happiness, the schools do so little to promote it.

Ed: Well, I promise to think more about it. (Shaking his head) I just don't see what we can do.

In this chapter, I have argued that aims-talk plays a vital role in sustaining a rigorous and relevant program of education, and I've tried to show how it has done this in the past. Today, with recent changes in social thought and massive changes in technology, it is more important than ever to consider why we are promoting certain goals in schooling and why we continue to neglect education for personal life and for happiness in our occupations.

PART 2

Educating for Personal Life

At the end of Chapter 4, Ed promised to think about the Visitor's ideas. That is what we will do now. Almost no one would argue against the claim that personal life offers our greatest opportunities for happiness. What can education contribute to the enhancement of personal life?

One of the most important tasks for every human being is that of making a home, and much of a child's fortune depends on the sort of home into which he or she is born. Our visitor from another world is baffled by our educational neglect of homemaking. How did it happen that something so central to our lives has been so consistently ignored in schools? If we were to redesign our curricula, what might we include about homemaking?

In addition to making a home, most of us also become parents, and that task is another one that is largely ignored by schools. If one's home and parents are more important than any other aspect of life in predicting school success or failure, it seems odd that schools do not teach something about parenting so that more children can have a better start in life. Today we seem to take the attitude that the schools should help all children learn enough for economic success. Then, it is supposed, they will be able to provide better homes for their own children. It is not clear, however, that mere economic improvement will guarantee better homes. Further, children from poor homes now in school have a difficult time learning, and so the odds are against their improving either their economic condition or their future home lives.

Again, many of us derive deep pleasure from our connections to a place and its natural forms, and yet the study of natural history has fallen off – displaced by the systematic study of special sciences such as biology, physics, and chemistry. Instead of educating for love of place, we educate for a global economy.

Then there are matters of spirit and character that we have already identified as significant in attaining happiness, but it is a struggle to include even these in the regular curriculum. Character education is experiencing a revival today, but its advocates make the mistake of supposing that character can be taught directly, virtue by virtue. In fact, the development of character may be very like the attainment of happiness itself; it may have to be aimed at indirectly.

Finally, we know that people with certain social virtues and pleasing personalities are likely to be happier than those lacking such qualities. It makes sense, then, to consider whether these virtues can be cultivated through education. These are the topics to which we turn in Part 2.

5

Making a Home

As we observed in Chapter 1, homemaking has never figured prominently in the general education of Western societies, although home life is a major source of happiness for most people. Because educational programs were designed by men, they were directed at preparation for public life – male life. Homemaking was taught at home and in some schools exclusively for women. The widely held belief that homemaking is women's work helps to explain why it has been so neglected in public education. It also explains why, when homemaking has been taught to girls, the subject has been treated superficially and technically. The deepest philosophical questions have not been engaged.

What does it mean to make a home? What does it mean to have a home? Wallace Stegner describes one of his characters, agonizing over a coming move, as she looks at "the Franklin stove which had been their hearthstone." On it, she reads, "O fortunate, o happy day/When a new household finds its place/Among the myriad homes of earth."[1] A few sentences later, Stegner's narrator muses, "Home is a notion that only the nations of the homeless fully appreciate and only the uprooted comprehend."[2] Surely, home is a topic worthy of serious study.

Home as a Basic Need

Whether people dwell as residents or wanderers,[3] they associate themselves with some physical and social attributes called *home*. Nomadic tribes carry their homes with them as they move from place to place. People, animals, implements, tents, customs, and usually routes of travel then define home. In Western society, many people move about but, at any one time, all but the homeless possess a physical location they call home. Some transients in Western society have a weaker sense of home than nomadic peoples who never settle in one place. This observation leads us to wonder about what makes a home.

Although home is rarely listed as a basic need, I claimed (in Chapter 1) that it should be. Home is the place where all the other basic needs are gathered under one roof and where, in addition, many wants are satisfied. Not every basic need is completely met in the home; we have to go outside for medical care and the purchase of food and clothing. But needs are identified and planned for in the home. Appointments are made, shopping lists created, advertisements studied, wants evaluated, and dreams shared. The home is a place where needs are unified. Without a home, an individual has to seek a different source for the satisfaction of each basic need.

Does this unifying function provide a sufficient reason for classifying the need for a home as a basic need? One can survive without a home so long as food, water, medical care, and shelter are available when needed. However, a home also gives us a safe place to store our possessions, and some homeless people reject public shelters precisely because their belongings are not safe in these places. Sometimes we make the mistake of supposing that homeless people do not really want a home. They seem to prefer living on the street. If we listen more closely, we may be convinced that most of the homeless do indeed want a home, but they associate *home* with a place that is safe for them and their possessions. As Robert Coates has pointed out, "A street is not a home,"[4] but it may meet the safety criterion better than some of our shelters.

A home has some stability in addition to its function in unifying needs. One not only has a place to store possessions but one has the *same* place to do so over an extended period of time. Further, one's entrance and exit are not questioned by strangers. Family members or others who share the home space may raise questions, but usually such questions are induced by their concern for us and by our own carelessness. We have forgotten to say where we will be, how we can be reached, or what time we will be home. The stability of a home is maintained in part by the responsible behavior of its occupants.

Having a place for our possessions, for example, may entail keeping them there and not leaving them all over the house. It also requires us to respect the possessions of others and keep their spaces inviolate.

To many of us, an important feature of a home is its provision for privacy. We enter home with a sigh of relief, shutting out the larger world. This is a relatively new feature of homes, and it shocks us to read of as many as four couples in the Middle Ages sharing one huge bed and surrounded by various individuals sleeping on straw mats.[5] In sharp contrast, by Victorian times, privacy was even equated with morality, and public rooms were sharply separated (usually by a whole floor) from bedrooms and other private spaces. Larry Ford comments:

> Victorian domestic architecture emphasized the relationship between proper spaces and proper behavior. Parlors, music rooms, dining rooms, and children's play areas were included in the Victorian house to encourage desired middle-class activities and etiquette. French apartments, on the other hand, were criticized as amoral, if not immoral, because they lacked hallways and usually had bedrooms on the same floor as more public rooms.[6]

Lack of privacy does not signify immorality, of course, and this is probably a lesson that all students should learn about homes and the ways of other cultures. Today, many immigrant families, out of necessity, share space in ways that would make others of us uncomfortable.

If the desire for privacy is culturally prescribed, we cannot regard it as a universal or basic need. However, we human beings do not live in a universal social environment; we live in a particular time and place. In today's liberal democracies, it is likely that even children will express a need for some privacy, and home members should try to satisfy this need.

Possibly the most important feature of a home – one that surely makes it a basic need in contemporary Western society – is that it supplies us with an address and thus an identity. Home is a place where people can find us and from which we can reach out to communicate with others. Consider how enormously difficult it is to apply for anything – a job, food stamps, mail catalogs, appointments – if one does not have an address. In our society, the address is even more important than stability or privacy. Without it, one cannot hope to acquire a place that possesses the other desirable features we have discussed. A home, however shabby, crowded, and unstable, gives us an identity. The need for an identity and the impossibility of separating this from an address is enough in itself to classify the need for a home as a basic need.

Consideration of the home and personal identity will lead us to a discussion of the physical home (or house) as an extension of self but, before addressing that topic, we should note that the material so far discussed has some bearing on education and happiness. We cannot be happy if our basic needs are unmet; that much is clear. We have already suggested, however, that we cannot be entirely happy if those around us suffer unmet basic needs. The fundamental aim for education in this regard, then, is a social or civic one – to understand how basic needs are in part culturally determined and to guide students toward a sense of discomfort when other members of the society suffer.

The Home as Extension of the Self

Built places may be regarded as extensions of our bodies, and the things with which we surround ourselves are part of our selves.[7] Even the poorest home may have a geranium blooming on a windowsill, and we know as we look at it that the woman who lives there is projecting an inner beauty. Traveling through poor rural areas, we are likely to see a proliferation of green and blooming plants thriving in old tin cans.[8] In some settings, these plantings are especially beautiful and strike us as authentic. In others, they seem contrived. What makes the difference? The answer seems to be that, in one case, the plantings are an extension of an authentic self – in another, a poor copy. We'll have to explore this more deeply as we move along.

Almost from the beginnings of a substantial middle class, writers have mocked the bourgeoisie. These people are supposedly (and often, in fact) concerned with property values, convention, and their own public reputation. If we believed in *true* selves, we might say that the bourgeois has sacrificed that self for a reputable but false self. I think it is a mistake to look at it this way. All selves are true or real selves, and there is no true self lurking somewhere within.[9] The question is what sort of self is under construction. Hermann Hesse said, "The bourgeois is...by nature a creature of weak impulses, anxious, fearful of giving himself away and easy to rule."[10] This is an important criticism and worthy of extended time in educational discussion, but it is not the whole story.

Communist philosophy was merciless in its attack on the bourgeoisie, accusing it – as a class – of contributing to the exploitation of the proletariat (working class) through its acquisitiveness and willingness to toady to the upper class. One does not have to embrace communism to see that there is some truth in this criticism. John Kenneth Galbraith has argued persuasively that a society marked by widespread economic prosperity is unlikely to enact the legislation required to relieve the misery of its poor.[11] Contentment, marred only by the nagging desire for still more material goods, is not a promising base from which to launch major social changes. This issue is worth extensive study from historical, political, and economic perspectives.

We are interested here in the connections between home and self and, although it is important to study society and social classes, it is also important to look at individuals and how they differ. Harry Haller, the protagonist of Hesse's *Steppenwolf*, hates the bourgeois life, yet is drawn to it. He wants to live in a clean, fresh-smelling house that is orderly and comfortable. He rents rooms in such houses. But his own room is a mess, with books, papers, and wine bottles scattered everywhere. The messiness, we are encouraged to believe, is a sign of Harry's wolfishness – something wild, lonely, and different from the rest of the house and neighborhood. The particular content of Harry's mess – books and papers – reveals him as an intellectual, a special form of lonely wolf.

Harry recognizes that he contains two warring selves, each consumed by hatred of the other. To reconcile them seems impossible, and he is driven to thoughts of suicide. Other characters in the novel try to teach him that every human being is a bundle of contradictions – that indeed he contains a great many more selves than two in conflict. Because, despite his hatred of it, he is drawn to bourgeois life – especially what passes for bourgeois intellectual life (another horrible contradiction) – he can see no way out. As he prepares to pay a visit that he both wants and does not want to make, he broods over the average way of life and the choices people make:

> Without really wanting to at all, they pay calls and carry on conversations, sit out their hours at desks and on office chairs; and it is all compulsory, mechanical and against the grain, and it could all be done or left undone just as well by machines; and indeed it is this never-ceasing machinery that prevents their being...critics of their own lives and recognizing the stupidity and shallowness, the hopeless tragedy and waste of the lives they lead, and the awful ambiguity grinning over it all.[12]

Harry's condition is very like that of Bill Chalmers in Lightman's *The Diagnosis* but, whereas Bill's body more or less decides on suicide with no conscious reflection, Harry clings to a hopeless but critical autonomy. Neither can analyze his situation in a way that might bring happiness without hypocrisy. Here we see an opportunity for education to confer a great gift. It can encourage the analysis that Bill and Harry so completely avoided. Indeed, in his condemnation of bourgeois hypocrisy, Harry ignores his own. Dependent on certain middle-class amenities, Harry has contempt for those who provide them. The desire to get away from trivia such as cleaning, shopping, and working set hours is in tension with his recognition that, as things are, someone has to do all of these things. One avenue of escape for the Steppenwolf is the world of drugs, and this too is important for teenage discussion. Can students see another way to resolve the conflict? Why might they want to escape from their own homes? What would they miss if they did so?

Communist philosophers, Hesse, and social critics in general often bring critical insight to the large social scene, but they miss the joy and goodness hidden in the details of everyday life. If it is true that the typical bourgeois is easy to rule and lives a boring life, it is also true that the woman who keeps the fresh-smelling house so admired by Harry Haller often loves her children unselfishly, cares sincerely for her husband, tends a few plants that add beauty to her rooms, nurses an elderly parent, and sustains a church that would fall down without her. Her harried husband sometimes completes work that does matter, and there are nights when he comes home satisfied. There is joy in watching children grow, in tending a garden, in watching the seasons change, in assisting a neighbor or coworker.

Not all members of the bourgeoisie are alike. Each has an individual life, an individual character, even if it is pressed and twisted by the forces rightly identified by the critics. The everydayness of bourgeois life – the loss of intensity – so condemned by Hesse is, for some, a way of life to be celebrated. The bourgeois home with its clean curtains, lavendered sheets, and kitchen fragrances dominates loving memories and imaginative longing. Fiction, poetry, and biography abound in images of the life so easily castigated by social critics. Nor is it a single way of life. There are dirty homes and clean homes; kind fathers and cruel ones; competent mothers and stupid, lazy ones; meals to remember and food eaten only to prevent starvation; houses that stay forever in memory and houses from which the occupants flee as soon as they are able to do so.

The task of educating for home life is enormously complex. The material is easy to come by; it is all around us in great literature, in the vulgar profusion of advertising, and in stories in the tabloids. The question is where to begin and how to proceed, and we encounter difficulties at every turn. Suppose, for example, that a teacher, Ms. A, decides to start a unit (must it be a *unit*?) on homes and homemaking with the reading of a few pages from Proust's *Remembrance of Things Past*. Most likely her choice would be the few pages in which Proust's remembrances are triggered by tea and madeleines – a marvelous episode that reveals the power of our senses to evoke memories.[13] After the reading, discussion of similar events in personal experience or remembered stories should flow easily. But everything is against us here.

In schools today, we rarely use bits of literature to launch discussion of existential questions. The system insists either that a work must be completely read (and often analyzed to its ruin) or that its author must simply be matched to a work, with no time at all given to the content. Success at the latter task is sometimes offered as proof of cultural literacy. The first way, complete reading, is often infinitely worse. Not long ago, I watched a class of teenagers suffer through an entire semester "studying" *The Scarlet Letter*. By the end of the semester, they hated the book, their teacher, and reading in general. Thus, an immediate question arises: Would the system as it is now constructed allow Ms. A to read a few pages of Proust, tell a bit more about the work, and invite discussion?

Another difficulty involves the real potential for personal harm when we encourage students to speak of their own experience. When we look at the school scene through the eyes of our Visitor from another world, we cannot imagine genuine education that neglects personal experience, and certainly there are educational theorists today who insist on its importance.[14] Personal experience is of central importance, but it is not mere stupidity that causes its neglect in schools. As students begin to discuss the homes they live in and the homes they dream of, they need assurance that they are not compelled to speak and even that their choice of silence on some things is admirable. We cannot know, when such discussions are encouraged, what will come out or how greatly a student might later regret having spoken. It takes sensitivity and pedagogical skill to conduct these discussions effectively.[15]

A similar caution is required, however, in conducting discussions on the topics of class, race, or gender. A great worry for critical theorists – one that should receive far more attention than it does at present – is that the efforts of critical pedagogues may induce anger, alienation, and hopelessness instead of wisdom and practical action. "Discussion" can deteriorate into venting and blaming, thus causing increased separation between groups.[16] From the perspective I am taking here, perhaps the greatest worry is the actual obliteration of personal experience. If identity is defined only in terms of class, race, gender, or ethnicity, individual personal experience is lost. Not only is memory distorted to fit the favored class description, so also are accounts of a hoped-for future. Still, critical theorists are basically right in wanting to open classrooms to discussion of class, race, and gender, but we must find ways to preserve personal experience as we analyze the conditions of oppression. Moreover, we must learn how to do these things more skillfully and sensitively.

Personal experience must be acknowledged, but it cannot be subjected to the standard forms of educational evaluation. If we use literature as a starting place, students should feel comfortable in staying with the literary experience, perhaps creating their own fictional stories. A teacher might tell her students that they will never be forced to say whether the stories they tell are autobiographical or fictional. This might relieve some anxieties.

Having recognized some of the difficulties we face, let's consider now what might be included in a study of homes as extensions of our bodies. We might start by asking what can be learned about various literary characters from a study of their rooms and possessions. What can we say about Harry Haller? About Proust? About Bill Chalmers? We can pick characters from almost any richly detailed book and infer much about them through the ways in which they have extended their bodies into built places and possessions. Somewhere along the way, students should be invited to explore the question, What do your rooms and possessions say about you?

Readers of David McCullough's biography of John Adams will notice that the descriptions of the houses and possessions of Adams and Thomas Jefferson contrast sharply. Adams lived a life of moderation and frugality, always as nearly as possible in situations similar to his origins on the Massachusetts coast. Jefferson spent money liberally and ended his life deeply in debt. Jefferson left behind a property and grounds still visited by tourists and students of architecture, and his property clearly demonstrated his aesthetic vision, but we know from an examination of his possessions that he was neither frugal nor prudent. Adams's possessions demonstrate both love of home place and the virtues so often associated with New England.[17]

An exploration of this kind brings the study of personal experience and the study of class up close and makes it, too, personal. Mention of class could be avoided, of course, but what if a student mentions it? Should one be proud or ashamed to be a member of the working class? How about the bourgeoisie? The upper class? It helps to have more stories at hand. On reading *Aunt Arie* (a Foxfire Portrait), students may feel that poverty is not the measure of a life.[18] In her story, we encounter flowering plants in old tin cans, a hand-cultivated vegetable garden, a woodsy location, exuberant hospitality, and a wondrous mixture of wisdom and superstition. There is no poverty of spirit. On one level, there is charm and a primitive romance about Aunt Arie's life, but how many of us would have the stamina and spunk to replicate it? Can we find stories of material poverty and rich spirit in urban America?

Whether students belong to the middle class or just aspire to belong to it, they need to know the weaknesses identified by Hesse and others. They also need to know that personal memories cross all class lines. Detailed descriptions of childhood homes, Grandmother's kitchen, and Grandfather's barn or study abound in literature. From poor, tiny houses to the fine grandparental house,

Laufzorn, described by Robert Graves,[19] houses are embedded in our memories.

We identify not only with our houses but also with other possessions. What does it mean if a teenager does or does not wear top name-brand clothing? Why do people spend their money on well-advertised clothing? What would people learn about you by looking at your room and belongings? What would you like them to think? What are your dreams for a future house and possessions?

Before the rise of bourgeois domesticity, living places (those that were not rude shelters or huts) were built to reflect the wealth of their owners. Little thought was given to what we today call *comfort*,[20] and the impression made by a house was more important than the comfort of its occupants. The tendency to build and decorate for the purpose of impressing others is still with us, and writers like Hesse would criticize the tendency as a characteristic of the bourgeois desire to conform. That desire, paradoxically, is often accompanied by a desire to stand out, but only as an exemplary case of what is already approved. How much of what students possess and exhibit can be explained in this way?

When we enter a living space that is built and decorated to impress, we often say that it doesn't look lived in, that we could not be comfortable there. What sort of people live in houses that reflect an advertised model rather than a family? Casey remarks, "As we feel more 'at home' in dwelling places, they become places created in our own bodily image."[21] Perhaps people who live in model homes never really feel at home, and perhaps too they have not yet acknowledged the selves they are becoming. This sends a challenge to people of every class: Am I just a thin image of my class – a paper doll of sorts – or am I a distinctive, interesting self? Perhaps both an acceptance of admirable qualities in one's class and genuine effort in building a distinctive self offer a special form of happiness.

Comfort

When we think of happiness at home, we usually think of warm and loving personal relationships. These are, of course, basic to our happiness unless we live alone by choice. All of us, however, whether living alone or in company, desire comfort, and comfort is closely associated with domestic happiness.

Comfort as we think of it today is a relatively new concept. Witold Rybczynski tells us that it originated with the bourgeois home.[22] Before that, comfort referred to consolation; a little later, *comfortable* indicated an adequate level of material resources. Our idea of comfort was not familiar to people in earlier times. Medieval dwelling places might have been ostentatious, for example, but most of us would not have found them comfortable. Too hot near the open fire, too cold everywhere else, even castles and manor houses were poorly ventilated, ill-lighted, and infested with rats and fleas. Furniture was not comfortable, and it was the custom for many people to sleep in one huge bed. Those who could not be accommodated in beds slept on a pallet of straw.

Even today people do not entirely agree on what is meant by comfort. Rybczynski points out that people in the Western world prefer to sit on chairs, while those in the East often prefer to squat or sit on the floor. Each is uncomfortable when forced to adopt the ways of the other. Despite our differences, however, it is clear that our physical selves are involved when we speak of comfort. We want to avoid physical discomfort.

The desire to impress others is sometimes at odds with the wish to be comfortable. The history of comfort reveals that wealthy landowners often put appearance over the comfort of a house's occupants. For centuries, of course, there was no feasible way to achieve comfort with respect to light and temperature, but it is hard to understand why people did not seek comfort in designing furniture and clothing. In a very real sense, the much maligned bourgeoisie opened the door to consideration of comfort, and it was middle-class women who drew attention to the relationship between efficiency and comfort.[23]

If we cannot agree on exactly what is meant by comfort, we may come close to agreement on the factors involved. Temperature is certainly one, and it is hard on the occupants of a home when some like it hot and others like it cold. Bachelard writes, as we noted earlier, that "the house we were born in is physically inscribed in us. It is a group of organic habits."[24] Starting in different houses, with different parents, we develop different organic habits, and a major problem for all couples beginning their adventure in shared housekeeping is just how to manage the differences in organic habits. Helping each other to achieve comfort with respect to temperature is one such problem.

Another is light. There are those who prefer a vampire-like existence in perpetual twilight. Others blithely ignore fading carpets and upholstery, happily bathed in the light from many windows. Some pull the shades or blinds as soon as dusk falls, and others let their light shine out into the darkness. Lamps and lighting fixtures have become important in home decoration, and nothing is a more obvious symbol of poverty than the naked light bulb. Certainly, appropriate lighting is necessary to our comfort in work areas. We can hardly imagine the struggle to read and write by candlelight. On the other hand, some of us find comfort in candlelight at the dinner table.

Our sense of comfort in work areas cannot be separated from efficiency, and here female domestic scientists made significant contributions. Work counters constructed at the right height for average women, the proximity of counters to stove and refrigerator, adequate ventilation, and efficient use of household appliances were all promoted by women as part of a thriving program in domestic engineering.[25] Today both women and men are interested in comfort while working at desks and computers, and there is much discussion of how to avoid the discomforts associated with repetitive motions such as those required by long hours at the computer.

Physical comfort surely is an important factor in our happiness at home, but so is psychological comfort. Because it does seem natural for us to make our living spaces into extensions of our bodies, we come to need a certain kind of housing environment in order to be psychologically comfortable. Many writers have described the features of rooms in which they work, but the need for a comfortable environment is not restricted to writers. We know more about the preferences of writers because they tell us about them in writing. Pearl Buck said that she had to have fresh flowers on her desk, and Robert Frost liked a rural environment for his writing; Sartre disliked greenery and preferred working in the city.

Artists and other creative people (and perhaps all of us) develop routines that add to our psychological comfort. Descartes did his best thinking while lying in bed in the morning. Winston Churchill read communiqués and signed memos on a movable tray in his morning bath. Pablo Casals started each day by playing Bach fugues. A few great artists seem to have been able to work under any conditions. Alexander Borodin, for example, worked effectively on either music or chemistry in conditions of near chaos.[26] The essential point is that the routines must be *ours*, the ones that give us psychological comfort. Copying the routines of others in order to acquire their powers doesn't work. James R. Newman, in discussing mathematical creativity, comments: "Alas, the habits of famous men are rarely profitable to their disciples. The young philosopher will derive little benefit from being punctual like Kant, the biologist from cultivating Darwin's dyspepsia, the playwright from eating Shaw's vegetables."[27] It seems likely, however, that the men who had these habits would have been less comfortable if the habits had been interrupted. Even Darwin's dyspepsia provided a measure of comfort since it gave him an excuse to avoid unpleasant confrontations.

Education might profitably include many of the things just discussed. Students should be encouraged to think about what makes them comfortable and what makes others comfortable. What helps them to learn? What is their vision for a future home? These are important questions, but it is also worthwhile to study the history of homes and comfort. Why is this part of human history so often neglected?

Domestic Science

> Housekeeping . . . is an accomplishment in comparison to which, in its bearing on women's relation to real life and to the family, all others are trivial. It comprehends all that goes to make up a well-ordered home, where the sweetest relations of life rest on firm foundations. . . . It ought to be absorbed in girlhood, by easy lessons taken between algebra, music and painting.[28]

This quotation from an 1891 book on practical housekeeping makes it clear that housekeeping was regarded as women's work. It was also regarded as important and complicated work. Today housekeeping chores are much eased by tools and appliances of all sorts and by the availability of inexpensive ready-made clothing. Not many women in the Western world spend all day Monday on laundry and ironing, another day on bread making, and every spare moment on sewing. Some of us still can or freeze our own vegetables and fruits, but we do this more for pleasure than from necessity. Given the enormous changes that have occurred over the past century, it is reasonable to ask whether anyone now needs the kind of preparation once recommended for girls.

One way to find out what every homemaker needs to know is to survey successful homemakers or to call a convention of such people. What do they all know? Surely, this is the material that should be part of the domestic science taught in schools. There exists a strong possibility, however, that important knowledge might be missed this way, and educators would be in the position of merely reproducing homemakers exactly like those preceding them. It seems reasonable, therefore, to seek review and additional recommendations from experts in the field.

Why not start with experts? This is the mistake we make too often with other school subjects. We allow experts to establish what *all* people should learn in every subject. It is a mistake because subject matter experts cannot control their passions. Even when they start out reasonably enough, they quickly move to recommendations that reflect their own interests and not the needs of their students. A combination of the material known and used by happy, competent homemakers and that suggested by experts who see room for improvement should provide the foundation for the curriculum. This approach should be used whenever we claim that *all* people should learn a set of topics. It provides a check on the passions of experts, and it allows room for surpassing the current knowledge of practitioners. I have often argued that it is the method we should use in constructing the mathematics curriculum.

We can be fairly sure that certain broad topics would be included in a domestic science curriculum for all students: nutrition (meal planning, basic cooking skills to preserve food values and taste, identification and selection of fresh foods); safety (checks on wiring, smoke detectors, child-proofing electrical outlets, storage of dangerous materials; knowledge about lead, asbestos, molds, and radon); care of pets; cleanliness and order; budgets and shopping; light and ventilation; basic home repairs, including the repair of minor appliances; care of clothing and linens.

In the quotation at the beginning of this section, it is recommended that young people get housekeeping lessons from their early years "between algebra, music and painting." When we teach domestic topics in schools, the risk is that each item will be assigned to a particular subject and grade, learned long enough to pass a test, and then promptly forgotten. Learned at home in a well-ordered household, lessons are marked by continuous practice. In schools, we would have to think seriously about a spiral curriculum that would be designed to repeat and deepen the most important concepts, and teachers of all courses should be asked to consider how their subjects can contribute to competence in the skills and concepts involved in homemaking. I have already suggested that the topics to be included should come from the repertoires of happy, successful homemakers, guided (and perhaps augmented) by experts in domestic science. As we construct the curriculum itself, we would do well to keep in mind the important suggestion made by Jerome Bruner:

> We might ask, as a criterion for any subject taught in primary school, whether, when fully developed, it is worth an adult's knowing, and whether having known it as a child makes a person a better adult. If the answer to both questions is negative or ambiguous, then the material is cluttering the curriculum.[29]

We have to be careful with such a criterion. Indeed, we might do better to think of it as a guide to reflection on curriculum making. As such a guide, it should be useful at every stage of curriculum work. For a given topic X, it might not be the case that X is essential in some form for every adult. Still, X might make a significant contribution to the growth of *some* adults. X might then be offered, and students who express interest might pursue it more fully. Others would go on to different topics.

This observation suggests that the methods we use as well as the topics we choose should be submitted to a Bruner-like criterion. For life in a liberal democracy, the capacity to make well-informed choices is paramount. Developing this capacity must start in childhood and grow into adulthood. Therefore we might add a corollary to Bruner's criterion: Looking at the curriculum as a whole, are there opportunities for significant student choice? If not, the curriculum should be revised.

One more question should be asked in connection with Bruner's criterion. Are there topics and activities that are appropriate, perhaps even essential, for children even though they are of no interest or use to adults? Surely there is more to childhood than preparation for adulthood. Here we have to do some thinking at what might be called the *meta-level*. A particular topic or activity might be of specific interest or value to children, not to adults, but the spirit accompanying it or the attitude toward a whole family of activities might be of great value to adults, and this Bruner recognized. The childhood activity, while not in itself relevant to adulthood, might facilitate a more competent (or happier) adulthood.

It begins to look as though Bruner's criterion is not so easy to use and may not sort topics out faultlessly. As we saw in our analysis of aims, however, the kind of discussion induced by invoking Bruner's criterion and my suggested corollary is enormously valuable. We are led to ask: Is this topic or activity essential for everyone? If the answer is yes (and that answer must be rigorously supported), the topic becomes a requirement. If not, we still ask, is it valuable for some people? How can we provide exposure without undue coercion, so that students can make choices on this and other topics? Finally, what lasting educational aims are satisfied by activities specific to childhood?

The reason for this brief discursion into curriculum theory should be clear. If we are serious about educating for homemaking, we have to employ methods of curriculum construction that are compatible with the ends we seek. This is demanding, exciting work. I am not suggesting a one-semester course in domestic science for seventh graders but, rather, a full curriculum to provide continuous growth in knowledge and practice throughout the precollege years.

I'll conclude this part of the discussion with an example of the kind of thinking that seems necessary. There was a period in American education in which adolescents were taught specific adult skills such as budgeting, reading an electric meter, writing checks, and the like.[30] These were largely futile exercises. Children of middle school years seldom write checks, do not have extensive budgets, and will not worry about the electric meter for several years. It is not specific adult-level skills that should be taught. It is basic principles and attitudes.

In an age of mass advertising, children should be helped to understand how they are being constantly manipulated. Even small children can understand that certain wants do not arise naturally, and they can be led to sympathize with children who live in poverty. As they get older, they can study more formally the effects of advertising, of movies and television, of peer pressure. Eventually, they can be involved in discussions of the sort I started earlier: How important is consumer spending in a capitalist economy? Are there ways to live that avoid both profligacy and wholesale condemnation of capitalism? What skills and virtues are needed to develop such a life?

Education for wise consuming and sales resistance may seem a bit removed from traditional domestic science, but today it is central. As I write, a major issue in the news is consumer indebtedness. Americans have greater debts now than ever, and yet representatives of our current federal government are urging people to spend the tax rebate they have received. This situation reminds us that the concerns Schumpeter tried so hard to dismiss are still with us. On the one hand, it is frightening to think what will happen to an already shaky economy if consumers cut spending drastically. On the other, it is even more alarming to think of what families and individuals will suffer if they continue the current pattern of spending. Serious consideration of these issues is important at every stage of life and brings with it the deeper study of many traditional topics in domestic science and economics.

In this discussion of domestic science, we must return to a consideration of efficiency. Many educators are quick to identify any talk of efficiency with factories and assembly lines, and I certainly do not want to promote the so-called factory model of education. But efficiency itself is not a bad thing. In an earlier section, we discussed the facilitative routines of some highly creative people. To teach children something about efficiency is very different from employing efficient methods to teach them. We still use a bit of caution; we do not want students to sacrifice reflective thought, exploration, and artistry in a quest for efficiency. Rather, efficiency should serve these higher purposes. Structuring one's life so that routine tasks are done efficiently provides more time for the activities we value and want to savor.

Domestic scientists made contributions to the efficiency movement. Lillian Gilbreth extended her husband's time and motion studies into an analysis of housework, and Ellen Richards emphasized the serviceability of a house and its arrangements.[31] The distinction between efficiency as facilitative, as a way of handling routines so that higher activities can be engaged, and efficiency for its own sake is illustrated in the attitudes of Gilbreth and Richards as contrasted with those of the male architect Le Corbusier.[32] Both women thought that style should be a matter entirely separate from efficiency and that women and their families should be free to choose their own styles, whereas Corbusier advocated a standard style that in itself

113

represented efficiency. A lesson in the history of domestic science would be very helpful here. It involves a lesson in the appropriate ordering of means and ends. A practical exercise might involve examination and discussion of real estate advertisements. Why do so many new houses look alike? What impression is the builder trying to make?

Today, when both girls and boys must be concerned with establishing and running a home, efficiency should be a matter of great interest to everyone. A careful study of time management should be part of general education; it is a topic that can be useful in every part of one's life, including student life. People who are efficient in routine tasks need not be robotic. Indeed, they may be more relaxed, flexible, and reflective than less structured people because they are not haunted by tasks undone. I often find it a relief to renew my to-do list and see that each of the many tasks awaiting me has been, roughly, assigned a time. My free time is delightfully free – not stolen, not riddled with guilt.

Women have not always been on the "right" side with respect to efficiency, however. Laura Shapiro argues strongly that many female domestic scientists were carried away with ideas of efficiency and standardization, and she claims further that American cuisine suffered a regrettable setback as a result.[33] Not only were the meals suggested by these women often unappetizing – appealing more to the eye than the palate – but some women derived little pleasure from eating them. Their cookery and their concern for their figures were in considerable conflict. Under such practices, preparing and eating food contributed little to happiness. Again, it might be helpful for young women today to learn that they are not the first people tempted to starve themselves for the sake of some female ideal of beauty.

Greater skill and efficiency, more reflective thought, and the development of virtues such as frugality and moderation are all called for in current domestic science. In helping us to avoid pain, they are part of our pursuit of happiness. However, homemaking is not simply a matter of efficiency and the avoidance of pain; it is also an arena of pleasure. We turn to that possibility next.

Pleasure in Homemaking

Books with titles like *The Joy of Cooking* remind us that homemaking can yield pleasure.[34] Homemaking is not just a set of dreary tasks.

For those who love cooking, gardening, entertaining, or decorating, homemaking can be an enterprise in which the lines between work and play become blurred. It is not necessary today to grow one's own vegetables, can tomatoes, make soups from scratch, or bake bread, but many women and men gain enormous satisfaction from doing these things. Further, the connections between food and place, food and art, and food and season are all worth exploring. I can imagine schools offering an interdisciplinary unit on food that would involve cooking, art, geography, history, mathematics, biology, religion, biography, and chemistry. Every classroom should contain maps and at least a few cookbooks to be discussed and enjoyed.

As I look over the cookbooks in my own collection, I spot *Monet's Table*.[35] Children can be introduced to many standard-like questions during an examination of such a book: Who was Monet? When did he live? What school of painting did he bring to its heights? Where is Giverny? What are the names of some of his great paintings? Beyond the standard questions, however, there are wonderful points to ponder. Monet was "a demon for punctuality,"[36] and he insisted not only on having lunch served at the appointed time but even that his vegetables be picked exactly at their prime. He rose early and went to bed early, making best use of the light that was essential for his painting. Was his penchant for punctuality and efficiency unusual in an artist or is it a myth that efficiency and creativity are somehow in opposition? Students should be invited to study other biographies (some mentioned earlier) to answer the question. Depending on the interests of teacher and students, a great variety of issues might be discussed. Monet enjoyed roasted or stewed venison, partridge, pigeon, and rabbit. Is hunting ethically acceptable? Should we eat meat at all? Do students find a double-page photograph of a whole poached pike attractive or repulsive? Why?

Hospitality is another topic triggered by *Monet's Table*. Our customs of hospitality differ widely, but few of us consider ourselves obligated to provide hospitality to strangers. Yet it was once the custom – virtually everywhere – to do so. Theodore Zeldin writes, "This kind of hospitality [opening one's house to strangers] has been admired and practiced in virtually every civilization that has existed, as though it fulfills a basic human need."[37] Perhaps it did fulfill a basic human need centuries ago. Now a generous giving and receiving of hospitality adds immeasurably to our pleasure, but it is no longer a basic need.

The brief history of hospitality provided by Zeldin is both interesting and instructive. Because travel was once so difficult and travelers so scarce, strangers were enthusiastically welcomed. By the twentieth century, however, hospitality was either purchased or offered only to and by acquaintances. Zeldin comments:

> There were few places left where all comers were entitled to take fruit from orchards, as they once could in colonial Virginia, where it was an honour to give, a pleasure to see a new face. The pedlar who sold unusual goods, the wanderer who told amazing stories, the stranger who brought interesting news, were no longer needed in the age of television and supermarkets.[38]

Zeldin points out, however, that a new, deeper form of hospitality arose as travel and communication became rapid. Now hospitality involved "admitting new ideas and emotions"[39] into one's mind. Needless to say, we have not yet mastered this deeper hospitality, and we have lost many features of the old, more personal forms. The physical hospitality of individual homes is no longer a basic need, and the intellectual hospitality described by Zeldin rarely appears as an expressed need. Home is now a private place for regular residents, a place to be opened occasionally to chosen visitors.

Not all household tasks give pleasure in the doing. Although many of us enjoy cooking and providing hospitality, we may not enjoy cleaning bathrooms and vacuuming. Still, pleasure may arise in enjoying the result of work that itself often seems drudgery. The sight of gleaming fixtures, the fragrance of a stack of freshly folded laundry, sparkling counter tops, clean rooms are all deeply satisfying. Of course, we might – like Hesse's Harry Haller – experience enjoyment of these things without doing the jobs ourselves and even with some contempt for those who think these jobs important. Some people do undergo Steppenwolf-like conflicts, and they need a form of education that puts greater emphasis on self-knowledge.

One of the great pleasures of homemaking is the creation of beauty. Most of us are not content to live in merely efficient surroundings; we want our homes, rooms, or corners to be attractive. As we noted earlier, our living places become extensions of our bodies and selves. Our homes are not just shelters for our bodies. Bachelard said that the house is a shelter also for the imagination.[40] It is the place where we daydream, engage in privileged conversation, pursue our hobbies, and grow more skillful in the activities we value. Beauty is best created not from a photograph or blueprint but from the things we love. Those who love books, plants, children, and pets can create lovely homes, but those homes will not look like unlived-in models. Where in schools do we ask these questions: Does it matter if our surroundings are lovely or ugly? How would you describe a room you would like to live in? What makes a home attractive?

In addition to the real pleasure experienced in some tasks, in hospitality, and in the creation of beauty, happiness is often identified with the privacy and informality of home. Peace and quiet are sought at home as safe and respectable escapes from the noise and contention of public life. It is obvious that physical comfort plays a role, and informality augments that role. Not only should the furniture be comfortable but our bodies can be shoeless, formal garments hung away, sleeves rolled up, ties and makeup abandoned. At home we can relax – soak in a hot tub, put our feet up, enjoy physical pleasure.

Not every home, however, is free of noise and contention. For many centuries, it was thought to be the special task of wives to maintain a serene home, and when husbands or children went astray, the housewife was blamed. Today we are not so quick to blame women for everything that goes wrong in homes, but we have done little to educate boys and girls in the ways required to maintain cooperative and loving relationships. This will be a topic for a later chapter.

I did not set out in this chapter to develop a full and coherent curriculum on homemaking. Rather, my intention was to identify significant topics and questions that might be addressed in a variety of school settings. There is a civics lesson, for example, in recognizing home as a basic need, and there are history lessons in tracing the development of the modern Western home. The discussion of home as an extension of our bodies and selves is filled with possibilities for the examination of class differences, individual taste and authenticity, self-knowledge and conflict. Even comfort, so highly valued today, has a history, and it too is a concept holding much potential for self-analysis. Efficiency and the employment of facilitative routines were suggested as highly useful topics of study, and they too are ideas that can be explored in history and biography. Throughout the chapter, problems of curriculum making and teaching were considered as they became relevant. Finally, we talked about pleasure in homemaking and, after identifying several of its sources, left open the door for fuller discussion of some topics closely associated with happiness in home life. These topics, centered on the establishment of caring relations, will be the focus of later chapters.

Before turning to those topics, let's consider another large source of happiness – love of place. Our personal dwelling places are located in larger communities or regions with which we identify. Just as our houses become extensions of our selves, our selves shape and are shaped by the regions in which we live. How important is place to our happiness?

6

Places and Nature

At the beginning of the twenty-first century, policymakers are promoting globalization and a strong global economy. Schools are urged to adopt "world-class" standards and to produce graduates who will maintain the status of the United States as an economic leader. Where does a love of place fit into this picture? Should schools teach for an understanding and love of place or should they now offer curricula designed to transcend place? Is there a way to avoid the dichotomy built into these questions?

We'll start this chapter with a brief discussion of love of place and how that love has so often contributed to human happiness. Then we'll move to a more general level and explore the human connection to nature. Finally, we'll consider how schools might balance the tasks of preparing students for a global economy and of promoting the love and care of place that figure so importantly in human flourishing.

Love of Place

Many of us associate home more with a geographical region or community than with a house. Love of place is a theme that runs through fiction, poetry, and biography. John Adams, for example, had a life-long love of Braintree and the Massachusetts coast where he was born. His biographer, David McCullough, writes:

> Recalling his childhood later in life, Adams wrote of the unparalleled bliss of roaming the open fields and woodlands of the town, of exploring the creeks, hiking the beaches.... The first fifteen years of his life, he said, "went off like a fairytale."[1]

Years later, departing from London and his grueling diplomatic duties, he eagerly anticipated his return home:

Adams is not known to have recorded any of his thoughts during the voyage home, but earlier he had said his great desire was "to lay fast of the town of Braintree and embrace it with both arms and all my might. There live, there to die, there to lay my bones, and there to plant one of my sons in the profession of law and the practices of agriculture, like his father."[2]

Love of place adds to pleasure in everyday living, and it also contributes to pleasures of the mind. Everything associated with the beloved place yields a special pleasure. Thus, during their years in France and England, John and Abigail Adams found woods, fields, and gardens that reminded them of home especially beautiful. Similarly, Pearl Buck recounts how her mother, a missionary's wife, created an American garden in China.[3] It was not national chauvinism that led the Adamses and Buck's mother to favor such gardens (although some of that was present in them) but lasting love of a home place.

Stegner's narrator speaks of his grandmother as a *nester* – a person who makes a home and stays put. "Grandmother wanted her son to grow up, as she had, knowing some loved place down to the last woodchuck hole."[4] A bit later he says, "I wonder if ever again Americans can have that experience of returning to a home place so intimately known, profoundly felt, deeply loved, and absolutely submitted to? It is not quite true that you can't go home again. I have done it. . . . But it gets less likely."[5]

It becomes even more unlikely when schools insist on teaching to *transcend* place. The idea, not bad in itself, is to prepare students for economic life anywhere in the developed world. We can't teach narrowly for life in Vermont or West Virginia because our students are very likely to leave these places and seek employment elsewhere. But economic success is not everything in life; moreover, there seems to be no cogent reason why preparation for occupational life should be at odds with an education that respects and recognizes joy in the very place where it is undertaken. We need not *insist* that students love the region in which they grow up, but we should acknowledge the possibility and help them to develop an appreciation that may well bring them a lifetime of joy.

Much great literature reflects and is bound to a particular place. In a review of the poetry of Robinson Jeffers, Brad Leithauser writes, "No American poet seems more tightly bound to a fixed landscape than he to the California coast. . . . It's impossible to conceive of his career removed from the land associated with it."[6] Still, it is also hard to separate Robert Frost or Emily Dickinson from New England or James Dickey from the southern backwoods, and most poets have been at least in part inspired by particular places. The same is true of novelists.

It is not only great literature that reflects the widespread love for particular places. Cookbooks and gardening books do also. Many fine cookbooks are regional, and they contain stories, pictures, and folklore along with recipes. People who find pleasure in gardening usually also find pleasure in looking at seed catalogs. I say *looking at* because there is a pleasure of mind in looking at an illustrated seed catalog that is quite different from *reading* it and composing an order. Similarly, a well-illustrated cookbook is a pleasure to look at, and one containing stories is a pleasure to read. One may or may not actually use the recipes.

Love of place often marks a happy childhood. Bachelard describes the wonder children feel on finding a nest:

> This wonder is lasting, and today when we discover a nest it takes us back to our childhood or, rather, to a childhood; to the childhoods we should have had. For not many of us have been endowed by life with the full measure of its cosmic implications.[7]

What are these cosmic implications? Among other things, the nest represents a refuge. Bachelard quotes the painter Vlaminck:

> "The well-being I feel, seated in front of my fire, while bad weather rages out-of-doors, is entirely animal. A rat in its hole, a rabbit in its burrow, cows in the stable, must all feel the same contentment that I feel." Thus, well-being takes us back to the primitiveness of the refuge.[8]

Finding a nest, thinking of a nest, returns us to the safest places of our childhood. Sometimes the places are real, sometimes imagined, but they are always suffused with the feeling of contentment and well-being. To find a nest requires wandering forth, but the finding itself is a comforting reminder that one has a nesting place of one's own, a place to which we continually return in dreams. Perhaps our fascination with cookbooks and garden catalogs serves a similar purpose. It is at once a reflection of interest in real meals and seedlings and a longing for dreamed-about kitchens and gardens.

From the utterly practical, through daydreaming, arises the image, and the image, says Bachelard, begets a new being. As we noted in Chapter 1, Bachelard said, "This new being is happy man."[9] There is something in the image that contributes immeasurably to human flourishing, and it does not require deep forms of scholarship. Recall Bachelard's further claim: "It is the property of a naive consciousness; in its expression, it is youthful language."[10] Here we have discovered something that adds to our conception of happiness. It is an invitation to see that which is right in front of us, to go beyond in imagination, and to return to the everyday with deepened appreciation.

How can schools preserve and enhance the pleasure that children seem naturally to find in the places they love? Obviously, acknowledging and sharing this pleasure offer a starting point. We have to include happiness as an aim of education, and then we have to recognize all the major sources of that happiness and establish aims consonant with them. If we want children to be happy now and continue to derive happiness from their love of places, then somehow our curricula have to provide for this aim.

Like good parents, we can share poetry, fiction, music, art, and biography that enhance the knowledge and pleasure associated with places. In today's schools, however, sharing knowledge and pleasure is not easy and may even be actively discouraged. All teacher and student activities are supposed to be aimed at specific learning objectives. The idea is that children will do certain things as a result of our teaching, and there isn't much room for the more flexible parental approach that says, in effect, here's something you might enjoy, or see what you think about this, or let's listen and have fun together. Everything a teacher does has to aim at some fact or skill that will appear on a test, and the overriding goal of teaching has become higher test scores.[11] The reason for these pedagogical objectives is the acceptance of a still more pervasive educational aim – financial success.[12]

If, however, we were to take seriously the idea of happiness as an educational aim, we would establish very different guidelines for teaching. We would have more respect for incidental learning and for differential learning. Teachers would be encouraged to read stories and poems to their students with the understanding that a great variety of outcomes might be expected. Some students might simply come to love poetry (but there would be no insistence that they *must*); some might increase their vocabularies; some might learn the meaning of metaphor (but there would be no test on this); some might be inspired to write a poem or story of their own; some might want to paint or draw a picture; some might want to learn more about the writer; some might find and share related music; some might seek a loved place comparable to one described in the shared work; and some might "merely" feel that they have a teacher who cares for them.

I am not suggesting that all education should be conducted in an informal way or that we can depend entirely on incidental learning. A problem that has plagued educational theory for decades is the search for one best method to be used for everything. Thus we have taken polarized positions (you must, you must not) on the use of drill in arithmetic, phonics in reading, multiple-choice testing, tracking, homogeneous grouping, standardized testing, cooperative learning, student-centered learning, the use of rewards, project-based learning, direct instruction, open classrooms, interdisciplinary studies, social promotion, and a host of other topics. We have not done what we say students should do: think problems through carefully and match means reasonably with ends.

Should we use drill in arithmetic, spelling, and grammar? Of course, but not for everything in these subjects! Drill should be used judiciously – to routinize skills that will make the learning of important concepts easier and more enjoyable. The principle we used to argue for efficiency should be our guide in using drill as a pedagogical tool. Whenever we choose a topic or method, we should consider what it is we are trying to do and in what ways the choice might further our aim.

With happiness as an aim, there will be many free gifts in our teaching. We will not wreck the experience of poetry – which is supposed to bring us enjoyment and wisdom – by coercing students to memorize, by overanalyzing it, and by insisting that *all* children learn the names of rhythmical patterns and the exact meanings of metaphor, simile, and analogy. We will share the folklore of place, tell stories, and offer opportunities for students to describe their favorite places. We will restore a sense of the sacred to our teaching. By *sacred* I mean all those things that contribute to lifelong happiness and thus deserve to be preserved and encouraged. Love of place is, in this sense, sacred. Even more sacred is the expectation of children that adults will care for them and for their happiness.

Although we do not think deeply enough about educating for love of place, we do give some thought to teaching ecology and environmental sensitivity. What is the aim of such teaching? Is it to preserve the earth or to satisfy something innate in children? Both?

The Nature Connection

There is some evidence that a connection between people and nature, beyond the need for food, is inherently necessary. The biophilia hypothesis holds that human beings have a genetically based need to affiliate with nature.[13] For those of us who feel a strong affiliation with other life forms, water, rocks, and geophysical phenomena such as tides and sunrises, the biophilia hypothesis sounds right. We have to acknowledge, however, that there are people – increasingly many – who seem to feel no need to connect with nature and prefer to live as far from it as possible.[14] That so many people *do* feel the need and that others might if given the appropriate educational exposure is reason enough for us to explore how education should approach the human–nature relationship.

I have chosen to start with the human need and the joy many of us experience in connection with the natural world rather than the documented needs of the earth and our responsibility to reduce threats to its flourishing. Environmental movements are extremely important but, instead of starting with these, I think we might accomplish more by starting with our own needs and the happiness we experience in healthy relationships with nature.

One difficulty in starting our study of nature with environmental problems and responsibilities is that the approach is so quickly and easily made into standard lessons, and most kids hate lessons. Whitehead counseled that directed learning should start with *romance*, a period of exploration and delight that provides the intrinsic motivation to push further into study. At this stage, we are grabbed by something, having fun, raising questions. Whitehead says:

> This general process is both natural and of absorbing interest. We must often have noticed children between the ages of eight and

thirteen absorbed in its ferment. It is dominated by wonder, and cursed be the dullard who destroys wonder.[15]

The stage of romance is followed, Whitehead says, by a stage of – a need for – precision. The questions that have been raised in the first stage must be answered by careful planning and investigation. In one sense, then, the delights of the first stage are instrumental in providing motivation for the second, more systematic stage of learning. This is an insight used effectively by open educators and their successors.[16] Dewey certainly agreed with Whitehead on this, but he pointed out that we cannot easily tell when "messing about" expresses a real interest, and we cannot suppose that stage two will always naturally follow stage one. It takes considerable shared time and effort to know when to guide students into a second stage that will follow their interests.

For that reason, many impatient educators would simply scrap discussion of stages and go directly to a coerced set of lessons that resemble the stage of precision. Just teach them the facts, skills, and habits that should emerge in the stage of precision! The problem here is that the most important intellectual habits – curiosity, wonder, problem finding, hypothesis testing, and evaluation – may well be lost. Further, as facts become ends in themselves, they begin to clutter the curriculum.

Wise curriculum makers and teachers analyze situations and try to match aims, topics, and methods. When we ask Why are we doing this? we may well respond with more than one answer. Surely, we want to produce young citizens who will care for the places in which they live and for the earth itself. We want them to be aware of the issues and debates surrounding globalization and environmentalism, and we would like them to understand some of the scientific principles involved in studying the earth and its living organisms. In addition, however, we would like to contribute to the lifelong happiness many of our students might experience in connection with nature. When happiness is so directly involved, it makes sense to start with experiences that recognize and enhance the delight children find in the natural world.

Ideally, we would spend part of the day outside exploring with our students, but that isn't always possible. In this litigious age, it isn't only finding time that holds us back. We worry constantly about allergies, injuries, and threats from molesters. When we can't actually get out, we can bring nature in. We can show really good films, find and display collections, bring in small logs, branches, leaves, rocks, soil samples, shells, and seeds. We can provide magazines such as *National Geographic, Dolphin Log, Natural History, Ranger Rick*, and the like; then, of course, we must provide time for the children to read these publications. We can direct kids to library books that focus on topics in natural history and display such books in our classrooms.

Sustained observation and study should be encouraged. It is important to preserve wonder and delight, but it is also important to guide students beyond messing about. Not long ago, I read about a science teacher who set out to teach ninth graders about observation. She set up six stations (each containing a live creature), at each of which groups of three or four students were to spend five minutes and then write up their observations. There were no plans to follow up through reading or further observation. What could this teacher have been thinking? She seemed to be suggesting that scientists look at things and write down what they see. Our classrooms are cluttered with such busy work, and Bruner was right to suggest that clutter of this sort should be cleaned out. In this case, the observations are worse than clutter because they give a faulty impression of scientific work.

What might the teacher have done instead? One of the creatures to be observed was a cockroach. Suppose a group of four or so (maybe more) decided to learn more about cockroaches. Before making their decision, they would have been told to choose one of the six creatures displayed. "Which would you like to study?" Progressive educators (except for A. S. Neill) never said that teachers should leave kids alone. On the contrary, they talked at length about the need for teacher guidance, for sensitivity in deciding when to push a bit, for caution in giving or withholding instruction. So we press a bit. Which would you like to study?

One hopes that students who choose the cockroach would learn something about the evolutionary success of cockroaches. Despite human efforts to exterminate them, they have survived while many other creatures have disappeared. How long does a cockroach live? How do they reproduce? What do they eat? Do they bite human beings? Are they dirty? Is it true that if you put pots away wet, you'll "get" cockroaches? Why are we so bent on eliminating them?

For all of the students, whether their choice was cockroaches or ladybugs, we hope there will be encouragement to read the biographies of great naturalists and some essays on nature. We would also like them to hear about religious beliefs that forbid the deliberate killing of any creature. Think of the lively discussion that could be engendered by a consideration of Albert Schweitzer's "reverence for life." Schweitzer did not deny the necessity of killing some creatures to save others, but he regretted that necessity. A person who takes seriously the reverence for life "injures and destroys life only under a necessity which he cannot avoid, and never from thoughtlessness."[17] Because such a person regrets the injury, he or she will try to find a way to avoid it. Because this is not always possible, such a person develops a tragic sense of life, and that sense may, paradoxically, deepen the happiness one can find in relating to nature.

In insisting that nature study actually involve *study*, have I deserted the camp of those who see the child–nature relation as pure romance? Well, yes. For a thoughtful teacher, there is no pure relation, stage, or life. That doesn't mean that we ignore the romance of childhood. I am as charmed by anecdotes describing it as any nostalgic romantic. I love Robert Paul Smith's accounts of childhood freedom and ritual. Speaking of the folly of stuffing facts into kids, Smith writes:

> They don't want science. They want magic. They don't want hypotheses, they want immutable truth. They want to be, they should be, in a clearing in the jungle painting themselves blue, dancing around the fire and making it rain by patting snakes and shaking rattles.[18]

But someone has to be sure that the blue paint does not contain lead, that the fire is not too big (or full of poison ivy), and that the snakes are not poisonous. And at the end of the dance, lucky kids leave the jungle and go home to a good meal, a bath, and the assurance that home is *not* a jungle. This suggests, metaphorically, the kind of exquisite balance required by competent teaching. We treasure the wonder but guide it safely to knowledge and thoughtful appreciation.

Smith is fundamentally right, however. Children seem to need wild places or, at least, places that seem wild to them.[19] I can remember as a child crawling under a huge blackberry bush to retrieve a baseball. It was stickery torture to get in there but, once inside, it was like a cave. I didn't want to come out, and there was the feeling that nothing could get me. Such spots have served as wild places for generations of children.

Many children like gardens, too, if the gardens are not too formal and they are not made to work too long at tedious jobs. Every child should have opportunities to plant seeds and watch plants grow. In one of Rumer Godden's novels, a tough little girl, Lovejoy, longs for a real home and someone to care for her. Living in a poor section of post-blitz London, she discovers a hidden place in which to plant a garden. With her interest awakened, she begins to see pots and boxes of flowers everywhere. Near one of the houses, "a whole vegetable garden grew in boxes."[20] Receiving little care for herself, Lovejoy was determined to care for something that would respond to her longing for beauty.

As in so many areas of education, parents and teachers often make the mistake of putting responsibility for plants and gardens ahead of delight. "If you plant it, you have to take care of it" is the perennial parental warning. It is true that, for seedlings to thrive, someone must care for them, but this can be a shared task. Children love to walk around a garden and learn the names of plants. They often spot new growth or insect life before adults, and they make observant companions in the garden.

This "walking around" in the garden is a wonderful time to learn how to identify various insects, to admire spiders and their webs, to overcome a fear of bees and learn to work serenely among them. It is a time to feel the silkiness of poppy petals, the stickery stems of pumpkin vines, the puffiness of seed capsules from love-in-a-mist. We do not specify a set of learning objectives before starting our walk and we are not sure what will catch our attention, but these "untaught lessons" may last for a lifetime.[21]

The same approach should be taken with pets – start with delight and move to responsibility. Parents will have to remind a child that "Boots is hungry" or "Lucky needs to go for a walk," but the animal is never left to suffer, and wise parents do not threaten to "get rid of that animal." Through our own care and delight, we show children that the relationship between human beings and pets can be a lifelong source of happiness. I'll say more about this relationship in the next section on environmentalism.

Experiences with nature are often tied closely to a home place. Flowers, trees, dog, cat, and brambles form an integral whole with a remembered home. Just as we want to preserve this home place in our memory, the educational hope is that we will act to preserve actual places that we and others love, and commit ourselves to care for the earth.

An intimate connection with the natural world is a continuing source of happiness for many people, and it is possible that the bio-philia hypothesis is right – that we are genetically disposed to need this connection. The natural world is not all fun and joy, however. It is loaded with fear, pain, and horror as well. William James writes:

> The lunatic's visions of horror are all drawn from the material of daily fact. Our civilization is founded on the shambles, and every individual existence goes out in a lonely spasm of helpless agony.... Crocodiles and rattlesnakes and pythons are at this moment vessels of life as real as we are;... and whenever they or other wild beasts clutch their living prey, the deadly horror which an agitated melancholiac feels is the literally right reaction on the situation.[22]

I would not press the horrors of nature on children but, as they get older, I would acquaint them not only with the suffering of animal life in the wild but also with philosophical views that culminate in pessimism or asceticism. Although I wouldn't emphasize the fearful side of nature with young children, I wouldn't deny it either. When children see natural calamities, we should discuss them honestly. While writing this, I was interrupted by a grandchild who had just rescued a baby mouse from our cat. This cat is the gentlest of creatures – a cuddler who never scratches a human being or even a curtain. But she would certainly have killed the little mouse, and it probably will die. It is lying on a bed of damp grass now under a steamer basket. An eye dropper lies next to it, ready to use in feeding it, if it lives for even an hour. (It struggled for thirty-six hours to live. How does one explain this to children?)

This is the sort of incident from which children learn about the paradoxes and conflict in our relations with nature. We do not want mice in our house or even in the brush pile behind the compost bin (where this little one was caught). Sometimes we have to exterminate them. And yet one baby rodent lying helpless with its small heart beating visibly calls forth a response of care. How else can we respond when a child watches and whispers, "We can save it, can't we?"

In working with children and their connection to nature, we have to ask ourselves questions, pragmatic questions: What good does it do to adopt the view we are considering, for example, to save a little mouse? Can we do something to relieve the pain we observe? Should the existence of suffering destroy our happiness or make us more keenly aware of its fragility?

As Smith said of children, they tend to want absolutes, not hypotheses. As they grow into adolescence, many are led to extremes in the interest of great causes. Thinking only of the trees they love, they treat logging communities with callous disregard for both a way of life and economic suffering. Seeing only pain in our domestication of animals for food, they fail to see that the alternative would be no life at all for these creatures. A major question for education is how to educate for a sensitive environmentalism that will extend care to all those involved and, at the same time, preserve and enhance human happiness. As Isaiah Berlin warned us, it may not be possible to realize all of our treasured values at once.

Responsibility and Happiness

In the Afterword to his popular *The Unsettling of America*, Wendell Berry tells us that people who love the land and want to preserve it think differently from high-level policymakers:

> They think so differently, I believe, because their motives are different. Their thinking does not begin with a set of predetermining ideas but rather with particular places, people, needs, and desires. This book's friends and allies began to think and to work not because they had careers to make or ideologies to serve but because they loved certain places, people, possibilities, and ways that they could not indifferently see destroyed.[23]

Berry speaks of motives, but his pattern of argument is very like mine in emphasizing aims-talk. Two groups may state the same aim – in this case, to feed the hungry – but they should be prodded to say what other aims they seek, and the next step is a check on compatibility among aims. After that, we have to defend our choice of means with respect to the stated aims. If a major aim is to make large profits, we should be alert for rationalizations on shoddy means.

Berry may be wrong in claiming feasibility for the methods he recommends, but if he is right on aims and in his critique of contemporary agribusiness, then his methods deserve a trial. It is frightening to hear a potato farmer admit that he does not eat potatoes freshly dug from his own fields – that, for his family's use, he plants a small area without chemicals.[24] Commercially grown potatoes are soaked in poisons, and the soil in which they are grown is a grayish powder, not the rich loam we usually associate with soil.

For our purposes, however, one of Berry's recommendations is especially interesting. He writes:

> I am convinced that the present concentration of the best educated and most able people in centers of power, industry, and culture is a serious mistake . . . the best intelligence and talent should be at work and at home everywhere in the country. And therefore, my wishes for our schools are opposite to those of the present-day political parties and present-day politics of education and culture. Wes Jackson has argued that our schools – to balance or replace their present single major in upward mobility – should offer a major in homecoming. I agree.[25]

And I agree with Jackson and Berry. We must educate for love of place, and then we must gather and disseminate the knowledge required to preserve the places we love. Love alone is not enough because, through ignorance, we can unintentionally destroy what we love. With happiness as a primary aim of education, we have another strong incentive to teach for both love and knowledge of place.

One of the most interesting and useful things we could teach in suburban schools is, in the words of Sara Stein, "restoring the ecology of our own back yards."[26] Huge and useless lawns that require gas-guzzling machines to mow them and poisons to keep them free of weeds could be, at least partially, replaced by trees, shrubs, thickets, vegetable gardens, and wild flowers, and these plantings would provide homes for birds and other wild life. They would also provide the wild places so loved by children and now largely missing in the suburban landscape.

When children live in contact with nature, they gradually come to know that the relations among living things and their environments are enormously complex. The gentle, much loved cat becomes a killer when mice appear. Some seedlings fail to thrive even though we have

131

not neglected them. Some plants will not do well in the presence of certain others. Killing one set of marauders may deprive a beneficial insect or spider of food. An ugly, scraggly plant may be the main food for the larvae of a beautiful butterfly. Problems are seldom simple, and we have to work observantly and thoughtfully in the environment we wish to preserve.

Understanding the complexity, observing the mixture of beauty and horror, and accepting the feelings of happiness and sadness engendered by their connections to nature, young people should be less prone to either carelessness or fanaticism. To cultivate our happiness, we must enjoy situations and relationships that are less than perfect but, as we are open to them, yield moments of great joy. Our commitments should not turn us into grouches, violent protestors, or single-minded proselytizers. For example, a young woman committed to conserving water may insist on taking short showers, but she may make everyone else miserable by harping on her virtue and the vice of others. A hot shower is a sensuous luxury to be enjoyed. One can avoid excessive use but still take delight in what she *is* using. Similarly, one can be dedicated to recycling without going into fits of guilt over occasional lapses.

The joylessness of some activists reminds us of Augustine's pronouncement on sex – the act is acceptable so long as one keeps in mind the original purpose and doesn't enjoy it too much. That attitude persists as an Augustinian legacy into today's efforts to be responsible. It emphasizes responsibility and remains suspicious of happiness. The message in this book is that the possibility of happiness is more likely than the self-congratulation of grim duty to attract converts to worthwhile causes. We'll see evidence for this in the next chapter on parenting.

Young people today face environmental problems that were rarely discussed years ago. (One could argue, of course, that if they had been discussed and treated effectively, the problems of today would not be so acute.) Some of today's more tender attitudes would have worked against survival years ago. The cat would have been congratulated on her kill then, and not only that – we would have tracked down the nest and destroyed mother and brood before they could invade our grain supply.

If the problems of today are in part products of prosperity and leisure, they are not entirely so. We have the time now to recognize and ponder the lives of animals, for example, but their suffering has always been part of the natural condition. Our relationship to non-human animals is a topic that education can no longer avoid, but it should be guided by the quest for balance. Raging sentiment, even on the "right" side of things, risks harm to some and may alienate more than it convinces.

How should ethical people relate to nonhuman animals? Many young people today are leading the campaign for vegetarianism. Is this the product of sheltered, even pampered, lives, or is it the precursor of more enlightened relationships between human and nonhuman animals? How should this topic be approached in schools?

One might start with horror stories likely to convert many of us to vegetarianism, or one might start with a careful analysis that leaves open a later examination of the horrors but also identifies the complexities involved in human interaction with nonhumans. Suppose we were to start with a quotation from George Adamson:

> A lion is not a lion if it is only free to eat, to sleep and to copulate. It deserves to be free to hunt and to choose its own prey; to look for and find its own mate; to fight for and hold its own territory; and to die where it was born – in the wild. It should have the same rights as we have.[27]

What can the writer mean by the last sentence? Surely lions are not to be granted meaningless rights such as freedom of speech and suffrage. What rights should they have, then? Any right that requires capacities that an organism does not possess is irrelevant for that organism. Can we agree on this? Rejecting highly sentimental and emotional beginnings, we might arrive at characteristics shared by lions and humans. Both feel pain and avoid it whenever possible. Both exhibit a will to live. Both care for their young. Both seek pleasure as well as sustenance in food, rest, and sex. Both need a home place that provides for basic needs and, possibly, the sort of growth characteristic of it as an ideal type.

An analysis of capacities should forestall much of the emotion and exaggeration we hear today in talk of rights. Indeed, students might abandon the doubtful idea of *natural rights* and proceed from the understanding that rights arise from needs and capacities.[28] This beginning still leads us to agree with advocates of animal rights that the infliction of unnecessary pain on sentient beings is wrong, that confinement in small, unnatural housing is wrong, and that the premature separation of mothers and babies is wrong.

Careful study of contemporary farming methods uncovers many abuses, but the situation is complicated. If we were all to become vegetarians, it seems clear that farm animals would – except for a specimen few – become extinct. People would cease to breed these animals, and almost certainly their natural breeding would be severely curtailed. Much suffering would be eliminated, but so would whatever happiness accompanies the natural lives of these animals. Humans could avoid suffering in roughly the same way; that is, we could deliberately reject the will to live and refuse to reproduce.[29] However, even humans capable of making such a decision would protest if it were made for them, and most of us find life worth living. Might animals feel the same way if they were capable of making the choice? If the horrors of factory farming were abolished, might animals choose to live and reproduce even though their ultimate fate were to be, as it is now, to provide food for humans and other animals?

Students should consider, too, questions of natural habitat. When herds of deer multiply and their habitat becomes too crowded, we kill some of them (for the good of the greater number, we say). We rarely consider expanding their territory. In contrast, when humans multiply, we think it not only necessary but right to expand their territory. None but the most vicious misanthropes would consider "culling" the herd of humans. Some do advocate limiting population through birth control, of course, and it is possible that similar methods could be used on nonhuman animals. Notice, however, that the decision would necessarily be ours, not theirs.

Just as students must come to grips with racism, classism, and sexism, so must they at least explore what might be meant by *speciesism*. Peter Singer writes:

> Speciesism . . . is a prejudice or attitude of bias in favor of the interests of members of one's own species and against those of members of other species.[30]

A statement like this can be adopted too easily without thought. Even those of us who agree wholeheartedly with Singer that cruelty should be condemned and that animals should not be made to suffer for trivial human interests should encourage careful analysis of his definition. To associate speciesism with racism, sexism, and classism is a powerful emotional move, but it may involve a category mistake. At least in principle, each of the big human "isms" applies to all the entities involved – all human beings. We usually think of racism in connection with the oppression of blacks by whites, but clearly, if power relations were reversed, the oppression of whites by blacks would still be racism. The same can be said of sexism and classism. Such a reversal is, however, meaningless with respect to species. All species give special consideration to their own, and we would not think of criticizing nonhuman animals for this preference, nor would it make sense to accuse them of speciesism. They are not capable of such discrimination.

The generous convictions of animal rights advocates may blind them to the truth that, no matter how respectful and gentle our handling of nonhuman animals, we humans remain in charge. It is we, not they, who decide when there are too many of them, and it is we who decide to limit their reproduction. Humans who advocate the forced infertility of other humans are accused of violating their rights, and this is true even when the victims of our coercion are as unable as nonhuman animals to make a rational choice. Students should notice that this argument can be carried into several conclusions: (1) Perhaps the right to reproduce should be granted to all animals; (2) perhaps there is no "right" to reproduce, and rationally competent humans should control the reproduction of mentally incompetent humans as well as that of nonhuman animals (with their interests in mind); (3) perhaps there are irreconcilable differences with respect to moral issues across species, and humans must therefore be treated differently from nonhumans.

Our relationship to nonhuman animals is one of the most perplexing and important problems in contemporary moral life. Perhaps people centuries from now will look back on our times as a period of incredible moral obtuseness. Or perhaps people will still blithely consume meat with little or no concern for the suffering of the live creatures whose bodies are killed and eaten. It is not the job of conscientious teachers to convert their students to vegetarianism. Rather, it is their job to present the issues with full attention to their complexity and significance. If, as Smith said, children want absolutes, educated adults should have developed a tolerance for unresolvable ambiguity and a tragic sense that we cannot always be sure of what is right or best. The hope is that students will agree with Peter Singer and Tom Regan that the interests of animals should not be callously disregarded – that, at least, their lives should not be made miserable and that their desire to live should outweigh trivial human interests such as improvements in cosmetics.[31]

They should also consider the mounting evidence that factory farming and large-scale agribusiness are polluting our waters, destroying the soil on which we all depend, and wrecking the places with which many of us identify. Love of place cannot in itself overcome this trend, but it can provide the motivation for serious study and responsible action. Concern for our own happiness requires us to accept responsibility for the natural world.

Before closing this chapter, we should return to the question with which we started: Should schools teach for a love of place or should they now offer curricula designed to transcend place? My answer is to reject the dichotomy and to embrace an inclusive sense of *or*. I respond with a wholehearted yes to the first part of the question; we should teach enthusiastically for love of place and the happiness that accompanies it. The second part is more difficult, and my response is a cautious yes, but.... Many of our students will live and work in a global environment, and schools must prepare them for such life. Appropriate education for a particular place may play an important part in modifying our ideas about globalization. It may make us more sensitive to the effects of our economic activities on other environments and people.

What should students learn about the growing conflict over free markets and globalization? What do the governments of rich countries claim as benefits? Is there some truth to these claims? What do the protestors claim? Which of their objections seem most warranted and cogent? Can we find a nonviolent way to settle the dispute, preserve local integrity, and share economic benefits? What stands in the way?

It is somewhat disheartening to reread today Charles Reich's 1970 *The Greening of America*. It would be wrong to say that nothing has improved since then. The ocean waters along the Atlantic coast of the United States are far cleaner, many states have worked hard to reduce air pollution, more young people are entering postsecondary educational institutions, and a valiant effort has been made at affirmative action to redress abominations of the past. This last effort, however, is now under attack. The larger picture is not a happy one.

Consciousness III, identified by Reich as a celebration of individual acceptance and excellence, not only failed to develop, its constituting ideas – the refusal to evaluate people by general standards . . . to classify or analyze them, acceptance of "freaky friends" in the community[32] – have all been rejected. Instead of the Corporate State, we now have the Corporate World in which children are judged by world-class standards and many feel so left out that violence is chosen as a way of getting attention.

Reich ends his paean to Consciousness III (the new generation) this way:

> We have all been persuaded that giant organizations are necessary, but it [C. III] sees that they are absurd. . . . We have all been induced to give up dreams of adventure and romance in favor of the escalator of success, but it says that the escalator is a sham and the dream is real. . . . For one almost convinced that it was necessary to accept ugliness and evil, that it was necessary to be a miser of dreams, it is an invitation to cry or laugh. For one who thought the world was irretrievably encased in metal and plastic and sterile stone, it seems a veritable greening of America.[33]

Perhaps it is this lost vision that the protestors against world trade are trying to regain. At the disastrous meeting in Genoa (2001), it was reported that French President Chirac commented that the presence of 150,000 protestors must signify something of importance. Perhaps we should listen.

In this chapter, I have considered the role of place and nature in human flourishing. I have explored the fascination of cookbooks and garden catalogs, children's apparent need for wild places, and the possibility that we are genetically predisposed to affiliate somehow with nature. With respect to education, I suggested that joy should usually precede responsibility and that we should have more faith in both incidental learning and the choices children make in exploring the world. I gave considerable space to our relationship to nonhuman animals because they bring us happiness and because their suffering from human cruelty calls forth a sense of responsibility. Finally, I discussed the present trend toward globalization and suggested that the trend may be a real threat to human happiness.

7

Parenting

Possibly there is no human task more demanding, more rewarding, and more universal than parenting, and yet our schools apparently think that algebra and Shakespeare are more important. Parenting is supposed to be taught at home but, as our Visitor pointed out, if parents are not very good at the job, how will they teach it to their children? How will parenting improve?

In this chapter, we will consider three large topics associated with parenting and happiness. First, we will look at birth and the miracle of parental love. Second, we will consider the growing child and his or her relationship to parents. Finally, we will discuss parents as educators.

Birthing

Romance and love, at least in today's Western world, usually precede pregnancy and birth, but for many centuries love had little to do with marriage, and often the first great love in a woman's life was that for her child. A vestige of this attitude remains even today. Increasing numbers of women are having children through artificial insemination, and many teenagers have confessed to engaging in sex not for love of their partner but out of longing for a baby to love. None of this suggests that romantic love between women and men is a thing of the past, and we will look at romantic love in Chapter 9, but relationships have changed and continue to do so. Here we will concentrate on that special love of mother for child.

The biology of sex and pregnancy is fairly well taught in today's schools, although critics complain that not nearly enough attention is given to ethics and values in sex education. I would add that schools neglect the history of birth practices and the influence of religion and politics on birthing. Still, we can be glad that the number of teenage births has started to fall, and there is some evidence that prenatal and postnatal care have improved. We have a long way to go on the latter; many young women still do not have medical insurance and, therefore, suffer inadequate care.

When we consider that giving birth is nearly a universal experience among women and that being born is a universal experience for all human beings, it seems odd (astonishing and baffling to our Visitor from another world) that schools give it so little attention. Birthing has a fascinating history – at least as interesting as the history of great battles and the succession of kings.

From the care perspective and our concern for happiness as the reduction of suffering, the shift from female attendants (midwives) to male physicians as birth assistants is especially interesting. Before the seventeenth century, most women in childbirth were attended by women who performed this service regularly. When male physicians began to invade the field, puerperal fever became a virtual epidemic. This devastating disease was transmitted to the mother by the unclean hands of the physician who delivered the child. It is not that men's hands were more obviously soiled than women's, but physicians came to the birthing directly after treating others for a variety of communicable diseases. Their hands were dirty in the epidemiological sense. Further, they moved quickly from one patient to another, spreading germs as they worked. In contrast, midwives tended to stay with their patients from the start of labor well into recovery. In telling this tale, Adrienne Rich points out that *midwife* means literally "with woman."[1]

This history yields an important message for today's practitioners. Physicians no longer bring dirty hands to the birthing experience, but they are often hurried and impersonal in their attitudes. In contrast, nurse practitioners more often get to know their patients and stay with them. Moreover, they seem more willing to empower their patients and listen to their life histories.[2] Establishing a relationship between practitioner and patient may even reduce the number of malpractice suits brought by unhappy patients because one doesn't sue someone who is liked and trusted. If something goes wrong, a tragic outcome is mourned by both mother and practitioner.

The story of physicians and dirty hands is filled with suffering. Not only did thousands of women die unnecessarily, but one physician who diagnosed the problem and informed his colleagues about it suffered scorn and calumny. Ignaz Philipp Semmelweis was driven from his post in Vienna after writing a book on the problem. Perhaps Semmelweis was too sensitive, too passionate in his convictions. He died in the Vienna Insane Asylum. Some years later, when his theory was shown to be true, a statue was erected in his honor.[3]

Students should hear, also, about the role of religion in adding to the suffering of childbirth. When anesthesia became available to relieve the pain of childbirth, some religious leaders and physicians objected to its use on the grounds that the suffering of childbirth was ordained by the Bible. This history and analysis must be handled carefully. It is easy to say that the objectors were wrong and that no one subscribes to such a position today, but the problem is much deeper. The Bible (Gen. 3:16–19) *does* say that God would multiply the sorrow of women in childbirth and condemn men to endless toil in feeding themselves and their families. Does this mean that men should not be allowed to use powerful technology in farming and husbandry? Such verses raise important questions about a God who is held to be all-good and all-knowing. Would a good human parent inflict lasting pain on his or her child for one act of disobedience? On *all* children for the disobedience of one? Do students know that the doctrine of original sin was invented by Augustine (it is not in the Bible) and has caused untold human suffering?[4]

It should be possible to discuss the Adam and Eve story as a powerful myth.[5] Although such discussion is fraught with difficulty, it is important to find a way to do this. So much of the oppression of women has been supported by this story that analysis and critical discussion of it should be considered essential to the education of free and happy people. Teachers need not say, "Now here's the truth" in either defense of or opposition to the biblical account. Instead, they should refer to what many reputable scholars have said and leave the conclusion open to student judgment. The rich and conflicting stories should become common knowledge.

Our Visitor might well ask how we dare to say that critical thinking is taught in our schools when we rarely allow it to be used on matters central to our lives. Thus, the first thing to be gained by an analysis of the Adam and Eve story is a true exercise in critical thinking. Students will learn that there are good thinkers within traditional religions who accept the mythical status of such stories. They should also hear from those who, while accepting such great stories as powerful myths, reject religion entirely.[6] Can anyone reconcile logically the existence of an all-good God with that same God's decision to inflict lasting punishment on generations and eternal punishment on some unfortunate souls, or does one have to move beyond such beliefs in order to live happily with (or without) religion?

Another thing to be gained by critical study of the Adam and Eve story is a deeper understanding of myth. Myth should not be taught as falsehood but rather as a powerful symbolic construction designed not only to explain natural phenomena but, more important, to bind people together in communal ritual and celebration. Here again teachers might read (or just tell about) three or four pages from Frazer's *The Golden Bough*.[7] Open-minded listeners cannot avoid seeing that Christianity shares a long, long tradition of myths with earlier religions. Might young people "lose their faith" as a result of such study? They might but, alternatively, they might deepen it in a realization that they are connected to a host of human beings who preceded them and their own religious faith. In a sense, critical thinking can contribute to the rebirth of more rational religious life.

What I am trying to show is that, when we start on a topic that is centrally related to human happiness – in this case, birth – we quickly connect with many other topics of deep existential interest. As we study the story of Adam and Eve, we see a dramatic reversal of the natural order. It is women who give birth; yet, in this story, woman is created from man (who is anesthetized during the "birth"!). Then a question arises as to why this creation story rather than the first (Gen. 1:26–28) has been so widely accepted. This question was raised by Elizabeth Cady Stanton and answered forcefully: The second story – the Adam and Eve story – better served the political purposes of men who wanted to maintain the subordination of women.[8] The first suggests strongly that there is a feminine aspect to God's image and that much of Christian theology has been politically constructed and used for nonreligious purposes.

The male construction and use of religion is vividly illustrated in an astonishing omission in the Ten Commandments. There is no commandment that Thou shalt not rape.[9] The commandment against adultery does not forbid rape, and its primary aims are to protect men's property and overcome the inferential nature of paternity. Historically, women have been much more severely punished than men for adultery, and there are places in the Bible where rape seems actually to be endorsed. Young men and women need to know about this history and the culture that has grown up with rape at its center – a culture that allows the powerful to take what they want even if it means leaving women and nature in degradation and ruination.[10] Half the human population cannot live happily if it must fear for its dignity and safety; nor can any of us live happily if the attitude of rape shapes our relation to the natural world.

Because women's lives and bodies have been controlled for millennia, the present determination of women to control their own bodies is important. Abortion has to be discussed from both practical and historical perspectives. There will be no consensus on this issue in the foreseeable future. Those of us who favor giving women the choice to abort or to carry a fetus to birth can still agree heartily that abstinence be taught and endorsed. But young people should also be well informed on methods of contraception and where to turn if those methods fail. They should also be aware that governments have used (and continue to use) women shamefully for their own purposes – some forbidding the production of children during times of overpopulation and others urging continuous pregnancies when the state needs more soldiers.

In addition to topics in the history of medicine, feminism, and religion, students may become interested in the psychology of gender. They should hear and discuss at least the basic ideas of Freud, Jung, and Erikson, and they should be introduced to feminist psychology. Is mothering an instinctive female response? Is the production of babies the main purpose of female life?

Certainly motherhood has brought great joy into the lives of many women, and some have found birth an almost mystical experience. In recent years, female educators have begun to talk about birth, mothering, and maternal influences in education.[11] Madeleine Grumet writes: *"What is most fundamental to our lives as men and women sharing a moment on this planet is the process of reproducing ourselves."*[12] She speaks of the transformation that many women experience when they bear a child:

> "This child is mine, this child is me" is an index of relation that will vary with every speaker. What it means to be mine, to be me, depends on the way each speaker knows herself. The maternal ego reaches out to another consciousness . . . and self-knowledge grows in this process of identification and differentiation with this other, this child, "my child." The process of thinking through the world for and with the child invites a mother to recollect her own childhood and to inspect the boundaries of her own ego.[13]

We'll say much more about the process of "thinking through the world" in the section on parents as educators. For now, staying close to the theme of birth, we must admit that the experience is not always a joyous one. Grumet worries about the inexperienced mother who is herself a child; Rich documents the violent feelings and actions that sometimes displace maternal love in even very good mothers; and Sara Ruddick, in describing a tradition of nonviolence among mothers, admits that there are numerous exceptions both in individual women and in the course of any one woman's mothering.[14] I, too, have discussed the effects of heavy responsibility and frustration on the responses of mothers to their children's demands and behavioral infractions.[15]

At this point, we should return briefly to the biblical verse in which God is said to have instituted the pain of childbirth. This story has all the earmarks of a myth designed to explain a frightening natural phenomenon. Sometimes that function of myth is harmless and even charming. In this case, however, it has laid the foundation for the destructive notion that our suffering can always be traced to our own sin – that we "did something to deserve this." An education for happiness must reject this pernicious notion.

Thus, when we talk about birth and infant care, we have to avoid both the romantic picture of rapturous maternal perfection and the one of pregnancy as barbaric, the very root of women's oppression. The latter view has been passionately expressed by Shulamith Firestone.[16] Whereas some women have been persuaded to try *natural childbirth* (methods that rely on exercise and psychological support – no painkillers), many have rejected it, and Firestone states simply, "Childbirth *hurts*."[17] It does indeed, but many women find the result – "my child" – worth it.

At this point, we should return briefly to the biblical verse in which God is said to have instituted the pain of childbirth. This story has all the earmarks of a myth designed to explain a frightening natural phenomenon. Sometimes that function of myth is harmless and even charming. In this case, however, it has laid the foundation for the destructive notion that our suffering can always be traced to our own sin – that we "did something to deserve this." An education for happiness must reject this pernicious notion.

If we set aside both the "pregnancy is bliss" and the "pregnancy is hell" views, we can find convincing evidence that many women do experience a wonderful sense of well-being during much of pregnancy and that the majority of us also experience considerable pain and discomfort. Young women who are not well informed about these ups and downs may feel odd or even guilty when discomfort threatens what was advertised as a blessed experience.

Education on pregnancy and birth should give special attention to the perils of postpartum depression. Many new mothers experience periods of "feeling blue" and may break into tears for no apparent reason; they need both reassurance and real help with the tasks of mothering when this happens. Real depression, however, is serious and may have tragic consequences for mothers, babies, and other family members. Recently, the country was shocked by the case of Andrea Yates, a young mother who killed all five of her children by drowning them in the bathtub. Rereading Rich's *Of Woman Born* reminded me of a similar case – that of Joanne Michulski – in 1974. Michulski killed the two youngest of her eight children and left their chopped-up bodies on her front lawn.

The similarities between the two cases should awaken us to the need for education and timely help for struggling mothers. Both Yates and Michulski, middle-class women, were known as good mothers who kept their children clean and safe; neither, apparently, used physical punishment. But both kept incredibly messy houses, lost track of what was in the refrigerator, gave up real cooking, and often found it impossible to "get going." Both have been described as "quietly desperate." A reasonable, compassionate society would see that the depression of these women made it impossible for them to cope. It was not some moral weakness in them that made coping impossible and led to depression.

It is disheartening to realize that our society has become less understanding and compassionate over the thirty-year period from the Michulski case to the one of Yates. Michulski was tried for voluntary manslaughter, acquitted by reason of insanity, and committed to a mental institution. Prosecutors for the state of Texas say that they will seek the death penalty for Yates. She may, of course, yet win acquittal on grounds of insanity, but the decision to make hers a capital case is horrifying. No morally decent society would allow capital punishment for *any* crime.[18] For a crime so obviously the product of despair, the decision shakes one's faith in the rationality of our criminal justice system.

It is possible that these desperately unhappy women could have been helped if someone had told them that many other mothers have experienced fatigue, that others have occasionally felt hatred for their children. Depressed mothers are not *entirely* different from undepressed mothers. They need not suffer self-loathing in addition to exhaustion, but they do need special help. If young women come to understand that feelings defying the notion that motherhood is bliss are quite common but *may* be signs of depression, they will not be ashamed to seek the help so badly needed.

The Growing Child

As Grumet points out, parenthood invites us to revisit our own childhood and think through the world with our children. I'll talk specifically about the parental role as educator in the next section, but let's think here about what teenagers might profitably learn concerning the growth of children and even their own development as adolescents. I suggest here that the study of child development may be an especially effective way to get teenagers to think about their own lives and well-being.

In developing a curriculum on the growing child, we have to be careful not to commit the Bobbitt-like sin of requiring the mastery of particular tasks that are as yet irrelevant to young adolescents. These are probably best learned in practice situations, and opportunities should be provided for teenagers to care directly for young children under the supervision of competent adults.

The classroom experience should be organized at a somewhat more abstract level. Categories of the sort offered by Sara Ruddick are especially useful and rich with potential material for discussion. Ruddick suggests that maternal interests arise from three great needs of children: preservation, growth, and acceptability.[19] Parents must first preserve the child's life and see to its physical and psychological health. Next, they must promote the child's growth and, finally, they must shape the child's behavior by some pattern of acceptability. The initial reaction of some liberal-minded people (both adults and teenagers) to this last is that such efforts violate the child's freedom. However, honest parents admit that they want their children to

145

be good people. Some of us are more specific and rigid than others about the meaning of *good*, but we all have some vision of goodness in mind.

To maintain life, basic needs must be met; for example, children need food. Oddly, satisfying this basic need – feeding their children – often causes modern parents some confusion. Should the baby be on a schedule? Must children eat everything on their plates? Will a child become malnourished if he refuses all vegetables? How many sweets should a child be allowed?

This is a good place to illustrate the basic pedagogical principle of avoiding the kinds of specific information that are best left to practice. What is wanted here is an attitude or a basic outlook. Food is a lifelong source of pleasure that requires both freedom and self-control. We want to eat food that tastes good to us, but we also want our bodies to be strong and attractive. It seems reasonable to start out by following a baby's lead on when to nurse. Not only does such a practice help to avoid an obsession with food, it may also increase babies' sense that they have some control over their environment – that their caregivers can be summoned when needed.

Students should hear about the confusion caused by the recommendations of experts. When my mother was young, experts recommended forcing a feeding schedule on babies. Some time after that, *demand feeding* became all the rage. When I had my babies, Dr. Spock more or less argued against both practices.[20] The sensible way, he said, was to feed babies when they are hungry but, at the same time, to work toward regular feeding times. Parents might play with or sing to a baby who cries too early for food; they might gently awaken a baby who threatens to miss a feeding and, as a result, scream in the middle of the night.

Teachers should encourage stories and discussion, and this is a good place to emphasize the role of fathers. For example, my husband always took over the last feeding of the night so that I could go to sleep early. He tried to make that feeding as late as possible. When it was still around 10 P.M., I usually had to respond to a call for food at 2 A.M., but this did not last long. Our babies usually slept through the night after only three or four weeks. Dad was up late, and Mom was up early, but no one was disturbed in the middle of the night. Does this always work? Of course not! Again, the point of such stories and discussion is to establish an attitude of respectful solicitude toward the child and each other, to reduce blind dependence on experts, and to remind one another that parenthood is a source of happiness.

Instead of talking about specific formulas for infants and precise diets for young children, it is probably better to talk about wise and pleasurable eating for everyone. Teenagers often indulge in junk food, and many may have little experience with family meals and well-balanced menus. Preaching doesn't help much on this topic, but the exploration of cookbooks, discussion, and practice in planning meals may contribute to real interest. Here again is an opportunity to discuss historical, geographical, and economic aspects of meeting basic needs.[21] If teenagers become interested in food and the various customs surrounding mealtimes, they may well seek out the specific information they need when the time comes for them to exercise responsibility.

In discussing responsibility, I would be inclined to invite exploration of the widespread interest of human beings in alcoholic beverages and other mind-altering substances. Instead of talking incessantly against the use of alcohol and demanding abstinence, we should study the history of its use. In the Middle Ages, for example, something called *mead* was widely imbibed, particularly in regions where it was difficult or impossible to grow grapes.[22] How and from what was mead concocted? What other drinks are made through fermentation? How did people invent distillation? From what familiar fruit did the pioneers in the American Midwest make an alcoholic beverage?[23]

The history of apple growing in America is especially interesting. Until the end of the nineteenth century, apples were more often drunk than eaten. Cider was the drink of preference, and without refrigeration, the adjective *hard* was meaningless. As Michael Pollan points out, "virtually all cider was hard,"[24] and most people – even children – drank it. Protestants, who often condemned the use of wines (because of their association with Catholicism), welcomed cider and made themselves feel more righteous by noting that the Bible has nothing bad to say about the apple. Pollan writes:

> It wasn't until this century that the apple acquired its reputation for wholesomeness – "An apple a day keeps the doctor away" was a marketing slogan dreamed up by growers concerned that temperance would cut into sales. In 1900 the horticulturist Liberty Hyde Bailey wrote that "the eating of the apple (rather than the drinking of it) has come to be paramount...."[25]

Everyone understood, however, that the earlier lively interest in apples derived from their use in cider making:

> When Emerson, for instance, wrote that "man would be more soli-
> tary, less friended, less supported, if the land yielded only the useful
> maize and potato, [and] withheld this ornamental and social fruit,"
> his readers understood it was the support and sociability of alcohol
> he had in mind.[26]

John Adams, a sober and somewhat puritanical man, is said to have drunk a gill (about half a cup) of hard cider every morning before breakfast, and this "salubrious" habit started in his college days at Harvard, where everyone seems to have done likewise. Later in life, he developed a taste for fine wines.[27]

No reasonable teacher will suggest that students rush home to con-
struct a still or begin the process of fermenting hard cider. Indeed, part of the discussion should focus on the reasons why the Women's Christian Temperance Union was founded. Were these women (Carrie Nation in particular) just moralistic prudes, or did they have important arguments? Is alcohol abuse a symptom or a cause of social disorder? Might it be both a symptom and a cause? How should we approach the problems associated with the use of alcohol? Can the same arguments be applied to, say, marijuana?

This may be a good place to introduce a topic to which I will return repeatedly. If we value critical thinking, if we commit ourselves to encouraging it, then we must allow it to be exercised on critical matters – that is, on issues of keen interest to students. Certainly students should hear about the value of abstinence with re-
spect to alcohol, drugs, and sex, but they should also hear about the long and fascinating history of human interest in these activities.[28] Drugs far more dangerous than marijuana are prescribed regularly by physicians, and it is simply not true to say that, despite their dangerous potential, they are somehow safer simply because they are prescribed by doctors. If we really believe that knowledge and critical thinking contribute to living fuller public and private lives, then we must allow the study and discussion of such critical and controversial issues.

The discussion should also include consideration of what our stu-
dents might want for their own children. Do they want their children to be fully and critically informed or to be protected from realities

that might frighten them or lead them astray? In this last part of the discussion, they should hear about Plato's recommendations for censorship. Was Plato right or wrong? What about the people today who insist on "abstinence only" in school-sponsored programs? Is this censorship of material students need? Students might want to consider other types of censorship. What about those who would remove *Harry Potter* from the school library?

It may seem a bit odd to spend so much time on food and alcohol in a chapter on parenting. However, both are sources of pleasure in human life, and full discussion is relevant to the present lives, as well as the future lives, of teenagers. Because of this double relevance, the topics here have special importance. It makes sense, in preparing students for eventual parenthood, to work through topics that are important to them now and through which they may develop lasting attitudes that can contribute to their happiness.

Another topic that holds this double relevance is the conflict between preservation and growth. Every good parent worries about how to protect children without impeding their growth. When should Susie be allowed to climb trees? When it is safe to allow Jake to cross a street on his own? What competencies signal growth, and what experiences associated with being a grownup are best avoided?

It was once considered normal for late-adolescent boys to gain some sexual experience. At the same time, such experience was forbidden to young women, and the boys who bragged of their experience would not consider marrying girls who had any prior sexual experience. For many young men, an introduction to sexual activity was considered a rite of passage, part of growing up. Students should now be encouraged to ask: Is such activity a genuine sign of growth? If it is, should young women be admired for engaging in it?

After the discussion has proceeded for a while, teachers should ask whether students would want their own children to experience premarital sex as part of growing up. My guess is that many will say no. Some may add unhappily, "But they probably will anyway." The important issue here is why adolescents might hope that their children will abstain from sexual activity. There might be a pregnancy. They might catch a sexually transmitted disease. They might be emotionally hurt. They are not ready for the responsibilities that accompany sexual activity. Now we can ask about the nature of these responsibilities, and we can ask also what is meant by growth.

Growth, we might decide, is a manifestation of competence that leads to fuller and richer experience. John Dewey used the competence of a burglar as an example that does *not* represent growth.[29] Although a burglar may increase his skill at picking locks, choosing victims, and escaping with valuable loot, he risks shutting down opportunities for the future, and few of us would predict a "richer, fuller" life for him. On roughly similar grounds, perhaps held only intuitively, adolescents might fear that early sexual activity (for others) does not represent growing up in a way that forecasts a fuller, happier life.

Discussion of this sort avoids preaching, and it avoids a direct assault on the behavior of adolescent students. With a shifting focus from their future lives as parents to their lives now and back again, they may figure out for themselves what constitutes growth and what impedes it. The discussion should, of course, include issues other than sexual activity. Is the child who spends most of her time at the computer growing? How about one who watches television for hours? How much hanging out is compatible with growth?

The opposite side of the issue must also be examined. Can parents be overprotective? Lots of examples and complaints are likely to arise here, but many students may agree with protective parents that children should not be allowed to wander freely about their neighborhoods. This claim presents an opportunity to do an analysis of the safety and dangers in a given community. With careful study, students might conclude that their own communities are surprisingly safe and that children are actually deprived of valuable experiences by being so closely supervised. They might even read Robert Smith's book and debate whether such experiences would be safe for children now.[30] Were they safe even then? For whom?

It is obvious that these discussions will vary greatly in different settings. Some neighborhoods are demonstrably unsafe, and students should be invited to explore how they might be made safer. What would you do if you were a parent now? In other settings, students might well complain about being oversupervised and restricted. In some affluent communities, students might come to see that their parents' ambitions for them and their own "grade grubbing" are actually impeding growth – producing a distorted increase in apparent competence that promises more and more stress, not happiness.[31]

Students might begin by defending their parents – "they want the best for me" – but, encouraged to imagine how they themselves would behave as parents, they might be more open and honest in analyzing their own situations. In turn, the hope is that they will guide the growth of their own children more intelligently and sensitively.

Parents as Educators

So far, we have discussed the birth experience and the growth of children. On the latter topic, I suggested a powerful technique – getting at the problems of teenagers by posing problems for them as future parents. Now I want to discuss more directly the role of parents as educators. Facilitating the growth of children, sharing knowledge with them, and learning with them are among the great joys of parenting.

Parents do some direct, formal instruction, but most of what we do is informal, and often our "teaching" has no clear objective. We may spontaneously recite a poem or piece of doggerel, tell a story or joke, identify an insect, suggest a book we loved as children, invite participation in the kitchen, criticize a film, select a video for family viewing, play a game of pinochle. Most of us can tell stories about the effects of such informal learning in our own lives. I know, for example, that a cousin and I became whizzes at division of whole numbers by playing dice-baseball and keeping batting averages. We both learned something about negative numbers by playing pinochle with our grandmother – who certainly could not have explained the formal operations with negative numbers. I am not sure what we learned from countless games of Monopoly, but I suspect there were many benefits beyond counting money – among them, estimating spaces, planning ahead to buy houses, plotting deals with other players, and negotiating changes in the rules.

I remember learning the names of flowers from my mother and grandmother, and it was a special delight to pass on this information to my children and then to watch them pass it on to their children. I remember, too, learning the names of many insects because my children were interested in them. I don't recall having such interest as a child, but – thanks to my children – I now find many insects both interesting and beautiful, and I have taught my grandchildren how to work happily, and without fear, among bees.

Sometimes at the dinner table, we take turns reciting the lines of a poem. One person will say, "Whose woods these are I think I know," and someone else will give the next line. And kids seem to like it when, as we are walking on the boardwalk, I recite, "A wonderful bird is the pelican/Its beak can hold more than its belly can...."

In none of these situations do we establish learning objectives or give tests afterward. We exchange gifts and delight in the sharing. The effects on children are incalculable. Dinner table conversation has long been recognized as educational, but recently I read an account that criticized praise for the *dinner table model* as insensitive to the fact that many families do not eat together. Many children have no experience with conversation at the dinner table. Such criticism is rather like criticizing a nutritious diet on the grounds that some people are not fortunate enough to have a good diet. If there is something valuable in dinner table conversation, then parents should be advised to make room for it in their busy days or to think creatively about a worthy alternative.

Some years ago, when my own children were young, I fell into conversation with a neighbor who had just one young son. As neighbors do, we commiserated over the cost of clothing, dental bills, future education, and the like. Then I mentioned that it was also expensive to take the kids camping, on trips to museums, and to participate in various recreational and educational activities. "I never thought of that," she said, and indeed it was clear that she had not. While our kids went everywhere with us (and added tremendously to our enjoyment), her little boy stayed home with a babysitter. Her idea of parent-as-educator was one of controlling her child's behavior and saving money for his college education.

There are cultural differences, too, in parenting, and discussion of such differences has become a sensitive topic. So-called deficit models are properly frowned on today. Educators should not assume that students whose native language is not English are therefore suffering a cultural deficiency. Nor should we assume that youngsters who use Black English are lacking in intelligence. But we should not be afraid to advise students and parents that some lacks *do* represent deficiencies with respect to particular purposes and goals. To avoid giving this advice is not a sign of respect but of moral weakness. Children should not be told that their cultural knowledge is a deficit; it is a resource, sometimes even a treasure. But lack of proficiency in standard English *is* a deficiency, and children's cultural resources should be used in overcoming the deficiency.

Similarly, in contemporary liberal societies, certain parenting styles are more effective than others. We need not claim that one style is better than another in an absolute sense, but an authoritative style seems better for educational purposes than either authoritarian or permissive styles.[32] An authoritarian style keeps control in the hands of parents and insists on obedience from the young; the parent makes all important decisions unilaterally. A permissive style allows the young to do as they please, with little interference or guidance. In contrast, the authoritative style requires guidance, shared activities, and lots of practice in both talking and listening. As we teach parenting in schools, we should not be afraid to promote this style. We need not say that it is absolutely best, but we certainly can say that the weight of evidence favors it at this time for successful life in a liberal democracy.

Language figures prominently in authoritative parenting. Authoritative parents talk *with* their children, not just at them. Here again, there are cultural differences. In some cultures, adults and children do not engage in conversations. They exchange needed information and give and take orders, but they do not share words in the ways that seem to prepare children well for the usual patterns of schooling.[33] Teachers have to learn how to draw on the individual and cultural strengths of children without labeling either a culture or a parenting style deficient. At the same time, we should find a way to educate children for parenting so that they are aware of the effects of various styles and patterns of conversation.

We know that the informal learning characteristic of rich home environments provides many children with a good part of what the school regards as cultural literacy – knowledge highly regarded by the dominant culture. These children are ready for school learning. E. D. Hirsch, a strong advocate of cultural literacy for all children, comments:

> The readiness-to-learn principle cries out for generalization: In a democracy, all students should enter a grade ready to learn. True, the requisite skills, background knowledge, and vocabulary for such readiness are very unequally provided by the children's home environments. But precisely for that reason, it is the duty of schools to provide each child with the knowledge and skills requisite for academic progress – regardless of home background.[34]

153

Hirsch would use direct instruction as a remedy for the differences in readiness. However, it is not at all clear that this will work. Parents as well as teachers run into resistance when they insist that their children learn particular skills or bits of information as a result of planned activities. There seems to be something of great importance in selecting what one wants from certain experiences and in feeling that he or she is participating in shared life. Moreover, children learn much more than facts and skills from parents and teachers.[35] At best they acquire – without real awareness – an attitude of openness to learning and a sense of control over their own learning. They adopt habits of mind quite different from those who see learning as a set of specific tasks. I grant that this difference is somewhat mysterious, but I am quite sure it exists. If I am right, immersion in an atmosphere of shared exploration, rich in language and opportunities for decision making, should provide the basic framework. Within this framework, direct instruction would be used judiciously, just as it is in good homes.

One of the activities that has tremendous potential for shared pleasure is reading aloud. Most children love to have someone read to them, and I've found that even older children enjoy such sessions, especially if the listeners include people of different ages. On summer evenings, we often hold such sessions. Whoever is visiting our seaside house joins the group of listeners. After reading Thurber's *The Thirteen Clocks* (a favorite of kids in the six to thirteen age group), the kids may run about threatening to "slit you from the guggle to the zatch," but the end result is hilarity, not slaughter. Other favorites include E. B. White's *The Trumpet of the Swan*, May Sarton's *The Fur Person*, and T. H. White's *Mistress Masham's Repose*. The Pooh books (A. A. Milne) delight younger children, and all of our kids insisted on playing "Pooh sticks" after hearing the stories. Participants find sticks near a stream and simultaneously drop them on the upstream side of a bridge. Then everyone runs to the downstream side to see whose stick comes through first. (Often, having failed to distinguish them in any way, we have no idea how to match stick with player.)

We read poetry, too, and the younger children recite poems they have learned in school. But poetry is not just for children. One evening, after discussing World War I poetry with adults, I remarked that it was hard to understand how any further war could be waged after the publication of that poetry. How could reasonable people not be moved by the terror, horror, insanity, destruction, and waste described in that poetry? A child who had been listening said, "But, Grandma, maybe lots of people didn't read that poetry." Indeed. Perhaps, also, schools do not treat poetry in the way families do. We listen to and imagine the fear and horror, whereas schools focus on rhyme, meter, stanza construction, and metaphor. Who does the better job of educating?

Parents have an advantage over school teachers. They can work effectively in the mysterious realm of informal and incidental learning. I have used the word *mysterious* before, and we should say a bit more about the mystery. Why do we learn some things better informally than formally? And what do I mean by *better*? Consider grammar. If we set aside the poorest schools, most children receive roughly the same instruction in grammar. Many people who use poor grammar in their speech can probably identify correct constructions on paper – although this is by no means certain. Recently, I overheard a conversation in the post office between a postal clerk and a construction contractor. Both are (at least) high school graduates. The contractor was asking about a neighbor:

Clerk: If you came up from the beach, you should have saw him.
Contractor: No, I didn't. Oh, well, it don't matter.

I suspect that both know better, but their informal education has not been consonant with the formal. In contrast, people (even fairly young children) from homes in which the match is isomorphic are likely to adopt correct usage. Years of formal instruction may have little effect on everyday language. This familiar result casts significant doubt on the wisdom of Hirsch's recommendation to teach directly to "deprived" youngsters that which lucky children get indirectly.

We really do not understand why some things are learned so much more effectively in informal settings. One could argue that it is a matter of practice, and surely practice has something to do with it. But practice does not explain the myriad trivial and disconnected facts that we pick up informally and remember. There is something else operating. Perhaps we are, paradoxically, more attentive in informal settings. Perhaps the freedom to select what we wish contributes to our remembering. Perhaps the happiness that often accompanies informal learning helps to make that learning more nearly permanent.

155

In any case, the power of informal learning is clear, and schools might do well to provide settings in which it can occur more often. I am not suggesting that everything can be taught this way. Many important concepts and skills must be taught formally, but a foundation of cultural literacy may best be established through informal learning. Teachers and students should *live* together in the time allotted by the school. Lunch time could be used as an educational opportunity – one that would be satisfying in conversation as well as nutrition. Similarly, shared experience on the playing field, in extracurricular activities, and service learning might all add to the store of knowledge built up in informal learning.

Educators need to think carefully about how schools might increase opportunities for informal learning. They also should ask whether their interactions with parents increase or decrease the informal learning characteristic of good homes. The practice of involving parents in their children's homework may, for example, actually reduce the parents' enthusiasm for informal learning. Forced to act as taskmasters, parents may begin to feel that their proper role is to enforce formal learning instead of enjoying moments of shared experience with their children. I am not suggesting that parents should not help their children with homework if children ask for help. Children who see their parents as congenial companions and facilitators may indeed ask them for help. I would be cautious, however, in enlisting parents in the role of enforcers. I would be more than cautious and say right out: Don't do it! Encourage parents and children to enjoy their time together.

In this chapter, we have discussed the history and experience of birthing and both the joys and trials of caring for infants. Then I suggested a form of education for parenting that might help us to get at the current problems of teenagers without preaching or direct instruction. Finally, we looked at the role of parents as educators and explored the wonders of informal learning. So far, I have said nothing about what is possibly the most important task for parents as educators – that of raising their children as good people. In an earlier chapter, we discussed the connection of goodness and happiness. Just as there are differences of opinion on the meaning of happiness, so there are differences on what constitutes goodness. We turn to that topic next.

8

Character and Spirituality

Philosophers have long insisted that a measure of goodness is necessary for happiness or human flourishing. These days, however, we hear many cynical comments about the purported unhappiness of the rich and wicked. "I'd like to be so unhappy," a scoffer may comment on the wealth and high-living style of some enormously rich, not very nice person. Still, we know that the rich are not always happy, and the forms of happiness we admire – those derived from mutual relationships, respect in public life, inner serenity – require a depth of character and spirituality. As parents, we want our children to be good, not only so that they will succeed financially but, even more, because we believe in the connection between goodness and happiness.

Caring Relations and Character

Character education – the deliberate attempt to inculcate virtues – is the oldest and best-known mode of moral education. Now, at the beginning of the twenty-first century, after a lapse of just a few decades, it has once more become popular.[1] There are many thoughtful people, however, who object to the movement. Some dissenters doubt (with Socrates) that virtues can be taught at all; others object to how they are often taught – by indoctrination.[2] Still others, while sharing the doubts just mentioned, feel that most efforts at character education start with a mistaken view of moral life. Character educators seem to assume that virtues are possessions, that they are acquired and practiced by individuals in whom the accumulation of virtues eventuates in character. Sometimes character educators even advocate stern measures to discipline children so that the virtues will indeed be acquired.

In contrast, those of us who work from an ethic of care regard moral life as thoroughly relational. From this perspective, even the self is relational. We are, of course, individual physical organisms, but our selves are constructed through encounters with other bodies, objects, selves, conditions, ideas, and reflective moments with our own previous selves.[3] A relational view weakens and blurs the distinction between egoism and altruism, because much of what we do for others strengthens the relations of which we are part and, thus, our selves.

We believe that virtues are best learned in strong, happy relations. Happy children rarely become violent or cruel. One need not go so far as A. S. Neill, who said, *"I believe that it is moral instruction that makes the child bad."*[4] We might agree, however, that some forms of moral instruction do indeed make children bad, and we can usually predict the badness to come by observing that children so instructed are unhappy.[5] Happiness seems to be connected at both ends to moral character; it is a good start for moral life, and it is a welcome by-product of leading a moral life.

Happiness is construed here in the full sense that has been discussed so far. We are not talking about mere pleasure and certainly not about satisfying the restless flitting about so characteristic of children who seek to be continually entertained. Helping children to attain happiness involves guiding their intellectual and moral growth. It also involves helping them to develop a pleasing and well-integrated personality, and we will consider that task in the next chapter. For now, it is enough to recognize that a person may be highly developed intellectually and even have a deep and appreciative understanding of moral principles and still behave in ways that both he or she and society find abhorrent. This seems to have been true, for example, of the talented philosopher Charles Sanders Peirce. Louis Menand writes of him:

> He had a better nature, but he knew, even at twenty, that his personality was his enemy, and his entire adult life was a continual cycle of self-indulgence and self-rebuke.[6]

Peirce was not a happy man. His father taught him a great deal about thinking but, apparently, little about interacting positively with others.

Most conscientious parents are deeply concerned that their children develop the capacity to maintain caring relations. They show children first what it means to be cared for, and then they teach them how to care for others. Parents and teachers who use this caring alternative to character education do not give lectures on kindness, for example. Instead, they show what it means to be kind by modeling it. They also give specific, concrete lessons in kindness, but these are not lessons planned in advance and carried out as part of a formal curriculum. When a child is observed in an act that is causing pain, such parents intervene immediately and say, "You must not do that. That hurts." They make clear to the child that his or her act is wrong, and then they show the child a better way to interact – how to pick up a kitten, how to ask another child for an object, how to get Mother's attention.[7] All of this can be done in a firm but friendly manner. Children treated this way learn that some of their acts are bad (harmful, rude, hurtful), but they are not made to feel that they themselves are bad. Rather, they are treated as valued companions and, as Aristotle said, valued companions or friends help us to become better people.

So far in this discussion, I have assumed that the connection between happiness and good character is well established and widely accepted. But what exactly is the connection? We can start our search for an answer to this question by considering several generally approved virtues.

A Sample of Virtues

Let's start with honesty. Can we take it as obvious that chronic lying will almost certainly lead to poor human relations and thus to unhappiness? If this were a Socratic dialogue, my interlocutors would promptly answer yes. We can't be sure which is cause and which is effect, but we can say with some confidence that habitual liars are unhappy people. At the other extreme, however, those who are rigidly and unfailingly truthful may be difficult to live with, and they too may be unhappy. Who would want to live with the ancient Church Father who said, "I would not tell a willful lie to save the souls of the whole world"?[8] What sort of person would not lie to save the world, or his own child, or even the life of an innocent neighbor?

159

Neither the chronic liar nor the ruthless truth-sayer appeals to most of us. We do not trust the liar, and the ruthless truth-sayer makes us uncomfortable, especially if he continually reminds us of our own shortcomings. As Hume put it, "Who would live amidst perpetual wrangling, and scolding, and mutual reproaches?"[9] That is what life might become in the company of those who fail to exercise honesty in crucial situations or those who overexercise honesty. Both Hume and Aristotle argued that overzealous exercise often turns a virtue into a vice. The reason is that such vigorous displays of virtue tend to wreck human relationships, and our relationships are fundamental to our happiness. Unless we become hermits, seeking happiness in a relation only with God or nature, we need other human beings in order to be happy. Here is Hume again:

> A perfect solitude is, perhaps, the greatest punishment we can suffer.... Let all the powers and elements obey one man: Let the sun rise and set at his command: The seas and rivers roll as he pleases.... He will still be miserable, till you give him some one person at least, with whom he may share his happiness, and whose esteem and friendship he may enjoy.[10]

To be happy, then, children must learn to exercise virtues in ways that help to maintain positive relations with others, especially with those others who share the aim of establishing caring relations. They must be honest in the sense that they are trustworthy, but they must not hurt people by being brutally or priggishly frank. When someone tells the truth, we must grant that she is honest, but we do not have to grant that her honesty is virtuous.

Consider next the virtue of courage. This virtue has long been associated with military bravery, but an alternative to physical courage is "strength of mind, capable of conquering whatever threatens the attainment of the highest good."[11] Courage, to retain its priority as a virtue, must be joined to wisdom. Wisdom helps us to separate bravery from foolhardiness and, also, to make appropriate evaluations so that we exercise the virtue in pursuit of things that are worthwhile. The difficulty with this analysis, of course, is that wise people can differ on what they regard as worthwhile. Rationalists such as Aquinas and Kant would insist that the right use of reason is not a matter of dispute, but the real world reveals a different picture. In the year 2001, we experienced wave after wave of terror, deliberately inflicted on innocents in the name of great causes. Can we call the acts of suicide bombers cowardly? Surely we have to grant them great courage of a sort. Are they, then, lacking in wisdom? Most of us would say yes, but there are those who would defend them even on this – insisting that faith is a mark of ultimate wisdom.

To get a more satisfactory analysis, we must turn again to a relational perspective. If an act requiring physical or mental or social bravery tends to maintain caring relations with those immediately involved and does not destroy or greatly weaken relations in the larger web of care, then we may rightly say that the courage exercised is a virtue. But notice that, once again, this virtue does not seem to be the possession of an individual, one simply brought out and exercised at an appropriate moment. Rather, the label *virtuous* is better attached to the relational interaction.[12] An act is not virtuous, no matter how courageous the agent, if it deliberately or negligently harms others.

At this point, readers may object that my analysis denies the virtue of many acts of military courage. It does indeed. It does not deny the *courage*, but it suggests strongly that this form of courage should not be regarded as virtuous. War is not a virtuous activity. William James comments:

> Yet the fact remains that war is a school of strenuous life and heroism; and, being in the line of aboriginal instinct, is the only school that as yet is universally available. But when we gravely ask ourselves whether this wholesale organization of irrationality and crime be our only bulwark against effeminacy, we stand aghast at the thought, and think more kindly of ascetic religion . . . what we now need to discover in the social realm is the moral equivalent of war: something heroic that will speak to men as universally as war does, and yet will be as compatible with their spiritual selves as war has proved itself to be incompatible.[13]

James, like Hume, however, had little regard for the ascetic virtues. Happiness, from the ascetic perspective, is a desirable state for the soul, not the body, and I have already rejected this route to happiness. The paragraph from James raises another question: Must the moral equivalent of war avoid effeminacy? If by *effeminate* we mean too soft or self-indulgent, we might agree that effeminacy is best avoided. The problem is that the word also means *womanish*, and this suggests that the moral equivalent of war – if such an enterprise can be found – will not include qualities usually associated with women. From a relational perspective, such a decision is disastrous. It means persistently neglecting or avoiding the qualities that women have brought to caring relations.[14] It also multiplies the difficulties we face in overcoming violence because it suggests maintaining the masculinities that may lie at the root of violence.[15]

Without denying the heroism of warriors, educators interested in the happiness of their students must allow them to raise critical questions about war. For centuries, young men have been told that it is "sweet and seemly" to die for one's country.[16] Even mothers have urged their sons to bring honor on their families and nations by offering their lives in battle.[17] Appeals to honor have been highly effective, but they have often been backed up with powerful threats, and young soldiers have had to choose between risking their lives on the battlefield or being shot as cowards by their own troops. With respect to courage as a virtue, the question might be asked: Does a particular young man go into battle because he is courageous or because he is terrified of the alternative?

Teachers must handle this topic with exquisite care and balance. Nothing must be subtracted from the stories of heroism. Nothing should be omitted from the accounts of cruelty and destruction. Both warriors and war evaders can be credited with courage, but the virtue of war itself must be called into question. One can imagine the topic of courage taught through juxtaposition of strongly opposed views – leaving it to students to make their own carefully guided judgments. It is careful guidance that is so difficult, requiring teachers to ask: Have you considered X? Do you have the correct figures here? Have you read the biography of Y? Is there corroborating evidence for your claim?

How are teachers to do this? At present, and certainly for the foreseeable future, social studies teachers are tied to textbooks and a prespecified curriculum. The textbooks are very expensive, and there is rarely any money left over for supplementary texts. Further, although educators and parents extol the virtue of honesty and insist that children acquire and exercise it, they allow gross dishonesty to masquerade as objective knowledge in the school curriculum. Students today do hear about the evils of American slavery and our betrayal and destruction of Indians, but they are led to believe that these horrendous events were aberrations, uncharacteristic of the American way. Moreover, there are powerful voices that object to "too much emphasis" on even these well-documented episodes. It is risky and almost impossible for teachers to talk honestly to students about the horrors of present-day warfare and the ways in which the news media are forced (or choose?) to distort and underreport the realities of war.

Instead of slogging through dull texts, teachers should be encouraged to supply excerpts from outstanding books, excerpts that would help students to understand just how horrible war is and how military training coupled with actual combat experience can deaden or even destroy human moral resources. One chapter from Jonathan Glover's *Humanity* might do more toward genuine education than most "approved" texts could hope to accomplish.[18] It is not a matter of demonizing our own culture – and I agree with those who object to presenting our young with only the bad side of our culture – but of admitting with great sadness and some humility that, collectively, all humans have often behaved abominably toward other humans. No one can read Glover's account and come away with the notion that war is virtuous – no matter how virtuous the activating motives might have been.

What we need to do, and I have emphasized this again and again, is to educate the moral sensibilities, what Glover calls *human responses*.[19] Brought up and educated in an environment that promotes happiness, young people will remain in touch with those human responses we associate with caring: sympathy, motivational displacement (the desire to help and to share), tenderness, outrage and disgust at cruelty, generosity, a willingness to listen and be moved. They must also learn, however, that these human responses can be killed and that it has traditionally been part of military training to do just that. If there is no way to educate our children honestly and also to maintain a defensive military, we need to rethink what a *defensive military* might mean. No choice that sacrifices educational honesty should be acceptable.[20] Glover ends his informative and heart-rending work with these words:

> To avoid further disasters, we need political restraints on a world scale. But politics is not the whole story. We have experienced the results of technology in the service of the destructive side of human psychology. Something needs to be done about this fatal combination.

The means for expressing cruelty and carrying out mass killing have been fully developed. It is too late to stop the technology. It is to the psychology that we should now turn.[21]

Yes, to psychology but, more important, to education.

If happiness is connected to moral goodness, it is also influenced by intellectual virtue – by open-mindedness, critical thinking, and generosity of spirit. Thomas Paine said that he was committed to "doing justice, loving mercy, and endeavoring to make our fellow creatures happy."[22] He advocated nonviolence. To be nonviolent does not imply living in ignorance or allowing injustice to stand. One must seek the truth and recognize it even when it appears on the side less favored. This is possibly the hardest task of education – to bring students to a tolerance for ambiguity that will not paralyze them and prevent them from making commitments. Paine was castigated for his stand against violence. Many years after Paine's influential work was published, Theodore Roosevelt referred to him as a "filthy little atheist."[23]

In early 2002, we were faced again with a situation in which our leaders insisted that all others must be "with us or against us." Can education help people to understand that it is possible to be on both sides, seeing good and bad in each? We haven't made much progress on this. One reason is that, in a society that admires honesty as a virtue, we are unwilling to believe that some of our soldiers have cut and strung dried human ears as necklaces, murdered pregnant women, gutted living prisoners, and laughed at the obvious terror of their enemies.[24] Many of the boy-men who commit such crimes, like the young Nazi Karl in *The Sunflower*, are described by their mothers as "good boys."[25] What changes good boys into beings who can perform the cruel acts described in so many honest accounts of war?

Before examining one more virtue, we should return briefly to our earlier discussion of educational aims. There I said that it is dangerous to ignore aims-talk or to suppose that the analysis of educational aims is a finished task. Our Visitor from another world raised many questions about what we are doing. He might now ask why we are so intent on forcing standard academic subjects on all children when we have not even scratched the surface on the kinds of questions suggested by our discussion of courage. Shouldn't it be of great concern to us that young people finish high school with no knowledge of the kinds of acts they might perform in war? Brian Fogarty describes the changes that took place in military training after World War II:

> The major change was to de-emphasize physical skills in favor of psychological "motivation," that is the ability and willingness to kill automatically. Many psychological techniques were used, but most took one of two simple forms. The first is a matter of drill and desensitization: chanting "Kill, kill, kill, . . ." as a cadence while marching, for example. Or using the most explicit language possible when training to kill ("you want to *destroy* your enemy and send him home to his *mommy* in a *glad Bag . . .* ").[26]

If these techniques are widely used, it would surely be right for the public schools to prepare our young people for some form of moral resistance to them. The twentieth century provided us with a surfeit of horrors that could have been avoided if people were taught how to maintain their moral responses instead of how to overcome them. How is it that well-educated people – doctors, judges, mayors, philosophers – could participate in the torture, abuse, and even extermination of innocent human beings? In psychology, we are beginning to understand how these things happen,[27] and yet we rarely discuss what we have learned in high schools.

Failure to discuss the psychology of war is one more complaint we can raise against the contemporary character education movement. Courage is mentioned at least six times, for example, in Lickona's *Educating for Character*, and there are even several pages devoted to teaching about the Vietnam War. In the latter discussion, students are invited to examine both sides of the issue, to play the role of decision makers, and to "research the backgrounds of the persons who held the different views of the war."[28] They are never asked, however, to imagine themselves being so angry, confused, and terrified that they might slaughter women and children, torture prisoners, or gather dried human ears for souvenirs. But these are the things they need to consider if we are ever to establish a peaceful world.[29] If courage is to be a theme, the courage of those who have resisted evil nonviolently should be underscored.[30]

The last virtue to be examined here is perseverance. Perseverance is the ninth of thirty-one virtues presented in *Character Lessons*, a textbook published in 1909 for both teachers and parents.[31] As with the approach to other virtues, the section on perseverance starts with a definition and then moves to interpretation, elucidation and training, application, and inspiration. It recommends literature to be used with younger children and with older children. *Character Lessons* is a book rich in what E. D. Hirsch calls *cultural literacy*. It is filled with names, stories, anecdotes, quotations, and points to ponder. Today, it seems highly traditional, formal, even stuffy.

The lesson on perseverance includes many propaganda-style techniques such as having children recite "If at first you don't succeed, try, try, try again." But it also includes a bit of wisdom rarely heard today: "Keep to your specialty; to the doing of the thing that you accomplish with most of satisfaction to yourself and most of benefit to those about you."[32] It emphasizes that a "preconceived plan and a definite line of action are indispensable to perseverance."[33]

Choice and planning are highlighted. It is suggested that students should analyze their own interests and talents, plan accordingly, and then persevere in their plans. This is quite different from the usual message given in today's schools. Lickona, for example, speaks favorably of a first-grade teacher who has posted as the first rule of her classroom "Always do your best in everything." We give such advice to little children, and then we begin to grade them. What does this do to a child who does his best and regularly gets C's for his efforts?

Should we always do our best in everything, or should we choose intelligently and bravely those tasks to which we will give our best? For years I've advised graduate students to save their best for those intellectual tasks that arouse their passions. They must do an adequate job on everything required, of course, but doing uniformly well on everything is not the mark of a creative thinker, and trying to do so may well diminish creativity. "A 'B' is good for your soul," I tell them. "It helps you to decide what really interests you."

John Knowles has a wonderfully perceptive description of a student who becomes "exceptional" by carefully refusing to be really interested in anything but his grades. He has only one rival, Chet:

> But I began to see that Chet was weakened by the very genuineness of his interest in learning. . . . When we read *Candide* it opened up a new way of looking at the world to Chet, and he continued hungrily reading Voltaire, in French, while the class went on to other people. He was vulnerable there, because to me they were all pretty much alike – Voltaire and Moliere and the laws of motion and the

Magna Carta and the Pathetic Fallacy and *Tess Of the D'Urbervilles* – and I worked indiscriminately on all of them.[34]

It is this sad result that has recently been so well documented in real life by Denise Clark Pope.[35]

Thus, although the teacher described by Lickona deserves praise for getting 90 percent of her welfare-class children up to grade level, we wonder what will happen to them in later grades. If doing their best at tasks they have not chosen earns them C's, many will quit making the effort. If they push against the coercion – look for an interest and a plan – they may be defeated again. And if they buy their teacher's advice and, against the odds, make A's, they may become unhappy academic machines like Knowles's Gene and Pope's Eve. Such youngsters put their lives on hold – planning to be happy "some day" – while they obediently strive for the rewards attached to doing their best at everything.

Am I saying that we should encourage academic mediocrity? Quite the opposite. To expend equal effort – do one's best – on everything is a sure road to mediocrity. It is part of our job as educators to help students evaluate their own interests and work and, if possible, to find tasks at which they can work happily. They will have to do some tasks they might prefer to avoid, and we should not accept shoddy work, but we should guard against destroying the joy that accompanies a real passion for work that is chosen. Like honesty and courage, perseverance is not always a virtue.

We could spend much more time analyzing various virtues, but my aim is to establish an approach to the analysis. Insofar as virtue is connected to happiness, we must test each purported virtue to see under which conditions it actually shows this connection. We hope that the people produced by our educational efforts will be good people, and such people must be willing to sacrifice some episodic happiness for a deeper form dependent on a life of goodness. That hope suggests that we should spend time in discussing goodness in some depth, and the discussion must include critical thinking on critical issues.

For many people, character is closely connected to spirituality, and a fulfilled spiritual life yields great happiness. How might this topic be approached in public schools? In what follows, I will not discuss particular religions or, indeed, religion at all. I am not rejecting the spirituality connected to religion but simply showing that the topic can be taken up without risking a constitutional violation. We will look for spirit in everyday life.

Spirituality

Some who seek an enhanced spiritual life today join movements that promise escape from worldly concerns (even, occasionally, escape from the body); some turn to evangelical fundamentalisms as a way of recapturing lost souls, and still others study the contemplative life to learn its patterns and exercises. Without denigrating the first two approaches or rejecting the third (which I find deeply thoughtful and marked by great beauty), I want to suggest that enhanced awareness of certain features in everyday life can contribute significantly to spiritual life and to happiness.

Sometime between dawn and sunrise on days that will be clear, a red band appears across the eastern sky. My bedroom faces the ocean and, lying in bed, I can see this smear of red just above the sea. The actual sunrise is, until late fall, a bit north of the bedroom window; I have to get up and move to another room to see it. As I approach the library/plant room, even before a window is in view, I often stop – enchanted by the light across the bookcases on my left. The sea is to the right, and as I move ahead and turn, I'll see the full show of sunrise. But here, now, stopped in this passage, the pattern of light is magnificent. Some mornings it is gold, others pink. Once in a while, the whole wall and all the books are bathed in a reddish glow. The spirit soars.

Then there is the sunrise itself. When we think about sunrises de-picted in poetry and stories, we think of the gradual increase in light that is really dawn. Watching the sun rise, we realize that it is a phe-nomenon of suddenness. The sun bursts onto the horizon as though full of enthusiasm. One moment there is a mere curved line in the band, and in the next a full, fat sun. How many human beings share this moment with me? I marvel that, no matter what season of the year, there are always a few people watching on the boardwalk, or pier, or rock jetty just across the street from where I am watching. Perhaps we are all momentarily overcome with the immensity of the sea, its beauty in the sunrise, our tenuous place in the universe, and a continually renewed wonder at the start of a day.

Before I go further with accounts of spiritual moments in everyday life, I want to acknowledge what will be obvious to everyone. I live in a special place. Not everyone has such a view, nor a library/plant room. But I have read similar accounts of the spirit soaring in fishermen, in farmers, and in Navajos living in simple hogans – facing the east and the glories of sunrise.

The spiritual moments discussed here do not come as a result of detachment or meditation. They are, rather, moments of complete engagement with what-is-there. Martin Buber describes such moments as manifestations of relation, and they can happen in encounters with people, animals, plants, objects, or events. In describing an encounter with a tree, Buber points out the multitude of ways one might "contemplate a tree." In most of them, the tree is an object of scrutiny, of study. "But," he writes, "it can also happen, if will and grace are joined, that as I contemplate the tree I am drawn into a relation, and the tree ceases to be an It."[36] These are moments of surpassing wonder and contentment.

The sudden realization of relation does not always produce wonder and contentment. For Sartre's character Roquentin, an encounter with chestnut trees induces nausea:

> I sought in vain to *count* the chestnut trees, to *situate* them in relation to the statue... to compare their height... each escaped the relationship in which I tried to enclose it... the root... monstrous soft masses in disorder – naked, with a terrifying and obscene nakedness.

Feeling at one, blending, with the chestnut tree's root overwhelmed Roquentin and made him think that he was as irrelevant – as in the way – as a chestnut's roots:

> *And me* – flabby, languid, obscene, digesting, shaking with dismal thoughts – *I was also in the way*. I vaguely contemplated doing away with myself to annihilate at least one of these superfluous existences. But my very death would have been in the way. In the way: my dead body, my blood on the cobblestones, among the plants at the end of this smiling park... I was in the way I was in the way forever.[37]

Many spiritual encounters induce fear, horror, or nausea, and these should not be ignored but, as a teacher, I would not overemphasize these experiences; I would be careful to balance them with accounts that bring peace and joy. However, the accounts of horror are vivid.

William James provides several that are more devastating than that of Roquentin. He, too, calls a halt:

> There is no need of more examples. The cases we have looked at are enough. One of them gives us the vanity of mortal things; another the sense of sin; and the remaining one describes fear of the universe; – and in one or other of these three ways it always is that man's original optimism and self-satisfaction get leveled with the dust.[38]

If I were discussing this topic with high school students – the wonder and terror of spiritual experience – I might next show pictures that appear in W. G. Sebald's *Austerlitz*. Without mentioning Sartre and Roquentin or Buber, Sebald juxtaposes a photograph of a sprawling chestnut root with one of "windflowers covering the woodland floor."[39] The effects illustrate the extremes we are discussing. The I–Thou meeting described by Buber is wonderful. To connect, to be one, with another person, a tree, a work of art, or God is the height of spiritual life – if that other is perceived as somehow good. If that being is felt as evil, terrible, or disgusting, one feels terror or nausea, not a soaring of the spirit.

Sebald contributes something more. He tells how Austerlitz, as a child, learned about moths and how they occasionally lose their way in a house:

> If you do not put them out again carefully they will stay where they are, never moving, until the last breath is out of their bodies, and indeed they will remain in the place where they came to grief even after death, held fast by the tiny claws that stiffened in their last agony.[40]

This is painful enough for those who love nature, but the next passages invite a literary-spiritual experience:

> There is really no reason to suppose that lesser beings are devoid of sentient life. We are not alone in dreaming at night for, quite apart from dogs and other domestic creatures whose emotions have been bound up with ours for many thousands of years, the smaller mammals such as mice and moles also live in a world that exists only in their minds whilst they are asleep ... and who knows, ... perhaps moths dream as well, perhaps a lettuce in the garden dreams as it looks up at the moon by night.[41]

Students might be encouraged to check the scientific status of some of these remarks but, more important, they should ponder the ideas. How do we feel about the possibility of consciousness in a lettuce? If it can dream, it can have nightmares as well. Our wonder and terror may well deepen.

Ordinary everyday life – the life in which we encounter trees, moths, and lettuce plants – is more often associated with boredom and drudgery than with spiritual experience. Housework, for example is not usually spirit-enhancing work, but it can be occasionally. It is easy to forget that the house, in sheltering our bodies, also protects our spirits and imaginations. Literature and poetry are filled with descriptions and reminiscences of childhood homes and with longings for homeland and home region. However, the objects in homes are rarely mentioned (except, interestingly, clocks and portraits, which often figure prominently). But Bachelard reminds us:

> How wonderful it is to really become once more the inventor of a mechanical action! And so, when a poet rubs a piece of furniture – even vicariously – when he puts a little fragrant wax on his table with the woolen cloth that lends warmth to everything it touches, he creates a new object; he increases the object's human dignity; he registers this object officially as a member of the human household.[42]

Thus it happens sometimes, if not pressed by time and other tasks, if the light is just right, if the spirit is receptive, there can be this spiritual moment when the polished furniture gleams as though with appreciation, and the human spirit glows, too. It need not happen every time one dusts or sweeps, any more than any other spiritual exercise consistently produces epiphanies, but it does occur. As with other such exercises, one must be prepared and aware.

In previous paragraphs, where I have described the spirit as soaring, I might as easily have described it as indwelling. It is not so much that spirit transcends body as that body becomes consciously flooded with spirit. Both interpretations contribute to our understanding. The soaring I have described might be named *ecstasy*. As Carol Ochs defines it, "Ecstasy . . . is the standing outside of oneself (*ex stasis*). This means that the normal self, which includes our usual ways of thinking, judging, and evaluating, is displaced. We are brought outside the self through an irruption in our life."[43] From a relational perspective, however, my experience as described is more nearly a full realization of self than a standing outside of self. It is a momentary and exquisite realization of relatedness. It cannot be summoned, and yet one must be prepared in order for it to happen.

Ochs is right, I think, when she warns that experiences of this sort cannot be directly sought. Her remarks echo Buber's:

> Once we realize that experience is not a goal, we must reaffirm its importance as a means when we learn to trust ourselves and to be true to ourselves.... If spirituality is the process of coming into relationships with reality, then it must include a relationship with the reality of our own experiences.[44]

Everyday experience continues into night. For example, I may retire early and read, alternating among dissertation chapters, mystery novels, book reviews, modern novels, and classics that I missed in my student days. As the evening progresses and I grow sleepy, the cat Lulu joins me. Most nights she simply sleeps at the foot of our bed, but sometimes she snuggles tightly against me, under my right arm. It becomes hard to turn pages. I turn off the light and give my attention to petting her; she pets me back, "making biscuits" on my shoulder, and purrs with a gentle rumble. And I think, as I rest my hand lightly on her head and the happy rumble continues, about the meaning of such interspecies affection. Trust seems absolute. Why is so much love manifested in relationships the world considers insignificant?

Most nights sleep comes easily – for at least a few hours – and the pile of reading is always at hand for the wakeful hours. But, when the eyes are too tired to read, the cat has retired to the foot of the bed, my husband is gently snoring, and sleep still will not come – perhaps held off by the night fears that afflict moths and humans – I sometimes silently recite poetry, a bit from Frost or Hardy. Things, troubling fears and annoying details, fall away, and I sleep.

I ask myself often why we do so little in schools to promote spiritual well-being. Do we suggest to our students that the soul rises with the sun, that it is worth the effort to drag one's weary body out occasionally to lift the soul? Do we invite students to look at their houses and ask how many objects have been "registered officially" as members of the human household? Do we encourage reflection on interspecies affection as we pursue politically correct lessons on environmentalism? Do we acknowledge the uneasiness and fear that often arise at night?

Do we help students to memorize poetry, not for official performances or grades, but to build a repertoire of spiritual exercises? If we do not, why don't we?

Spiritual experience, as I have been describing it, is intensely personal, but there are some common experiences, other than the traditionally religious ones that I have said I would not discuss here, that many people have associated with spiritual happiness. Gardens have long been recognized as places that turn the human spirit to "virtue and sanctity."[45] They are also places of retreat – spots to which we turn to escape both the chaos of the larger world and the hubbub and stuffiness of the house. At the extreme of world weariness (and rejecting Pangloss's notion that the world's horrors were somehow necessary for the goods he now enjoyed), Voltaire's Candide said, "We must cultivate our gardens."[46] Those who have gardens to cultivate are fortunate.

Gardens, however, are not merely retreats; they invite kindred spirits. Many gardeners find gardening a spiritual experience, and what they share there is very like what a congregation shares in church. In this age of body consciousness, gardening can also be regarded as fine exercise, and it is: bending, stretching, lifting, and digging long enough and hard enough to produce sweat and an increased heart rate. But gardening is, even more, spiritual exercise. Among thousands of expressions of this truth, I particularly like E. B. White's tribute to his wife in the introduction of her book:

> Armed with a diagram and a clipboard, Katherine would get into a shabby old Brooks raincoat much too long for her, put on a little round wool hat, pull on a pair of overshoes, and proceed to the director's chair – a folding canvas thing – that had been placed for her at the edge of the plot. There she would sit, hour after hour, in the wind and the weather, while Henry Allen produced dozens of brown paper packages of new bulbs and a basketful of old ones, ready for the intricate interment. As the years went by and age overtook her, there was something comical yet touching in her bedraggled appearance on this awesome occasion – the small hunched-over figure, her studied absorption in the implausible notion that there would be yet another spring, oblivious to the ending of her own days, which she knew perfectly well was at hand, sitting there with her detailed chart under those dark skies in the dying October, calmly plotting the resurrection.[47]

One complaint I have long had against some churchmen is that many of them search constantly for miracles of a supernatural sort. They should get out, like Katherine White, into their gardens, where miracles of this world abound. Every time I brush aside the mulch on a garden bed in spring and find new seedlings – tender, green-red, or yellow-green, perfect in form – I sit back for a moment and just feel the miracle. Even more potent in producing this feeling is contact with a new human baby. What ecstasy in snuggling a newborn! As miracles go, these recurring events are quite sufficient.

Porches, like gardens, are earthly places of resurrection. Beaten, soaked, and scarred by the winter rains, ice, and wind, they stand bare and dead-looking in the late winter. But when spring arrives, the porches come alive and neighbors pause in their painting, scraping, hammering, and scrubbing to greet one another and see how each has fared over winter. We encounter one another, and we realize at least momentarily that Martin Buber was right when he said, "All actual life is encounter."[48] Spring brings a renewal of encounters with people, plants, the exterior of one's house, and the lovely intermediate spaces that both shelter us and give us confidence to wander forth.

For me, and for many others, the seaside is another place for spiritual exercise. The ocean is a splendor for all the senses. It is wonderful to look at, to listen to, to smell. I also love the feel and taste of it. Its buoyancy and active movement induce playfulness. As the spirit says, "Play!" The body obeys, and we body surf, swim underwater to surprise one another, do easy flips, swim, bob, dive under, and then float in the sun. And while the body is at play, the spirit says, "Thank you." To whom? To what? That I do not know. I only record the experience.

My account so far of spiritual experience in everyday life may suggest that the solitude so often prescribed for spiritual exercise is unnecessary. This would be a mistake. Although I do not believe that long periods of solitude are essential for spiritual awakening, I do believe that moments of solitude and quiet are necessary. When I am deeply affected by a sunrise or its spectacular pre-glow, there is always a moment of reflection, time to simply "be with." Even when the spiritual sense is aroused while playing in the surf, it is the quiet moment of floating in which the spirit is most fully actualized.

174

Anne Morrow Lindbergh recommended reasonable periods of solitude for everyone: "Every person, especially every woman, should be alone sometime during the year, some part of each week, and each day."[49] She observed that, despite mechanical improvements of all sorts, women at midcentury seemed to have less time, not more, for solitude. She feared, rightly many of us think, that the "spirit of woman is going dry." Too often, "With our pitchers, we attempt sometimes to water a field, not a garden. We throw ourselves indiscriminately into committees and causes. Not knowing how to feed the spirit, we try to muffle its demands in distractions."[50]

How much more true is this today? In contrast, Lindbergh noted, our foremothers – who had so much more physical work to do – had, at least, some seclusion:

> Many of their duties were conducive to a quiet contemplative drawing together of self. They had more creative tasks to perform. Nothing feeds the center so much as creative work, even humble kinds like cooking and sewing. Baking bread, weaving cloth, putting up preserves, teaching and singing to children, must have been far more nourishing than being the chauffeur or shopping at supermarkets ... the art and craft of housework has diminished; much of the time-consuming drudgery remains.[51]

This is especially true today when so many women work both at home and outside. Home tasks must be rushed because so many other responsibilities press us. There simply is no time to savor the *doing* of tasks that were once necessary but now are avoidable. One might actually enjoy baking bread or putting up strawberry preserves, but can one justify the time these jobs take up?

There is another insight from Lindbergh that is valuable. The perfect moments I have described are temporary, fleeting, and are to be treasured for their very evanescence. Like happiness itself, these moments must be handled gently. It is clutching them, trying to hold on to them, that destroys the joy we might have got from them. "It is fear," Lindbergh wrote, "that makes one cling nostalgically to the last moment or clutch greedily toward the next."[52] In part, this is why we need solitude and silence as well as encounter. In moments of solitude, we can feel the wonder of the sunrise, the new seedling, the rising bread, the last wave that swept us onto the beach. The moments have passed, but their memory has become part of us, and the solitude given to reflection refreshes us and prepares us for the next moment of spiritual awakening.

Finding the spiritual in everyday occasions may lead us to withdraw from public life; that is, without retreating as fully as Voltaire's Candide suggested, we may live in the world and yet be apart from it. Although such a life is often extolled in religious doctrine, those who live it may be lost to political action. When everyday life is full and satisfying, participation in that part of the public realm demanding debate, confrontation, and action may be unattractive. Hannah Arendt remarked on this tendency in a whole people:

> Modern enchantment with "small things," though preached by early twentieth-century poetry in almost all European tongues, has found its classical presentation in the *petit bonheur* of the French people. Since the decay of their once great and glorious public realm, the French have become masters in their art of being happy among "small things," within the space of their own four walls, between chest and bed, table and chair, dog and cat and flowerpot, extending to these things a care and tenderness which, in a world where rapid industrialization constantly kills off the things of yesterday to produce today's objects, may even appear to be the world's last, purely humane corner. This enlargement of the private . . . does not make it public . . . but, on the contrary, means only that the public realm has almost completely receded.[53]

Arendt made an important point, but she did not carry that part of her analysis far enough. Enchantment with the small things of everyday life may indeed be accompanied by disenchantment with public life in its mass action forms. One may shun mass displays of public grief or triumph, endless meetings that underscore seemingly irreconcilable differences, and political "debates" marked by incivility, empty slogans, and outright lies. One may indeed go too far in retreat. But if one remains hospitable and generous in personal encounters, the fault may not be so terrible. After all, semi-isolated villagers in Le Chambon-sur-Lignon provided a lesson in charity to a more sophisticated world in their sheltering of several thousand Jews during the Nazi persecution.[54] Maybe, after all, the French are well rid of their "great and glorious public realm."

Many of us recognize in ourselves this temptation to retreat to a manageable and deeply satisfying world. This is a topic to be considered in the chapters of Part 3. How big can the collective be before one loses confidence in understanding what is actually going on? There may be no reliable resolution of the conflicts that arise in this tension. Perhaps the best response is recognition and wary observation of both the collective and oneself. When does the enchantment with everyday life become mere self-indulgence? When does the enhanced spirituality associated with this enchantment provide the courage to wander forth and make one's voice heard in the public realm?

Whether we wander forth as positive contributors to the public realm or turn inward selfishly may depend on what we experience inside, in our "corner of the world." The love of place from the minutest detail – the bottle of sea glass on my desk – to the "winds and wide gray skies" described by Edna St. Vincent Millay not only enriches our lives and invites spiritual awakening; it also increases our sensitivity to the larger world and its inhabitants. Drawing on Merleau-Ponti's ideas about the connection between individual bodies and the "flesh of the world," Casey writes:

> We care about places as well as people, so much so that we can say *caring belongs to places*. We care about places in many ways, but in building on them – *building with them*, indeed *building them* – they become the ongoing "stars of our life," that to which we turn when we travel and to which we return when we come back home.[55]

It should be an aim of education to provide children with such "stars" to guide them to richer private lives as well as more generous and thoughtful public lives.

In this chapter, we first looked at the relationship between character and happiness and then considered the happiness often associated with spirituality. As the analysis proceeded, it became clear that some commonly named virtues – courage, honesty, and perseverance, for example – are not always virtues. We decided to credit some agents with honesty, courage, or perseverance even though we had to say that these labels do not automatically signal virtue and may even represent evil.

In the discussion of spirituality, we concentrated on everyday spirituality – the sort that certainly can be discussed in schools without violating any rules on the teaching of religion. Moreover, everyday spirituality has the capacity to contribute significantly to happiness. We noted, however, that the deep satisfaction gained in spiritual relationships may induce us to avoid or fail to promote interactions that may be basic to human flourishing. Before examining public life, we look next at the role of close human relationships in the promotion of happiness.

9

Interpersonal Growth

Human relationships are perhaps the most important single in-
gredient in happiness. In the previous chapter, we discussed
character and spirituality, both of which contribute substantially to
human flourishing. There will surely be some overlap in what we
explore in this chapter, but the emphasis here will be on interpersonal connections and how they enhance or detract from happiness.

We begin the discussion with an exploration of those agreeable
qualities associated with a pleasant personality. What qualities are
perceived as agreeable by most people? How are these qualities developed? Then we will look at two areas that are especially important
for happiness: friendship and romantic love.

Agreeable Qualities

It is intuitively plausible, and now substantially backed by empirical evidence, that people who possess the following qualities are
found agreeable: physical attractiveness, good manners, a capacity
for (decent) pleasure, wit, modesty, a certain grace of manner, self-
esteem (balanced by modesty), and extraversion.[1] We could no doubt
name others, and we should not forget, in our present attention to
personality, character traits that are greatly admired – traits such as
kindness, generosity, honesty, and fidelity. Indeed, it is hard to separate character and personality traits completely, and the separation
here is largely one of emphasis.

Physical attractiveness seems more closely related to personality
than to character. Perhaps it belongs to neither, but we know that it
plays a strong role in an assessment of agreeableness, and empirical

179

studies show that attractive people tend to be happier than unattractive people.[2] On the one hand, this finding could be taken as an indictment of humanity's character; on the other, we might ask how attractiveness is defined before we pass judgment.

Genetic factors play a part in physical attractiveness, but it is still reasonable to ask how this agreeable quality is developed. Many women and men without exceptional physical features – and even some with features that would be regarded as ugly in others – are nevertheless said to be attractive. Cleanliness is part of attractiveness; lack of it, Hume said, creates in others an "uneasy sensation."[3] Although it may be a small fault (Hume again), lack of cleanliness suggests that a person does not care enough about others to avoid exciting that uneasy sensation. If it is not overdone, attention to grooming, style, and posture is a reasonable way to achieve a level of attractiveness.

Once again we perceive a degree of circularity in an attempt to connect a quality with happiness. Physical attractiveness does seem to promote happiness, but happiness also contributes to attractiveness. Children who are well loved and happy are more attractive than those who are neglected and miserable. This is true for adults as well. David Myers comments, "In Rodgers and Hammerstein's musical, Prince Charming sings to Cinderella, 'Do I love you because you are beautiful, or are you beautiful because I love you?' Chances are it's both."[4] People who display other agreeable qualities and make the best of their physical features – without making a fetish out of that project – are likely to be perceived as attractive.

Children have to believe that it is both desirable and possible to develop agreeable personal qualities. Parents and teachers should notice when such qualities are displayed and spend some time talking with children about the acquisition of agreeable traits. It now seems likely, for example, that acting as if we are happy may actually make us feel happier. "Put on a smiley face" is sometimes good advice. If acting "as if" is carried too far, however, the actor may be seen as giving a performance – or worse, as deceitful and untrustworthy. Further, if children are *required* to smile when they are unhappy, they become unable to evaluate their own feelings. Such children grow into confused adults, out of touch with not only their own feelings but everyone else's as well. After all, if a person regularly smiles when she is miserable, how can she tell what a smile means on others?

Hume discusses qualities immediately agreeable to ourselves and qualities agreeable to others, and he points out that there is considerable overlap in these qualities. "A relish for pleasure, if accompanied with temperance and decency,"[5] is a quality we enjoy in ourselves and appreciate in others; "others enter into the same humour, and catch the sentiment, by a contagion or natural sympathy."[6] We like to be with people who make us feel good, who add to the pleasure of the activity at hand.

Qualities of personality, like those of character, comprise a system that requires a balance. An exaggeration of any one may diminish the overall effect of agreeableness. For example, most of us appreciate a healthy self-esteem in others as we do in ourselves. A person who really thinks of herself as inferior makes us uncomfortable. But so does a person who thinks too highly of himself. Similarly, we admire an appropriate level of humility, but Uriah Heep–like groveling disgusts us. Even cheerfulness, which we greatly admire in most situations, can be shockingly out of place. Sometimes we need tearful sympathy, not hearty encouragement to "cheer up."

How is the balance so essential for an agreeable personality achieved? This is a question of paramount importance to parents and educators. We now know that there is a significant heritability factor in personality qualities.[7] Babies are born with personality characteristics or, at least, tendencies. This does not mean, however, that parenting and teaching have no effect on the development of personality. Indeed, we might well argue that the existence of innate personality differences demands more sensitive and skillful education than would be required if personality development were entirely a matter of socialization and education. If the latter were true, we could seek and recommend one best way of raising all children. Since it isn't true, we have to find different ways to guide different children.

Does this suggest that our earlier identification of authoritative parenting as better than either permissive or authoritarian parenting might be mistaken? Might some children do better under authoritarian parenting? I think we have to admit this possibility. It is more reasonable, however, to look for alternatives within the pattern that seems overall to be best. Authoritative parents and teachers have considerable leeway within that approach to respond to individual differences. Without becoming authoritarian, a parent may occasionally use authoritarian methods with a child who responds to them.

Similarly, the same parent may be more nearly permissive with another child.

Possibly the most important single factor in the development of a healthy personality is self-esteem. This is especially true in a liberal democracy – not so important in collectivist societies.[8] John Rawls, who uses *self-esteem* and *self-respect* interchangeably, names self-esteem as "perhaps the most important primary good."[9] It is so important, he writes, because

> [i]t includes a person's sense of his own value, his secure conviction that his conception of his good, his plan of life, is worth carrying out. And, second, self-respect implies a confidence in one's ability...to fulfill one's intentions. When we feel that our plans are of little value, we cannot pursue them with pleasure or take delight in their execution.[10]

I think Rawls puts somewhat too much emphasis on a person's plans and the ability to carry them out and not enough on the person and his or her personal characteristics, but his judgment about the importance of self-esteem seems right. Some children never develop the capacity to make real plans because they are not accepted by either family or community as persons worthy of love and respect. Toni Morrison tells the story of a little black girl, Pecola, who begged for, prayed for, blue eyes – thinking that the possession of blue eyes would make her into a person worthy of love and attention. In the end, when Pecola has gone mad in order to find a self, the girls who scorned her realized:

> We were so beautiful when we stood astride her ugliness. Her simplicity decorated us, her guilt sanctified us, her pain made us glow with health, her awkwardness made us think we had a sense of humor. Her inarticulateness made us believe we were eloquent. Her poverty kept us generous. Even her waking dreams we used – to silence our own nightmares. And she let us, and thereby deserved our contempt.[11]

One must have some self-respect in order to get respect from others, but one must first have a free gift of love and respect as a starter. Pecola had no one's love and, without it, she was lost not only in the sight of others but even to herself.

Educators recognize the importance of self-esteem, but we do not always agree on how to promote it. Schools in California were the focus of mean-spirited jokes when they adopted programs specifically designed to raise the self-esteem of students. The attempt was mistaken, but not because the goal is unworthy. Self-esteem, like happiness, can serve as an educational aim, but it has to be nurtured indirectly. We can't establish self-esteem as a learning objective and teach directly for it. Instead we have to ask about the conditions under which self-esteem is nourished. Here, again, extremes must be avoided. Students do not gain healthy self-esteem through undeserved praise, but whatever self-esteem they have can be destroyed by teacher cruelty. Such cruelty is by no means rare. Possibly there is no worse pedagogical crime than that of making a student feel stupid. Hume points out that human beings, constituted as thinking, planning creatures, suffer terribly under the epithet of *fool* or any of its equivalents.[12] We hate the one who labels us that way, and we devalue ourselves.

In my early years as a math teacher, I often tried to encourage students by telling them, "This is easy. Just look!" and then I would show them exactly how easy it was for me! But many did not find it easy. I learned that it is much better to say, "This may be hard, but you'll get it. I'll help." It makes a teacher feel wonderful when a child then says, "That wasn't so hard!" Similarly, it is better to say, "You've almost got it" than "You're still doing it wrong." At the other extreme, the habit of saying "good" to every student response rings false and fails to help students make sound self-evaluations. Honest appraisals accompanied by encouragement and recognition of progress support self-esteem.

Another factor that seems to contribute to personal happiness is extraversion.[13] The strong relationship between extraversion and measures of happiness may, however, be a result of the measures we choose to describe happiness. Because so many of us find our primary happiness in the company of other human beings, we may overlook the inner happiness achieved by many introverts. Indeed, many of the sources of happiness identified earlier – love of place, the company of pets, immersion in study and ideas, religion, gardening, a hobby such as fishing or hiking – are readily available to introverts. A child should not be shamed or scolded for being shy. It should be acceptable to seek and enjoy solitary pleasures so long as the introversion does not turn into hostility toward others or self-hate.

It is often hard for teachers to know how to judge the emotional health of quiet students. Some young people find deep happiness in solitary pursuits. Other quiet students are deeply unhappy loners – kids who want recognition from their peers and elders but fail to get it. Most of the boys who commit violent crimes in school have been described as troubled loners. Because outgoing students demand so much of teachers' time and do it so directly, even conscientious teachers often overlook the quiet ones. Occasional conversations with these students can be useful. How are you spending your time? What do you enjoy? What do you share with friends? These are questions we want to ask, but we may have to start more subtly. Precisely because these students are quiet, we may not know where to begin. We have to watch for clues.

When children are not only quiet but also alienated and angry, teachers must try to help. Sometimes special counseling is required. In general, teachers have to work toward the establishment of class-rooms as caring communities in which all students are included and respected.[14] Young people today often experience harassment from their peers, and this problem should be discussed openly in class meetings, but without specific references or accusations. Students should not be forced to disclose their own victimization; fictitious accounts can provide a lively start for group analysis. But the matter must be addressed. We know now that most of the boys who go on rampages and kill others have suffered for a considerable period of time. "The young killers themselves insisted that they were 'angry, not crazy' and that they committed their crimes consciously on behalf of all people who are mistreated."[15]

The understandable temptation of teachers is either to ignore quiet students – "he was never any trouble" – or to label and refer them for special help. Sometimes, of course, we do need to seek special help, but often the labeling itself – done with the best intentions – makes the situation worse. A boy who felt alone and "different" before may now feel confirmed in his low opinion of himself. The first remedy must be loving inclusion, and kids must be helped to develop and act on empathy for others. Why do students make life even more miserable for peers who are homeless, homosexual, obese, or in any way different from the norm of the day? What triggers such cruelty? How can students help one another when teachers or parents treat them badly? How can kids get adults to listen? These questions are every bit as important for classroom discussion as the usual academic questions.[16] As we saw in the previous chapter, our society's expectations for masculine behavior often lead boys who are different – or merely perceived to be different – to prove their masculinity in violent ways.[17]

It is easier for elementary school teachers to get to know their students than it is for middle and high school teachers. In self-contained classrooms, caring teachers can attend to each student as a person and recognize a wide range of interests and talents. This is much harder for the high school teacher, who sees more than 100 students every day, usually in the limited context of one classroom subject. It is not unusual for middle and high school teachers to judge their students almost entirely on how well they do in their particular courses. "Good kids" are defined by good grades. The teachers know very little about their students as persons. The shock of this kind of anonymity may explain why so many academic and disciplinary problems flare up at the middle school level.

It takes time and devotion to know one's students as persons. If we are serious about teaching for social learning, we might consider promoting arrangements in which teachers and students stay together for several years (by mutual consent). The limited amount of research available at this time suggests that students benefit both academically and socially when such continuous relationships are established.[18]

Programs of this sort at the elementary level are now called *looping*. This is an unfortunate choice of words, because it concentrates on the teacher's experience. He or she is the one who loops. Our focus should be on *continuity* and its benefits for both teachers and students. Another objection to looping is that it ignores the different but valuable potential for secondary school continuity. For example, as a high school mathematics teacher, I often taught the same students for three or four years. It was wonderful to have only one new class each year, and the returnees and I could pick up where we left off.

Other arrangements to provide continuity are possible. Some middle schools keep a team of teachers with a cohort of students for two or three years.[19] Theodore Sizer has suggested that it might be better for a teacher to teach two subjects to, say, twenty-five students instead of teaching one subject to fifty.[20] Deborah Meier has pointed out that multiyear relationships increase the possibility of sharing power and

185

authority in schools.[21] But, again, I would use the word *continuity* to focus our attention on the relational benefits we hope to gain, and I would invite educators to create a variety of arrangements that might promote continuity.

So far in this chapter, as in previous chapters, we have been treating substantial questions raised by our Visitor from another world. Without denying the importance of academic learning, we have seriously considered what schools might do to help students achieve agreeable personality traits. One reward for displaying such qualities is the acquisition of friends and, of course, having good friends contributes to the development of agreeable qualities. Do we give sufficient attention to friendship in schools?

Friendship

It is intuitively obvious that good friendships contribute to happiness, and there is now much empirical evidence to back up our intuition.[22] However, we need to ask what makes a good friendship, and we might also ask about the number of friendships one can maintain. Are we happier if we have lots of friends rather than one or two steady ones? This is an important question for teenagers, who often equate having friends with popularity.

The standard school curriculum contains no official course on friendship, but some teachers do organize units around the theme of friendship. If literature teachers keep the topic in mind, they can raise important questions within the discussion of most required books. Some examples of interesting friendships come immediately to mind: Gene and Finny in *A Separate Peace*, Huck and Jim in *Huckleberry Finn*, Caesar and Brutus in *Julius Caesar*, Holmes and Watson in the Sherlock Holmes stories, Lenny and George in *Of Mice and Men*.

A nice start would be to have the class read a few pages of Aristotle or, if that is not possible, teachers can provide a brief summary and a few quotations. Aristotle says that reciprocated goodwill is the main mark of friendship.[23] One wishes a friend well for the friend's own sake. Further, to be friends, both parties must be aware of the other's goodwill. (We may wish well for strangers, but this does not make us friends.) Aristotle recognizes that the idea of friendship changes as young people develop. He writes, "The cause of friendship between young people seems to be pleasure."[24] Most students will agree.

Next, Aristotle notes that the conception of pleasure changes as young people mature. Pleasure is always thought to be good, but the notion of good also changes. Deeper, fuller meanings of *pleasure*, *good*, and *happiness* develop. *Complete* friendship is the highest form of friendship and much to be desired:

> But complete friendship is the friendship of good people similar in virtue; for they wish goods in the same way to each other. . . . Now those who wish goods to their friend for the friend's own sake are friends most of all; for they have this attitude because of the friend himself, not coincidentally.[25]

There is much to discuss here. If we follow Aristotle, we will seek good people for our friends, and we will wish the best for them. This well-wishing includes the wish that they will continue to be good people and become even better. The best friends work at their friendship and help each other to develop their best selves. But friends also spend time together and enjoy one another's company. It is because they spend time together that they have great influence on each other. That influence can be good or bad. In *The Picture of Dorian Gray*, the artist Basil tries to shake Dorian from his immoral ways. He says, "You have not been fine. One has a right to judge a man by the effect he has over his friends. Yours seem to lose all sense of honour, of goodness, of purity. You have filled them with a madness for pleasure."[26] A true friend's effects should be positive, not negative. Basil was trying to be a true friend to Dorian.

The duties as well as the pleasures of friendship are great. Aristotle warns that "no one can have complete friendship for many people"[27] because friendship requires getting to know one's friend well. We can form "incomplete" friendships with many, and we can please many people, but deep, long-lasting friendships must be small in number.

This much of Aristotle provides a fine background against which to discuss questions that usually concern teenagers greatly: Is popularity a sign that one has many friends? Is it better to have two really good friends than to be popular? Can one have a complete friendship with a bad person? What if associating with a person makes us worse, not better, people? What do we owe our friends?

All of these questions deserve our time and attention, but the last may be especially important for teenagers. Suppose that a friend does something bad? Suppose, for example, that Joe's friend Bob begins to use drugs. Should Joe report Bob to an adult authority or does friendship require loyalty of the "no ratting," "no snitching" sort?

These are enormously difficult questions, although there are people on opposite sides who give simple answers with confidence in their positions. One person will say that the law should have our primary allegiance – no question. Another will say that friendship demands our loyalty, and we should not betray our friend. Reacting from feelings, as Aristotle warned they would, teenagers are likely to opt for loyalty to their friends. I have considerable sympathy for them.

If friends want the best for each other, Joe must want to help Bob. If Joe could be sure that Bob would get help and not some legalized punishment that might well make him a worse character, Joe might be willing to report the problem to authorities. At present, there are many illegal acts that might better be considered problems for treatment instead of punishment. Suppose Joe were to confide in a teacher, Ms. Jones. Today, Ms. Jones would put herself in jeopardy if she tried to help Bob without turning him in to the law. Knowing this, Joe may try to reform Bob on his own – a task that is almost certainly beyond his competence. Adolescent stories are rife with cases of this sort – often cases in which a girl tries to reform her boyfriend.

If teenagers want the best for their friends, we should make it possible and desirable for them to confide in us. That is the message that a caring society should give to its young. "We are here. We will help." In the absence of this message, young people are caught in a real dilemma. Turning a friend over to a system that may further corrupt him is not in the Aristotelian spirit of friendship.

Our society makes matters worse by offering rewards to people who will betray their friends and neighbors. For example, the New Jersey State Police regularly advertise in our local paper a reward for reports of marijuana growing – "inside or outside." What sort of person would report a friend or neighbor for a monetary reward? Similarly, citizens can profit by reporting tax evasion or fraud on the part of their relatives or neighbors. This is morally disgusting, and we should discuss the moral issues openly and fully with the young people whose citizenship education is placed in our hands.

It is odd that we fail to see the moral weakness in our own governmental practices when we so rightly condemn totalitarian regimes for encouraging the young to report the disloyalties of their parents. Is it only the political regime that should be condemned or is there something morally questionable about the practice, regardless of the form of government?

A similar question may be asked of the honor codes used at many colleges and universities. The idea of an honor system seems right and healthy. We pledge ourselves to academic honesty. But why do we insist that students must report the violations of others? They almost never do this. To encourage honesty on the one hand and what may seem like betrayal on the other is almost certainly a mistake. Cheating scandals at our military academies – schools with the most demanding codes – are evidence of this mistake. A code should be elaborated with lots of questions for reflection and examples to aid analysis. For example, students might be urged to discourage cheating, to speak out against it without invoking authorities and penalties. They might even be advised to alert a professor when cheating is going on, and the professor should be allowed then to proctor tests even though this practice is usually forbidden under honor codes. Discussion is required when things go wrong, and it is also required to keep things going right. It is not enough to require students to sign a simple code. Complicated issues – issues that involve a clash of moral values – require adequately complex discussion. A simply stated code of required behavior can cause confusion in conscientious students.

The Ten Commandments illustrate my point. "Thou shalt not kill." Does this mean that one must refuse military service? Must one refrain from killing even in self defense? Does it rule out capital punishment? Does it forbid abortion? "Thou shalt not steal." Suppose my children are starving? Suppose I live in miserable conditions in a clearly unjust society? Character educators sometimes suggest that the Ten Commandments be posted prominently in schools, but they do not suggest that students read Exodus 21 and 22, in which all sorts of exceptions are made to the commandment against killing – without stating that the commandment has been challenged.

The point is that morality is not simple. Young people know this, but parents and teachers often force them to make exclusive choices: remain loyal to my friend or obey the code, violate a code to help another or stand aside silently and do nothing, live a highly restrictive life of code and ritual or break free in a bid for happiness. In most cases, it should not be necessary to make such dichotomous choices. Students should learn that life is a continual moral quest. It requires asking, listening, analyzing, discussing, acting, reflecting, and making commitments that will always be subject to review. Living a moral life sometimes involves tragedy.

If we know that an act causing personal harm has been done, most of us will report it because we want (or should want) reparation for the harm and assurance that no further acts of harm will be committed. If the perpetrator is a friend, we do this with a heavy heart, and we certainly do not seek a reward for our compliance. Our legal procedures at present sometimes fly in the face of the moral lessons we would like to teach in schools.

The discussion of Joe's dilemma offers an opportunity to analyze another virtue – this time, loyalty. Is loyalty always a virtue? Young people may respond that it depends on to whom or what one is loyal. We do not usually consider loyalty a virtue if it is directed to the Nazi Party, the Ku Klux Klan, or a cult of terrorists. However, most of us have contempt for people who betray even these groups for a monetary reward or to save their own skins. Sensitive teenagers may say of a true believer in Nazism that, although we abhor the beliefs of this group, we have to credit such a believer with loyalty. Others will be convinced that loyalty to wicked groups is not really loyalty and should not be considered a virtue.

Another facet of loyalty – one in some tension with leading friends away from wicked associations – is standing by friends in time of trouble. We expect comfort from friends when we are in pain, and we are deeply hurt if they suggest wrongly that we deserve our suffering. The classic case here, of course, is that of Job, whose friends insisted that his suffering must be just punishment for his sins. Job reminded his friends: "To him that is afflicted pity *should be shewed* from his friend," and when they would not let up on him, he said, "miserable comforters *are ye* all."[28] Job's friends were worse than fair-weather friends. They deepened his suffering. Parts of Job should be read and discussed as great literature, but the emphasis on friendship should give the reading relevance for the lives of teenagers.

Sorting through the issues around friendship is challenging work. As teachers, we want students to identify problems and reflect on them. In contrast to many character educators who strive for closure on moral issues, care theorists and cognitive developmentalists want students to understand that not all moral problems have absolute, indisputable solutions. This understanding does not imply that we are relativists. It is a matter of finding out which commitments are so fundamental that a person lacking them must be considered a psychopath, which differ acceptably by individual or group, and which are revealed in ways that look different on the surface but contain common elements at a deeper level.

It is often helpful to lead students through a series of questions. Would you report a friend for smoking marijuana? Most students will say no, but they might suggest ways of helping the friend. Would you report him if he started selling drugs to young teenagers? On this question, we will probably hear about plans for reforming the friend. What will you do if your attempts fail? Can you remain friends with a person who sells drugs to children? With one who tortures animals? What kinds of behavior would make you break a friendship? Why? Then we can return to Aristotle's claim that good people want similarly good people as friends. What does it say about *you* if your friends do really bad things?

Teachers today have a wealth of material to draw on in planning these discussions. In addition to books on required reading lists, there are many collections of adolescent biographies. In one, a young woman tells how a group of her friends gathered one night to make a phone call harassing another girl who had made one of them angry.[29] The girls "took turns getting on the phone to say nasty things to her." The narrator continues:

> I sat there for about a half hour getting angry and embarrassed. I was ashamed that I was actually *debating* about leaving. Finally I did get up and said, "This really sucks." And I left.[30]

On the following day, the writer feared that she would become the victim of her friends' anger and resentment, but the other girls actually admitted that they respected her for leaving. Perhaps they just needed one of their own number to remind them that what they were doing was beneath them – that they were, or wanted to be, more like the friend who left. Reading stories like these, students may be persuaded that Aristotle was right when he said that true friends point us upward.

Many of the books available today focus on adolescents from a specific race or ethnicity.[31] These can be useful not only for students of the group depicted but also for those from other races and backgrounds. We know now that racial and ethnic relations are not much improved by simply putting different racial groups together in a school – by "integrating." What does make a difference is the formation of cross-racial and cross-cultural friendships. Stories of the kind we are discussing can help lay the foundation for these friendships.

Let's return briefly to Aristotle's contention that adolescent friendships are motivated by the desire for pleasure. To an important degree, pleasure plays a role in all friendships. It would seem odd, for example, to say that someone's company gives us no pleasure but we still treasure that person as a friend. We all expect to get pleasure from our friendships. Where we may differ is in how we define pleasure.

A careful, wide-ranging exploration of friendship gives us an opportunity to bring together many of the topics we have already discussed. We can return to the meaning of happiness itself, the relief of suffering and what it means for a friend to comfort us, the satisfaction of needs and wants, the qualities of character and personality that we find admirable, the possibility of finding happiness in nature and non-human relationships, and the great joy that can be found in spiritual experience. Perhaps no other topic has quite so much potential for a living curriculum.

Romantic Love

Romantic love is often thought to represent the very pinnacle of happiness and, indeed, it does produce a form of ecstatic happiness, as we saw in Chapter 1. However, like other types of ecstatic happiness, romantic love is seldom lasting. It may be episodic or it may just fade away. In the latter case, it may disappear entirely or it may be transformed into a deep and lasting friendship tinged with vestiges of romantic love. This seems to have been the case with John and Abigail Adams. In years of sometimes lengthy separation, Abigail started most of her letters to John with "My dearest friend."[32] Romantic love that deepens into friendship is likely to be a source of lasting happiness.

The mad joy of romantic love should be acknowledged. No one caught in its throes wants to be relieved of it, but teenagers should be encouraged to examine the phenomenon intellectually. Romantic love is often involved in tragedy. Understanding this will not make young people immune to the madness of love, nor should we want it to do so. They should understand that the opposition of family and friends to a particular romantic relationship is not always misguided.

Sometimes, of course, it is, and then we celebrate the young people whose love overcomes the opposition. Often, however, family and friends can see things in the loved one and in the relationship that the lover – blinded by love – cannot see. It takes sympathy and tact to remove the blindness, and often even these do not work. The hope is that a young man madly in love will be able to give a positive answer to the question "But do you *like* her?" A well-founded sense of friendship is an important factor in marriage or a permanent commitment.

We cannot prevent all of the tragedies and heartbreak associated with romantic love, but we can educate the young about the problems and challenges of constructing a shared life. Here we should return to the chapters on making a home, educating for a love of place, and parenting. All of this material becomes important in preparing people for intimate relationships. A couple must create a shared aesthetic, and they must understand what Bachelard called the *organic habits* of their partners. If too many habits are in opposition and these habits are well established, a couple may find it difficult to live together. Comedies such as *The Odd Couple* are fun to watch, but in real life dramatic differences in habits and personality can mean the end of a relationship. Most of us would find it difficult to live with either Oscar or Felix.

Living in an age that openly admires "letting it all hang out" – expressing one's displeasure, sharing intimate details, insisting that a partner divulge every dream or passing thought – people may make the mistake of talking too much. The biologist Lewis Thomas advised us to forget unpleasant thoughts and to keep still now and then:

> Forget whatever you feel like forgetting. From time to time, practice *not* being open, discover new things *not* to talk about, learn reserve, hold the tongue. But above all, develop the human talent for forgetting words, phrases, whole unwelcome sentences, all experiences involving wincing.[33]

It is good advice to avoid the words *always* ("You always leave dirty dishes in the sink") and *never* ("You never take the garbage out on time"). Dragging up every past sin is another habit that is best overcome. But how will partners ever improve if we don't tell them what displeases us? One strategy is to use humor instead of expressing annoyance. Another is to balance a mildly stated complaint with a compliment or positive incentive. Still another is to discuss complaints in a problem-solving mode – one separated from the actual agents and events. Finally, Lindbergh's advice to seek some privacy is sound: Go for a walk, retreat and reflect, let it be.

Lindbergh also reminds us that hanging on too tightly is bad for a relationship:

> A good relationship has a pattern like a dance and is built on some of the same rules. The partners do not need to hold on tightly, because they move confidently in the same pattern. . . . There is no place here for the possessive clutch, the clinging arm, the heavy hand.[34]

A complete, trusting friendship is essential to a lasting intimate relationship. Additionally, however, many couples want to retain as much of the original romance as possible. In today's commercial environment, people can be easily misled. Is it really necessary to escape home and children periodically in order to revive romance? Is it necessary to indulge in luxuries of various kinds because "you deserve it"?

The influence of advertising and other media should be discussed often and carefully in schools. False notions of eternal romantic bliss should be called into question. The need for escape should also be challenged. Not every couple feels that need. Some find an alternative form of romance in vacationing with their children, refurbishing an old house, or redesigning a garden. What matters is the effect. If shared activities lead to continued commitment, they contribute to happiness.

In this chapter, we have looked at interpersonal growth. What personal qualities do we find agreeable, and how can education help children to cultivate these qualities? What does it mean to be a friend, and what sorts of friendships should we cultivate? In this discussion, we uncovered a close connection between qualities of personality and the virtues associated with character. Finally, we discussed romantic love – a phenomenon often linked to happiness – and decided that, for a relationship to be lasting, friendship must complement romance.

There can be little question that interpersonal relations are necessary to the happiness of most people. Are such relations also sufficient, or do we need some form of involvement in public life to be truly happy? This question motivates the chapters of Part 3.

PART 3

Educating for Public Life

How might public life contribute to the happiness of individuals? If we are honest, most of us will admit that we derive little actual pleasure or fulfillment from our role as citizens. Similarly, many of us would not place community or civic life high on our list of sources of happiness. Still, life in a liberal democracy may contribute significantly, if indirectly, to human flourishing, and we will try to spell out its significance. Participating in the life of a healthy community may also add to our happiness, and for some people such participation is a major source of satisfaction. The discussion of community will give us an opportunity to revisit the topic of friendship at what Aristotle called the *incomplete* level.

There can be no question, however, about the importance of finding work in which we are happy. This part of public life – an occupation – is probably second only to home and family in making us happy or miserable. A fortunate few find happiness in both occupation and home life. The question in Part 3 is how education can promote happiness in occupational life and, more generally, in our public lives as neighbors and citizens. We'll start with occupational life.

10

Preparing for Work

The activities involved in making a living can bring us happiness, misery, or boredom. John Dewey said:

> An occupation is the only thing which balances the distinctive capacity of an individual with his social service. To find out what one is fitted to do and to secure an opportunity to do it is the key to happiness.[1]

Finding the right occupation is certainly one key to happiness. But how is it found? How much choice does an individual have in the matter? What sort of authority should the school system exercise in guiding the choice? In the past few decades, schools have been driven by economic purposes and by a social commitment to remove long-standing inequalities. Both of these purposes have been misinterpreted, distorted, and actively pursued without careful analysis. We seem to have forgotten entirely that work and happiness might be connected at a level deeper than the economic.

In their zeal to give every student an academic education, schools today neglect those students whose chosen work may not require a college education. However, they also neglect genuine intellectual interest – an interest that, if cultivated, may enrich both occupational and personal life. Intellectual topics centered on home, place, parenting, character, spirit, and interpersonal relations have already been discussed in appropriate contexts. In a section of this chapter, I address the cultivation of intellect in those who have special intellectual interests. Intellectual interests, like all special interests, should be respected and promoted.

197

Emphasis on Money

It is common to suppose that the strength of a nation's schools is closely connected to its economic success. As we saw in Chapter 4, two decades ago, *A Nation at Risk* pressed the point with alarmist language, declaring that the "rising tide of mediocrity" in our schools threatened the nation's capacity to remain competitive in a world market.[2] Shortly after this – well before reform movements could get underway – the nation enjoyed an era of unprecedented prosperity. It is demonstrably false that downward fluctuations in the economy can be traced to the poor performance of our schools. Obviously, if schools are so bad that ordinary materials and facilities are lacking and teachers are vastly undertrained, the education provided will not sustain a thriving economy. But it is only in the poorest economies that such conditions exist. Generally, when the economy improves, the conditions of schooling improve. Education is not the engine that drives the economy; it is the other way around. Arguments for higher academic standards based on the nation's ability to compete in a world market are mainly false and certainly simplistic.

When the argument is cast in terms of a need for graduates with greater skills, one has to analyze what is meant by *greater skills* and how widespread the need might be. Economists and labor analysts disagree on some fundamental issues. In 1997, the *New York Times* published brief statements by a number of people willing to make predictions about the future of work.[3] Paul Krugman pointed out that the growth of technology has usually meant a decrease of jobs in the areas affected, not an increase; job growth, he writes, tends to be largest in areas least affected by technology. It is obvious, for example, that technology has reduced the number of farmers and manufacturing workers. It is clear, also, that retail clerks today need fewer mathematical skills than their predecessors forty years ago. In contrast to Krugman's view, William Julius Wilson said that "knowledge-based industries will soon dwarf all other industries" and "the demand for low-skilled workers will plummet to the lowest depths in human history." But here's Krugman again, giving the Labor Department's list of highest occupational growth: "the top five categories are cashiers, janitors and cleaners, salespeople, waiters and waitresses, and nurses." Only the last requires a college education.

198

I am not an economist, and I will not try to sort through the claims and counterclaims. I can, however, point out some ways with numbers that bear watching. When growth is described in percentages, one needs to be wary. There may be a large percentage of growth in a relatively small field; the actual number of workers needed may be correspondingly small. In contrast, a small percentage of growth in a large field may suggest the need for many new workers. One should be cautious also in assessing claims about the need for greater skills. Perhaps the kinds of skills have changed. That is possible. But what is the nature of the change? Does it require more interpersonal skills or more individual initiative? And what exactly is meant by greater skill in these areas?

Policymakers have taken the faulty message of *A Nation at Risk* to mean that all children should have a stronger academic education. Perhaps this argument could be made on grounds other than the needs of our national economy. Another basis for the argument might be the role of the school in social mobility. Individual students do often profit financially by more years of schooling. College graduates on average make more money than high school graduates, and high school graduates make more money than dropouts. However, there are many exceptions to the general rule, and some of the disparities are produced arbitrarily. We simply decide to require a credential of some sort for entry-level positions; the credential may or may not have anything to contribute to the work itself. It is notoriously difficult to measure the increase in skill levels produced by an increase in the years of schooling.[4] An indifferent but persistent student might finish college with fewer job-relevant skills than an industrious, highly focused high school graduate. The economy is not necessarily served by an increase in college graduates, nor is a given student assured of a brighter future. Further, as we noted earlier, jobs that are now poorly paid will still have to be done; education cannot by itself solve the problems of poverty.

It is especially hard to understand why educators have joined policymakers in recommending more academic mathematics and science for all students. The country does not need more mathematicians and scientists, and almost certainly it can turn out enough engineers and computer workers by providing a fine scientific education for those whose interests and talents lie in these areas. Why insist on math and science for all? One reason offered is that all citizens in the twenty-first century should be mathematically and technologically literate. That goal seems reasonable, but is it best accomplished by forcing all students into standard algebra, geometry, and biology classes? If the answer to that question is no, then why are we doing it? Some possible answers involve the quest for equality, and I'll discuss those responses in the next section.

Another answer, one I rejected in Chapter 4, is the claim that, because academic mathematics has served as a gateway to higher education, all children must now become proficient in mathematics so that they will not be deprived of educational opportunities. The alternative, of course, is to remove mathematics as a gatekeeper and insist on proficiency only for those who need it in order to pursue their interests.

Let's return briefly to the first response – that all citizens need to be mathematically and scientifically literate. Why should this goal be emphasized when there are so many other pressing needs? Given the state of the world and the documented loss of happiness among individuals, perhaps we should be more concerned with understanding and preventing violence, offering more courses in peace education, understanding and treating substance abuse, promoting self-understanding and interpersonal relations, protecting the environment, teaching love of place, parenting, spiritual awakening, preparing for a congenial occupation, encouraging lasting pleasure in the arts, and developing sound character and a pleasing personality. If we respond to this list by insisting that these tasks are not the job of the school, we encounter the baffled countenance of the Visitor from another world. How can they *not* be goals of education when they are central to human flourishing?

I am not suggesting that mathematical and scientific literacy is unimportant. I am claiming that other goals are even more important. Moreover, it is entirely possible to integrate these concerns in ways that will enhance all of them. Instead of teaching all children standard algebra, we should be sure that they can do the sort of figuring required to spot the faulty arguments in articles on jobs of the future. Instead of teaching all of them the sophisticated vocabulary of cell biology, we should spend more time on natural history and on the possible effects of genetic engineering on agriculture and indigenous plant life. Instead of telling them that they will make more money if they stay in school, we should invite them to explore occupations that might make them happy.

Policymakers today seem to equate a brighter future with more money, but we saw in Chapter 1 that money and happiness are not so closely related.[5] It is hard to be happy in poverty but, once that threshold is passed, more money does not always bring a proportional increase in happiness. Further, such narrow concentration on more money through a college education overlooks the intrinsic rewards of work.[6] Many of us are willing to sacrifice some salary to obtain work we really enjoy.

Striving for Equality

Possibly the most attractive argument for insisting on algebra and geometry for all students is that equality of opportunity demands it. We have long required college-bound students to take these courses, and other students have a right to equal treatment. Let's set aside for the moment whether such requirements can be justified for all college-bound students (I have already confessed doubts about this) and concentrate on the effects of this decision. Surely the end – equality of opportunity – is admirable. Are the means likely to achieve that result?

The evidence available now suggests strongly that many students are failing these courses, and many more students may drop out of high school before graduation.[7] Advocates of the new requirements for all ask a challenging question when critics raise objections: If rich kids have been able to pass these courses, why can't poor kids? This attitude is accompanied by slogans such as "All children can learn" and "No excuses," sending the clear message that massive student failures are the fault of the schools. This accusation should not be brushed off lightly. We could do much more to help poor and minority children. But notice that it avoids two significant questions: Why should algebra and geometry be *requirements* for any children? What has made it possible for wealthier children to succeed in these subjects? I'll return to the first question a bit later.

Consider the second. Many relatively well-to-do children have had a hard time with academic mathematics. Often these students persist because their parents and teachers assure them that getting these credits is the ticket to college and a good life. Parents also assure their children that they "went through it, too" and survived, thus providing sympathetic models. Quite often parents hire tutors for their struggling students. Students are counseled to do their homework, ask teachers for help, show their willingness to do extra work when they flunk tests, and cooperate with their teachers. Huge numbers of these "successful" students finish their schooling with a fear and loathing of mathematics that will last a lifetime. Ask any well-educated audience or graduate class in the humanities!

The point for present purposes is that children need strong support to get through these courses, and the necessary support is not just financial – for example, money for tutoring, although that helps. Students need to be convinced that the game is worth the candle. They need models of educated people in their lives. Beyond these obvious supports, they must enter tough courses with adequate preparation, and that cannot be supplied entirely by the school. We are faced again with the massive difference traceable to informal education.

The first, most obvious, consequence of the requirement for equal academic standards is exactly the opposite of what was hoped; that is, more children are failing and dropping out. The second is that algebra and geometry courses in many schools are mere caricatures of those subjects. Well-intentioned teachers do not want their students to fail, and so they work hard to present material that students can handle. Students get credit for these courses, but they are not adequately prepared for college work in mathematics (why should mathematics be required for all college students?), and many must take remedial courses. The blow to self-esteem is enough to discourage many young people, and they drop out.

In schools or classes where significant numbers of underprepared, reluctant students are forced to take academic mathematics, there may also be considerable collateral damage to students who could profit from more rigorous courses. They do very well in comparison to their uninterested peers and have a right to suppose that they are ready for college, but they cannot compete with students who have taken more demanding courses. In the past few years, I have seen algebra classes in which students were asked to do no word problems of any kind – not one. Students who earn A's or B's in such classes are more poorly prepared than students who earn C's in more honest courses.

Another consequence of forcing a uniform academic curriculum on all students is that, unless that curriculum is very broad, they may have fewer opportunities to pursue their own interests in learning. The history of American high school curricula shows fluctuation between broad and narrow conceptions of courses deemed acceptable for college admission.[8] We are now in a period of narrow definition with respect to the names or labels of acceptable courses, but the actual content of these courses varies greatly. The variation does not usually reflect student interest, however. More often it reflects the teacher's assessment of the material (from the standard course) that a group of students can master. Students who might profit from a series of math courses concentrating on business, shop, and personal topics are thus doubly hurt. They suffer a loss of self-esteem by doing poorly in courses they did not choose, and they lose opportunities to learn material for which they have interest and talent.

We should also be concerned about how a focus on getting all students through the academic curriculum tends to distract us from difficult social problems. A well-intentioned drive for equality through better schooling recognizes that education has played a role in social mobility. It would be a mistake to argue that schools have not contributed to the financial betterment of many students. But, as I pointed out earlier, they cannot possibly serve this function for all students. I'll say more about this seeming paradox later. For now, notice that if the society will continue to need significant numbers of workers in jobs that do not require college education, such workers will necessarily be at the mercy of market standards for their wages. Education can't do anything about this. However, a caring society could do something about market standards; it could commit itself to the elimination of poverty. Arguing, as one legislator did recently, that a failure to hold all students to a high academic standard would prevent many from going to college and thus "doom" them to economic failure reveals a sad state of thinking in public policy. Why should anyone who works full-time at an honest job be doomed to economic failure?

It seems contradictory to argue that equal educational opportunity is provided by forcing all students into a curriculum appropriate for few.[9] Yet one can see reasons for moving in that direction. It is easier and less expensive to give everyone the same courses rather than constructing and polishing an attractive variety. Moreover, those of us who advocate a variety of tracks for high school students have to show how our approach can be better. For the most part, tracking has had devastating effects on poor and minority children, and we cannot ignore that history. In speaking of tracking here, I am referring to different courses of study – for example, college preparatory, commercial, industrial, or vocational – not to ability grouping within specific subjects.[10] I will outline what I take to be a defensible form of tracking in the next section. For now, we should note that it might not be tracking itself that causes the damage but the way we order and evaluate the tracks.

Before leaving this critique of present efforts to achieve equality of educational opportunity, I want to make clear that I do believe there are some things all students must learn, and I also believe that we have a responsibility to expose students to a wide range of material that may or may not interest them in the long run. I have rejected curricular and pedagogical sameness as a remedy and, because I believe strongly in happiness as a guiding aim for education, I am wary of coercion. How should we approach the problem of preparing students for work – and more generally for a life – they may find satisfying?

Respect and Relevance

Establishing happiness as a primary aim of education may well guide us to an approach more compatible than sameness with democratic conceptions of equality. I have argued that we should educate enthusiastically for personal life. If we were to do that, we would surely be led to reduce the present emphasis on the economic ends of schooling. With that reduction, we could conscientiously educate for a wide range of occupations, assuring children that liking what one does for a living and enjoying a rich personal life are more important than mere money in attaining happiness. Thus we have made a step in the right direction by deciding to educate for a full personal life.

Our resolve should be further strengthened by reflection on democratic principles. As Dewey said, democracy is (or should be) a mode of associated living.[11] Its strength is in the recognition of interdependence and open communication. It is not merely rule of the majority, nor is it simply a system that allows all individuals equal opportunities to defeat competitors. Further, it does not depend so much on a well-established common culture as it does on the commitment to create shared values. The *desire* to communicate and the willingness to do so across lines of culture and interest are more important than a common language that is produced by coercion.[12] It is, in part, this belief that explains Dewey's admiration for Walt Whitman (the "seer" of democracy)[13] and for Jane Addams, who demonstrated deep respect for immigrants and their original cultures.[14]

Dewey does not deny the power of a cultural tradition; he even speaks of the necessity "to transmit" the resources and achievements of a complex society.[15] But he does not make possession of this cultural knowledge a prerequisite for participation in democratic processes. On this, he differed dramatically from Robert Maynard Hutchins and Mortimer Adler, both of whom insisted that democracy depends on a common fund of knowledge.[16] For Dewey, communication and choice get things started, and democracy is a dynamic achievement – a mode of living continually under construction. Hutchins believed that the best curriculum was already known by classically trained scholars and that the public must simply be convinced of its rightness. In contrast, Dewey believed that the curriculum must be continually constructed through shared experience.

Dewey's emphasis on choice does not imply permissiveness, and I am not suggesting that we let students do whatever they please. Choices in a liberal democracy should be well informed, and becoming well informed requires some common experience and a substantial amount of guidance. Further, no choice made with the consent of a school should deprive a student of an education rich in the material and skills required for a flourishing adult life. There should be no junk courses.

What might the necessary guidance look like? The best educational guidance is a product of shared life, not of highly specialized assessment. Professional guidance counselors have much to contribute in school settings, but they are not best positioned to guide the selection of courses and tracks for particular students. For this task, we need teachers who know their students, and this is another reason why continuity is so important. Teachers who have worked with students closely should know something about their aspirations, work habits, talents, character, and personality. When a relationship of care and trust has been established, a teacher can talk frankly with students about their goals and plans. Is it realistic to aim at a professional education if one hates reading? Is it reasonable to plan a career in teaching if one has great difficulty with verbal communication? Is it feasible to plan a mechanical career if one is "all thumbs"? Guidance should be neither coercive nor definitive; that is, students should not be *assigned* to courses against their will, nor should they be led to believe that certain avenues are definitely closed to them. They should be allowed to reject the advice they are given, but they must accept responsibility for their decision.

Coercion has too often characterized guidance efforts in education. We test for placement, not merely for advisement. We scrutinize past achievement to sort children and assign them to classes and tracks. Our justification for coercion rests on the youthful ignorance of our clients. "They" do not know what is best for them; therefore, we cannot responsibly satisfy their expressed needs. "We" do know (this is Adler's argument); therefore, the needs we infer for them are the ones we should act upon.

This pattern does not offer sound practice for responsible and happy life in a liberal democracy. Continuous negotiation between expressed and inferred needs can help students make well-informed choices. Even if youngsters occasionally change their minds (who does not?) and need to spend time catching up on a new set of courses, the experience of pursuing studies they choose should be profitable. There is such a thing as learning how to learn, and confidence in learning is promoted by choosing and evaluating one's own course of action.

We can and should exercise some gentle and limited coercion. We do, after all, compel children to go to school. There are some things that all children must learn – for example, how to read, how to speak clearly, how to write an intelligible message, how to understand a simple graphical display, how to use technology for ordinary purposes, how to exercise one's rights and responsibilities as a citizen, what constitutes good character, what characterizes a happy personal life – and these topics and skills should appear across the curriculum, in every subject that gets serious attention.

Beyond those things we regard as essential for everyone are topics and skills that many of us cherish. Although I do not believe that all children must master standard courses in algebra and geometry, I would like them to be exposed to these subjects. I would like them to "try out" the study of mathematics, physics, the visual arts, great music, fine literature, and other subjects that have been forced on students in the past. The middle school years are ideal for such exposure. However, if we are serious about exposing students to material so that they can make well-informed choices, we should not ruin the experience with coercive grading procedures. Our message should be that these courses (or mini-courses) are offered for personal exploration, to open avenues of possible study in the future, and for enjoyment. These middle years should be three glorious years of risk-free exploration.

Evaluation in these years should be formative. The idea is both to help children do better in whatever they study and to evaluate their own talent and progress.[17] By the time children reach high school, they should be able to make intelligent choices based on solid experience. Teenagers should be aware of the opportunities they may lose by deciding against academic mathematics, but there should be attractive alternatives that they can choose proudly. Under a well-developed scheme of exposure and formative evaluation, educators can be honest with students. We should not have to rely on the propaganda so popular now – that everyone needs algebra, everyone should go to college, everyone should work hard at everything the school requires. We can say instead, if you want to do X in the future, you will need to study Y. We can say honestly to a struggling student, so far you haven't done very well with Y; you'll have to work very hard if you still want to do X. And we can say, you are really good at W; you should consider a career in Z.

Exposure, as I am describing it, is a form of coercion but, without the usual competitive grading, it is a gentle coercion. It should depend heavily on informal learning – lots of free gifts for children to pick up or set aside. As we plan such a program, we should continually ask why we are offering each topic. Why, for example, do we offer poetry? If our answer is that poetry may become a lifelong source of delight and wisdom, then it must be offered as a source of happiness *now*. The same is true for music and the arts.

Exposing children to subjects we take to be valuable is a superb example of negotiating between expressed and inferred needs. Children can rarely express a need for something about which they know nothing, and we should not abdicate our responsibility as adults to open doors for them. Many children would have no idea that their interests might be intellectual if the school does nothing to introduce them to the life of the mind. But the purpose of opening doors is to

207

invite children to explore so that they can find out how these new ideas fit their own purposes. It is not to slam other doors. It is not to sort and assign them. It is not to destroy their self-esteem by showing them that they are not very good at the things that have traditionally mattered in school.

What things really matter? There are at least two useful ways to answer this question. One is to say that every topic, attribute, or skill that contributes to human flourishing matters educationally. Practically, it is impossible to expose children to everything that matters in this sense. A second answer is that while everything just mentioned matters, the most important things for schools to treat are those that provide a foundation for further learning and growing. This seems right, but educators do not agree on what these things are. Advocates of the traditional liberal arts, for example, insist that those subjects provide just such a foundation, but we know that many people succeed beautifully without training in the liberal arts. Sometimes the foundation is described in terms of the "disciplines."[18] This approach is very much like the first, but it challenges new subjects to prove their disciplinary worth. Sometimes the foundation is described in terms of human components: body, soul, and mind.[19] Then we have to decide what studies will contribute to growth in each. Howard Gardner's multiple intelligences are useful here, although there seems to be some disagreement on how to use them.[20] Gardner often emphasizes their use as pedagogical hooks to help students learn the standard subjects. I would prefer to develop them for their own sake, cherishing each as an end in itself and also as a stepping stone for children who find their talents in one area or another. However we begin, we are faced with the problem of deciding what should be considered basic for everyone and what should be assessed as basic for children with well-identified talents.

This kind of debate is essential in considering a curriculum of invitation or exposure. We should want students to try their hands at mechanical tasks, at dance and sports, at spiritual exercises, at interpersonal skills. As Dewey said, it is quite wonderful to find out the sort of work for which one is suited. Through exposure of this sort, children can also acquire an avocation – another source of happiness. And, from the perspective of democratic education, children can gain a genuine appreciation for a host of skills they do not themselves find easy to acquire.

208

The spirit of exposure and exploration should continue into high school even though the structure of classes and requirements becomes more coercive. Once students have chosen a curriculum to study, they will encounter requirements and standards of performance. There are things they must do if they are to attain the goals they have set for themselves. Challenging goals and high standards are appropriate when they are coupled with choice. Most of us work happily at tough tasks if they are demonstrably connected to the ends we seek. Within the required courses, however, there should be lots of room for free gifts, enjoyment, and optional exploration.

When children are ready to specialize in a general line of study (this is not as paradoxical as it sounds), every choice the school makes available should be rich and relevant. No child should be assigned to a program in mechanics because he wasn't good enough to handle the preferred academic program. Nor should he be assigned to a narrow specialty within the general field of mechanics. He should be able to choose a program in mechanics because he is good at that line of work, and there should be options from which he may eventually choose a particular occupation. Within the program, he should encounter topics rich in possibilities for both personal and public life.

A Rich Curriculum for Every Talent

W. Norton Grubb points out that early American schools did not differentiate between academic and vocational education.[21] All pupils got the same curriculum so long as they were in school.[22] From one perspective, this sounds like a thoroughly democratic policy, and twentieth-century thinkers such as Adler and Hutchins continued to recommend it. From another, as I have been arguing here, it is highly undemocratic. Educating students with very different talents with the same curriculum cannot be regarded as equal treatment. While the traditional policy was in effect, most young people dropped out before finishing high school; many did not even enter high school. Many factors contributed to the school-leaving phenomenon. It was possible to obtain gainful employment without a high school diploma, and families needed the financial contribution of their teenagers. The classroom atmosphere was often coercive, and children who found the academic curriculum hard were frequently humiliated, not encouraged. Then, too, as progressive educators argued, the traditional curriculum ignored the real world and its demands, and many students simply lost interest.[23] Contemporary educators who take the traditional approach should be credited with trying to change these last conditions.

The history of America's comprehensive high school is a mixed story in which people on opposite sides have both claimed the democratic high ground. Traditionalists continued to argue for a single academic curriculum and progressives argued for a differentiated curriculum, both in the name of democracy. Some facts, however, are clear. High school attendance in the era of progressive influence increased considerably, and so did graduation rates. The downside, from the perspective of democratic ideals, is that curriculum differentiation came to mean hierarchy. The old academic curriculum was still the "best," and vocational curricula were thought of as alternatives for those who couldn't handle the "better" courses. For those of us today who want to advocate curriculum differentiation, the hierarchical ordering of tracks represents a real problem.

We cannot deny that vocational and commercial tracks were often explicitly designed for those whose destinies were thought to be in the blue- or pink-collar workforce. The fact that arguments could be made on the basis of democracy for both a uniform academic curriculum and curriculum differentiation is illustrated in the statements of Charles W. Eliot, president of Harvard University. As chairman of the Committee of Ten, he had argued strongly for an academic curriculum for all, one not geared to probable destinies. Sixteen years later, he argued the opposite position. Not only did he now recommend differentiated curricula, he even argued that elementary school teachers "ought to sort the pupils and sort them by their evident and probable destinies."[24] Recognizing that he might be criticized for turning his back on the earlier, professedly democratic position, he responded:

> If democracy means to try to make all children equal or all men equal, it means to fight nature, and in that fight democracy is sure to be defeated. There is no such thing among men as equality of nature, of capacity for training, or of intellectual power.[25]

This seems to me indisputably correct. However, it is a bit of reality that is still widely denied. We accept as facts that people differ in stature, in color, in personality, in genetic attributes related to health, in physical strength. But we just cannot accept as fact that people differ also in intellectual capacity. As Hume said, nothing upsets a person more than having his or her intelligence impugned. But if it is a fact that people differ not only in intellectual capacity but, even more, in intellectual interests, then the first task is to rid ourselves of the notion that intellectual capacity in the form of abstract mathematical-linguistic talent is the capacity to be valued above all others. Were it not for this faulty valuation, all talents could be accepted and nurtured. Further, we need not agree with Eliot that teachers should engage in sorting children. We can insist that students be allowed to make the choices governing their occupational destinies.

With the positive evaluation of all morally acceptable human capacities, we would be comfortable in advising students about the destinies among which they might choose. What comes to mind here is how odd it is that choice is so infrequently mentioned in these disputes. The concept is at the very heart of philosophical liberalism, which, in turn, is a major foundation block of modern democratic theory. The idea of democracy is rooted in the combination of cooperative social life and free, well-informed, individual choice. Yet great educators such as Eliot, Ellwood Cubberley, and many representatives of the social efficiency movement persisted in using the language of sorting, assigning, and training. Student choice was not central to the discussion.

Liberal philosophy has long been stymied by the problem of children and choice. It has been developed as though the rational, mature adult springs somehow fully formed into the social world.[26] Dewey was a rarity among liberal philosophers in his insistence on recognizing the power of immaturity (its openness and flexibility) and on identifying the need for young people to practice the skills required by a liberal democracy.[27] From the Deweyan perspective, children must be given age-appropriate choices not only for optimal individual development but also as part of their education for citizenship.

Our project is made more difficult by those who appear to sympathize with genuinely equal treatment but do so at only the rhetorical level. I have been arguing here and elsewhere that all honest work should be appreciated.[28] But this kind of talk is sometimes mealy-mouthed. There have been – and still are – people who speak of the nobility of work but care nothing about the condition of workers. Similarly, there are those who advocate vocational education but

211

care nothing about its quality. Herbert Kliebard's remarks on this are deeply moving. Speaking of the worry and exhaustion experienced by his father working in New York City sweatshops, he writes:

> It is in this regard that I hope I can be excused for reflecting a touch of skepticism about the so-called dignity of work. Undoubtedly, satisfaction may be derived from the work of the hands, but I sometimes think that the conviction that all work has dignity regardless of the circumstances has served to inhibit attempts to improve conditions in the workplace and to stave off efforts somehow to humanize it. When all work, even under the most degrading conditions, is declared to be ennobling, the need to reform the workplace somehow seems much less urgent.[29]

This simple, enormously powerful statement must guide our thinking on vocational forms of education. Of course, all honest work *should* have dignity. Walt Whitman and Seamus Heaney have given it dignity in poetry. Karl Marx gave it dignity in philosophy. But we cannot deny the kinds of experience described by Kliebard, nor can we deny that children have too often been relegated to a life of labor by educators who predicted their destinies. There were pernicious assumptions involved in this sorting of children – first, that children of certain races and ethnic backgrounds were destined for manual labor and, second, that people who did this sort of work were intellectually inferior to those who could master an academic curriculum. Both the work and the worker were devalued.

We have properly challenged the first of these assumptions but, by adopting the new assumption that all children can master an academic curriculum, we have reinforced the second assumption. Common sense should tell us that much essential work does not require a college education. The task of social policy is to establish the dignity of labor as a reality. That means the elimination of poverty, and it also means enriching the school curriculum for students who prefer to enter the workforce after high school.

How is this to be done? The usual pattern is to add more academic work to the vocational curriculum.[30] Where the topics are chosen because they seem to have particular value for the students concerned, this approach makes sense. But it upholds the regrettable notion that topics from the academic curriculum are somehow important in themselves – that they are better and more challenging than topics

212

that might arise in the vocations and be pursued with intellectual vigor.

There are some examples of the latter approach. Mike Rose has described a graphic arts curriculum in Pasadena that illustrates the basic idea.[31] Students encounter the need for scientific principles as they try to perform the work in their lab. The problems they meet are intellectually challenging, and the need for sophisticated concepts and principles is pervasive. In such settings, thinking arises in direct connection to doing. Instead of force-feeding their students a set of predetermined scientific principles and then encouraging them to apply those principles, teachers help students to pursue genuine intellectual challenges as they do the work they have chosen.

The humanities need not be neglected in such programs. Students can be invited to read the novels of Hemingway, Steinbeck, and Faulkner. They can read Laura Hobson's *First Papers*, which describes the plight of laboring people and the reasons for their interest in socialism and their resistance to the draft in World War I. They might learn about Dorothy Day and the *Catholic Worker*. Perhaps they could discuss her contention that we should "keep in mind the duty of delight."[32] They might read and discuss Myles Horton's *The Long Haul*, Paulo Freire's *Pedagogy of the Oppressed*, and Orwell's *Down and Out in Paris and London*. And how about Doris Lessing's *The Golden Notebook* or *The Diaries of Jane Somers*? They might enjoy Scott Nearing's *The Making of a Radical* and Eric Hoffer's *The True Believer*. I would use the method of exposure here, not coercion. I'd tell them something about the books and perhaps read a bit from several of them. I'd tell them about the tradition of working-class intellectuals and introduce them to Tolstoy.

One could argue that most of the books I have mentioned are too hard for these kids. Maybe. But we could tell the stories, invite their reactions, and put the feast of possibilities before them. The books listed are a product of my privileged education, but they also reflect my working-class origins. They are not necessarily better than other choices, but they do represent selections that are highly regarded by many academics. They should not be chosen simply because they might be part of the academic curriculum (most of them are not) but because they fit the interests of vocational students and because they are thought by many of us to be fine works. Both quality and relevance are important.

I am not suggesting that we should use a sort of reverse snobbery in looking at the academic curriculum. There are wonderful books in almost every version of the literary canon, and all children should be encouraged to read them – at least try them out and hear enthusiastic readers talk about them. I am suggesting a subtler distinction in the way we make curricular decisions. Too often, vocational programs are "enriched" by simply adding on or plugging in material from the academic curriculum. This is sometimes called *integrating* academic and vocational studies. But the vocational program should serve as a screen or lens for the choice of rich intellectual material. The academic material does not add value to a vocational curriculum merely because it is academic.

If we are really concerned about curriculum integration, we should also ask how topics and skills from the vocational curriculum might enrich the academic curriculum. What is learned in vocational studies that might improve the lives of all children? Are there topics or skills that might enhance academic studies? I think here of my decision as a high school junior to take a year of typing instead of a second language. I already had scheduled five academic majors, but the principal advised me strongly to take French, not typing. Stubbornly, I insisted on typing. Now, when we academics serve as our own secretaries, I am very glad that I have the keyboarding skills learned in the typing class. With serious study and some imagination, many more such topics and skills could be found.

Vocational students should certainly study the contributions of labor to the making of America. They should learn about labor unions – their successes and failures, ethical strengths and weaknesses. Without overemphasizing the weaknesses of American democracy, teachers can help students to understand the suffering of workers and the battles fought by working people – from the Pullman strike to the Wobblies, United Mine Workers, and American Federation of Teachers.[33] They should certainly hear about the role socialism played in Depression-era America and in pre-Nazi Germany, and they should be invited to learn more about the lives of working people in other parts of the world.

It would, of course, be easier to build a variety of respectable programs if, as suggested earlier, we emphasized education for personal life. Such emphasis would enrich our academic offerings, and it would serve as a common nucleus for all school offerings. It is not hard to persuade students that happiness is something sought by all human beings. We can provide, through appropriately differentiated materials, many opportunities for students to explore the sources of happiness in personal life. In addition, as we educate for occupational choice, we can help students to understand that loving one's work is more important than money, that there are boring white-collar jobs, that no one should be so poorly paid that enjoyment of her work is impossible, and that no occupational role precludes thinking deeply as a citizen or reading widely.

We should also consider, in particular, the occupational lives of women. Today women can enter almost any professional field, and guidance counselors sometimes steer bright young women away from traditional female occupations. "You are too smart for that," counselors may say to girls who declare an interest in elementary school teaching. One response to this is that no one is "too smart" to be a teacher; one has trouble being smart enough. But another response is to recognize and discuss the great happiness that many women derive from working with children. Why force a young woman into engineering just because she has math smarts and it is now possible for her to be an engineer when her heart calls her to teach?

Educational theorists – teacher educators especially – have argued strongly for teaching as a true profession.[34] We have tended to scorn young people who mention "summers off" as an attractive feature of teaching. But it is an attractive feature! It is especially attractive to people who want more time with their families, gardens, reading, and other hobbies, and all of these activities can enhance teaching. Teaching is a career – profession or not – that brings happiness to many of its practitioners. Apparently, those happy people have often passed on a legacy of happiness to their own children, for we have many autobiographical accounts of happy childhoods with parents who were teachers.

There is a dilemma built into the argument I've made on teaching. On the one hand, we want teaching and other so-called semiprofessions (for example, nursing and social work) to be fully recognized as professions.[35] But in pressing for professional status, we sometimes fail to look carefully at the internal commitments and requirements of an occupation, and we may neglect entirely the ways in which occupational life contributes to human flourishing. As we prepare students for the world of work, these are matters for careful analysis.

Intellect and Happiness

Topics can be relevant to everyday life and also rich intellectually. I've been trying to show this throughout the book. In this brief section, I want to emphasize what should be obvious – students whose interests are mainly intellectual should be encouraged in those interests. When I speak of *intellectual interests*, I mean those interests that center on ideas and thinking in any field. I do not mean to refer to particular subjects or to superior mental capacities. There are students who are captivated by the ideas latent in the standard subjects, and teachers should help these students to cultivate pleasures of the mind that can accompany engagement with ideas. Apparently, pleasures of the mind are hard to find in schools.

> If the respective experiences of Stephen Wolfram and Dean Kamen are any indication, hell on earth is spelled s-c-h-o-o-l.[36]

Both Wolfram and Kamen are in science and technology, and both spend time helping schoolchildren engage in real science. Their own school experiences were miserable, and they are trying to make things better for today's children. If their stories of misery were unusual, we could brush them aside as intellectual oddities, but the stories are not rare. Albert Einstein, Thomas Edison, John Dewey, George Orwell, Winston Churchill, and Clarence Darrow all found school boring and unsupportive of their creativity. We hear this again and again from creative thinkers in a host of fields.

It is not only the rare creative thinker who suffers in school. All children who have genuine interests are likely to have them dulled by the demands of routine work in the classroom. To make matters worse, some educators and policymakers identify the intellectual with the merely academic as it has been defined traditionally.[37] The harder something is to learn, the more intellectual it is said to be, and subjects that are feared and hated by many students stand at the top of the hierarchy. Thus mathematics is regarded as more intellectual than literature or art. The harm done by this evaluation is not well documented, but my guess is that it is substantial.

Much misunderstanding has arisen over the meaning of *intellectual*. Dewey was often accused of *anti-intellectualism* because he recommended practical, hands-on activity as a central feature of education. In fact Dewey did oppose *intellectualism*, an attitude that values abstraction and disconnected thought above personal and practical experience.[38] He certainly opposed, as I do, the identification of intellectual with the mere accumulation of facts and academic skills. If instead we define intellectual as I did previously – as pertaining to a sustained interest in ideas and thinking – then Dewey was surely not anti-intellectual.

It is fair to say, however, that Dewey had little to say about the education of those students whose interests are primarily intellectual. We can assume that he wanted their interests – like those of all students – to be respected and encouraged. But how is this to be done? I have been arguing against forcing all students into a standard curriculum. This does not mean, however, that *no* students can profit from courses in abstract mathematics, philosophy, or literary criticism. Those who are truly interested in the intricacies of academic subject matter should be encouraged to develop their interests. Many mathematically talented students enjoy unraveling trigonometric identities, for example, and they improve their skills in mathematical manipulation by doing these otherwise useless exercises. Such activity, like any other in which the mind is fully engaged, should not be despised.

Trouble arises, as we have seen, when mental activity is elevated above all forms of human experience. Then we are forced into one of three positions: to identify those who are good at it as society's elite; to scoff at it and regard its advocates as effete intellectuals; or to insist that everyone can engage in it. Some of what Dewey said came close to the second position, but his basic message was that the initial assumption was faulty. Intellectual (abstract, mental) activity should not be valued more highly than other forms of experience; neither should it be scorned.

If the false valuation is dropped, we need not insist that everyone can master a particular intellectual task any more than we would claim that everyone can learn to play the violin skillfully or repair an airplane engine. By insisting that everyone can and should engage in intellectual activity, we risk either depriving those who have genuine interest and talent of real opportunities or distorting the meaning of intellectual.

Perhaps an example will make my point clear. I have argued repeatedly that there is no sound educational reason for forcing all students to study algebra and geometry. Both subjects should, however, be offered to students who need or want them. (Recall, also, that I suggested that all students should be offered risk-free opportunities to explore these subjects.) An intellectually oriented course in geometry would certainly include proofs, some discussion of postulate systems, and the fascinating epistemological problems that have arisen in connection with geometry. I have taught such a course, and I know that there are students who enjoy the material and do well with it. They are not better than students who hate math and love art; they are different, and their interests should be satisfied.

Instead, insisting that all students need geometry and can do it, we have changed geometry. In some geometry classes, no proofs whatever are required. There is no discussion of postulate systems and the wonderful variations induced by a change in postulates. There is nothing on the history of mathematics, on logic, or on the intimate connection between mathematics and philosophy. These are topics that appeal to many students who have an intellectual interest in mathematics. Well, then, a critic may object: Shouldn't all students be introduced to such fascinating topics?

The answer should be clear. Not all students have an intellectual interest in mathematics, nor is there any reason to insist that they should. Perhaps as many as 20 percent do have such interests, and schools should cultivate their interests without imposing them on everyone else. Students who have genuine intellectual interests derive happiness – even joy – from their engagement with a chosen topic. Interested high school students can spend hours happily analyzing a proof that all triangles are isosceles, and they are deeply impressed by the fact that Euclid could not block this faulty result with only the postulates he had proposed.

High schools today do provide courses that are supposedly designed for students with high intellectual interest; Advanced Placement courses challenge high school students with college-level material. However, such courses are not always invitations to genuine intellectual experience. More often they are inducements to compete with other students, to obtain a higher grade-point average, and to impress college admissions committees. They are sometimes inspired by the desire to get a certain subject behind them, not to study it further. Deep intellectual interest may even impede the goals of those students who perceive Advanced Placement courses as instrumental to narrowly defined forms of success.

I think highly intellectual courses should be offered, but I'd like to see the external rewards for taking these courses removed – no additions to the grade-point average, no special honors. They should be courses for the passionately interested, and they should be so designed that students can devote considerable periods of time to problems or topics that intrigue them. The time spent and the end result should be characterized by wonder, accomplishment, and happiness.

In this chapter, we have discussed the role of work in happiness. I've argued that, in preparing students for work, we should tell them honestly that money is not the only – or even most important – factor in making work enjoyable. At the same time, all students should come to appreciate the value of all honest work in our highly interdependent society, and they should commit themselves as citizens to establishing a livable level of compensation for all workers.

As educators, we should question claims that work in the future will require more and higher levels of skill. Some growing occupations will indeed require more years of education, but many jobs will not and, thanks to advancing technology, some may even require lower levels of skill. We should concentrate on developing rich, relevant, and highly differentiated school curricula, and we should provide the quality of advice that will make it possible for students to choose any of these programs wisely and proudly.

Students who have keen intellectual interests should not be neglected. Courses for the passionately interested should be provided for students whose interests are academic in the best sense. Taking such courses does not make a student better than others. It marks an important difference that should be acknowledged.

I emphasized the importance of educating for both personal and occupational life. With that emphasis – fundamentally an emphasis on happiness – we should be able to create stronger curricula for both college and noncollege preparation.

11

Community, Democracy, and Service

It seems right to say that people get most of their happiness from personal relations, the development of individual talents, and congenial work. What, then, is the contribution of community to happiness? Sociologists have identified periods in Western history characterized by what seems to be alienation and fear that the culture is falling apart.[1] Such periods sometimes follow eras of rugged individualism. In one period, people are eager to escape the bonds of community; in the next, they may fear its loss and try to recapture it. In both, community may affect happiness in ways of which we are barely conscious. Similarly, life in a liberal democracy may support the pursuit of happiness indirectly. However, some people derive happiness directly from community work and participation in democratic organizations.

I'll start the discussion with a brief examination of the human need for community. Next, we'll look at the standard-setting and socialization function of community. It is this function that sometimes drives people away from community. Paradoxically, it is also this function that people dread losing. One person's freedom is another's chaos. We will also consider ways in which some of our happiness may have roots in a democratic form of life. Finally, we will look at the gifts given and received in volunteer work and the role schools might play in introducing students to such activity.

The Need for Community

Community is difficult to define, and perhaps it is better not to do so at the outset.[2] In connection with our main theme, happiness, we are interested in the needs satisfied by community. Why do people long for community? Why do they fear its loss?

One need satisfied by community is identity or recognition. One is recognized – has an identity – in an extended family, for example. Kinship is one form of community described by the sociologist Ferdinand Tonnies. He also identified communities defined by physical proximity and communities of mind or common intellectual interests.[3] Looking at a community of kinship, we notice other features that belong at least to some degree to all collections called communities. Individuals are not only recognized (have particular names and family identities), but they also *participate* in various community functions. The kinship group has a *history*, and common memories form the foundation for communication in such groups.[4] There is also a sense of security in belonging to a kinship community. If an emergency arises, one can call on the group for support. At their best, these groups exhibit *mutuality*; the promise of help is reciprocal. They also exert some pressure for conformity; in doing so, these groups and other communities provide *order*. In addition, Selznick names *integration* as one of the primary functions of community.[5] I'll say much more about this in the sections on standard-setting and democracy.

The same elements are found, to varying degrees, in communities of place or proximity. Perhaps the most common use of the word *community* appears in connection with our dwelling places, although it is less frequently applied to large cities or vast open spaces than to towns, villages, and neighborhoods. The reason for this is clear when we consider the elements of community named previously. In neighborhoods, we are recognized, and we can participate in various functions if we wish to do so. We may also share memories with our neighbors, and we often depend on those neighbors in emergencies. We also know, more or less, what is expected of us in these settings. There is order. When these features are absent in a physical setting – as they often are in new housing developments or large cities – people may suffer malaise, an uneasiness that is hard to describe definitively. This uneasiness – a form of unhappiness – may attack unexpectedly. For example, an individual who "couldn't wait" to put a small town behind him may, if he recognizes the source of his discontent, return to the old town with renewed appreciation.

Communities of mind display similar features. In academic communities, for example, a sense of belonging is essential. Newcomers to an academic society press (or wait nervously) for recognition. The warmth of a society is noted almost immediately by newcomers. Older members, secure in their identities, may or may not be aware of the plight of newcomers. It is sad to hear of young people dropping out of professional societies because they could not achieve a sense of belonging. Many instructive stories can be told on this problem. A strong professional community supports and nurtures its members. It assures them that they have a place, they belong, even if they have lost or not yet acquired a position in some institution. In such situations, participation may be a necessary condition for mutuality; that is, the newcomer (or person who has lost her job) may have to offer services in order to get the support needed. It takes courage to submit a paper or offer to serve at a meeting when one has no formal institutional affiliation, but such courage is often rewarded with substantial support.

The discussion of academic communities suggests a larger issue for education in general. Children need help in understanding the connections among recognition, order, participation, and mutuality. Few children have the courage to push themselves into groups they want badly to join. More secure members have to invite participation, and this too is something children must learn to do. We noted in an earlier chapter that a capacity for happiness includes a sensitivity to unhappiness; that is, our own happiness cannot be complete if people around us are unhappy. Our schools do not always teach this lesson well, and many children suffer years of unhappiness because they are not accepted by their peers. They are deprived of that much-needed sense of belonging.

Paul Tillich has written about the need for both individual liberty and group participation.[6] We all have a need to belong, but for some of us this need is satisfied so easily that we fail to recognize either the need or its satisfaction. Our families, friends, and neighbors provide us with the security we need to develop as individuals. It is unlikely that people with such supportive communities will become members of cults or gangs. It is possible, however, that such lucky people will neglect to participate in the affairs of the larger democratic community. It is easy to take for granted the very structure that may make individual life so satisfying.

Those who are unlucky with respect to close associations may seek community in whatever groups will have them. Young people who feel rejected at home and school may join gangs. Some may join cults, looking for something in which to believe and to which they may commit themselves. People longing for community and frustrated by injustice may join political groups that demand wholehearted engagement and promise eventual liberation. When political aims and religious zeal combine, we see an especially powerful and dangerous form of fanaticism. Eric Hoffer writes of the fanatic:

> The fanatic is perpetually incomplete and insecure. He cannot generate self-assurance out of his individual resources – out of his rejected self – but finds it only by clinging passionately to whatever support he happens to embrace. This passionate attachment is the essence of his blind devotion and religiosity, and he sees in it the source of all virtue and strength. Though his single-minded dedication is a holding on for dear life, he easily sees himself as the supporter and defender of the holy cause to which he clings. And he is ready to sacrifice his life to demonstrate to himself and others that such indeed is his role. He sacrifices his life to prove his worth.[7]

The school can play an important part in preventing the sort of fanaticism that arises from loneliness and rejection. Teachers must work toward the inclusion of all students, and they must help students to understand the lure of gangs, cults, and intolerant ideologies. The second task is more difficult, because it involves the promotion of critical thinking, and many in our society fear what may result from widespread and competent critical thinking. Critical thinking may lead not only to rejection of socially unacceptable groups but also to skepticism about the groups usually deemed acceptable, including those into which one was born. This possibility makes teachers understandably cautious in teaching critical thinking.

Indeed, our democratic commitment to tolerance and diversity makes the task of teaching critical thinking even harder. On the one hand, we want students to think critically – that is, to acquire the skills of thinking critically. On the other hand, we give them few opportunities to exercise these skills on critical issues, in part because raising critical questions about beliefs and practices may be misconstrued as intolerance. Critical thinking is necessary for intelligent tolerance, but it is threatening to many groups. Consider William Galston's statement on the teaching of tolerance:

> The state may establish educational guidelines pursuant to this compelling interest. What it may not do is prescribe curricula or

pedagogic practices that require or strongly invite students to become skeptical or critical of their own ways of life.[8]

Socrates would weep. But, of course, people who feared critical thinking in his time knew what to do with Socrates.

High school students need to grapple with critical issues, and they need assurance that raising questions about the actions of their nation does not make them disloyal, nor does questioning certain practices of their religion make them apostates or atheists. Morally defensible national policies and logically defensible religious doctrines have nothing to fear from critical thinking.[9] How will national communities and religious communities improve if their members cannot analyze their practices, detect flaws, and suggest improvements?

It may be especially important today to discuss critical issues involving communities of mind – if we include in these not only religious groups but gangs and other collections of like-minded people. Discussion is crucial because traditional communities of kinship and place have been weakened by population growth, increased mobility, and technology. Dewey noted this trend more than fifty years ago, and its pace has quickened with the advent of television and computer technology. He said:

> The local communities . . . found their affairs conditioned by remote and invisible organizations. The scope of the latter's activities was so vast and their impact upon face-to-face associations so pervasive and unremitting that it is no exaggeration to speak of "a new age of human relations." The Great Society created by steam and electricity may be a society, but it is no community.[10]

One might argue (and many do) that computer technology has, in a reversal of the usual effects of technology, increased opportunities for community building and participation. There is room for doubt, however. Communication in itself does not provide identity, history, order, or mutuality, and the participation it invites may remain impersonal, even faceless. Advancing technology has, as Dewey noted, liberated the individual, but it has had destructive effects on community. Indeed, we might even question the "liberation" of individuals. Severing the bonds of community may produce a state more accurately called isolation than liberation.

224

Standard-Setting and Socialization

In modern times, human beings have been torn between a longing to be free and a longing to belong. Some thinkers have even identified certain eras as times dominated by one longing or the other.[11] In communities, groups that expect conformity and monitor the behavior of their members (however gently), it is predictable that some will feel stifled and eager to escape. The novels of Sinclair Lewis and others of his time often used a train whistle as a metaphor for the desire to escape – to get away from dullness and sameness, to become an individual. In later novels, we often read of characters wandering aimlessly in a big city, wondering what happened to the anticipated glamour and adventure.

What is it from which people want to escape? There are, no doubt, many answers to this question. Some reasons are, of course, personal, but many point to a general discontent. In any given community, there seem to be limits on personal success, on the range of acceptable adventures one may seek, on the kinds of questions one may ask. Conversations become predictable in their form and content. Critical thinking is discouraged, and one who voices it may be given a label usually reserved for outsiders – *Commie, free thinker, hippie, fag,* or any of a number of very nasty terms. The constant temptation in many communities is to strive for as much wealth and status as possible while denying greed and envy as motives. Critics of bourgeois communities see youthful aspirations dampened, true motives cloaked in hypocrisy, and all of life reduced to a shadow of possibilities. Totally disillusioned by such patterns, critics – like the Steppenwolf in our earlier chapter – may miss the goodness and contentment in middle-class community life. Again, like the Steppenwolf, they may find themselves in a love–hate relationship with the traditional community – needing and enjoying some of its resources, hating and rejecting its hypocrisy and apparent smugness.

Education could help to reduce the shock of Steppenwolf-like discovery. Good families and schools should help children to understand the power of socialization and how it is accomplished. Every society socializes its members, and much of what is achieved through socialization is valuable. Under most circumstances, for example, courteous manners are welcome and facilitate the smooth workings of a community. Prescribed patterns of dress are in some ways facilitative, too; we are distracted when someone appears at a given function in clothing that is thought to be unsuitable. On one level, dress codes relieve us of personal choices and anxieties; on another, they may seem yet another example of community meddling. Why, after all, should a man spend a significant part of his life half-choked by a colored cloth wrapped about his neck? Why should a woman be confined to skirts that impede free movement?

When we bother at all to explain the workings of socialization to young people, we usually emphasize the positive side. We point out that rules and customs are meant to keep things running smoothly, and in large part they do exactly this. We point out the rewards of compliance. But teenagers often see in these rules a manifestation of adult coercion and hegemony. Because they have not been taught anything about the underlying processes of socialization, they may reject adult domination only to fall under the even heavier domination of the teen world. Socialization exerts its power on them, but they do not understand its workings. Neither, for that matter, do most adults understand the social forces that shape their lives. If they did, advertising would not be so profitable.

To be happy – to avoid nebulous bouts of anxiety over meaninglessness – we need to understand ourselves and the groups to which we belong. This can never be accomplished completely, and often the attempt at understanding and its partial accomplishment actually increase our unhappiness. We see what is being done to us (and imagine even more), and the effect is further alienation and cynicism. Appropriate educational approaches, however, can help us to choose our battles wisely, and the power to do this certainly contributes to human flourishing, to happiness.

Foucault has helped us to understand the nature of social power.[12] This power is impersonal, a force all around us from which we cannot escape. At certain times, in certain circumstances, individuals or groups seem to have this power and use it to coerce us. We should not ignore this aspect of power – its potential to be seized at least temporarily. Often, however, this is the only possibility that people see. Someone has power and, if we don't like what we see of its use, we must fight that someone. Fair enough. But that does not get at the sort of power described by Foucault. In that larger view, there is no way to escape, seize, or defeat power. One can at best seek to understand it and make sound choices.

I have used the example of teenagers rejecting adult domination only to fall under teen domination. Many more examples could be given. I have watched some feminist colleagues fall into a similar trap. Just two decades ago (and even sometimes today), young female professors complained of sexism "everywhere." I advised some who were continuously angry to choose their battles more wisely. Fighting every instance of apparent sexism just leads us into another stream of power from which we might not escape, and it might well lead the perceived perpetrators into an opposing stream from which they cannot free themselves. It is better to ignore minor infractions, build relationships, and call for support when a serious problem arises.

In *Starting at Home*, I offered several examples of ways in which society controls our bodies; these might profitably be discussed in high school classes: the behavior of a congregation listening to a preacher whose message they find objectionable (but no one expresses an objection aloud); a concert audience listening to music that makes the body want to dance (but no one does); an execution at which all participants have mixed feelings of disgust and revulsion (but they all "do their duty"); and the case of schoolchildren plodding through tests while the May month calls them to the outdoors (but none leave; all continue filling in blobs).[13] We might add other cases for students to consider:

John, a high school junior, is aware that he could save a lot of money by purchasing shirts and athletic shoes that are not widely advertised. Still, he insists on paying high prices for name-brand garments he can ill afford. Asked why he does this, he first says that the lower-priced articles are inferior. Given evidence to the contrary, he says that his friends would make fun of him if he showed up wearing "that stuff." Then he quickly adds that it is really his own preference. Is it?

Wendy, a teenager just entering high school, has added an eyebrow ring to her earrings and belly ring. She confesses that she is afraid of catching it on something and also that she has experienced infections from other piercings. Why did she do it then? "All the kids are doing it" is her first answer. But then, like John, she insists that she has made an autonomous choice.

What about the young woman described in Chapter 9 who walked out on her companions because they were verbally mistreating another girl? What did she fear? What helped her to muster the moral courage needed to walk out?

In all of these cases, from the annoyed but silent congregation to the girl who rebuked her friends, there is an awareness that something or someone is exerting control over our behavior. Often, as in church or at a musical event, we accept control as necessary for orderly community life. At other times, we are keenly aware that, for our own sense of integrity, we should violate the script. At still other times, we are not consciously aware that we are being controlled and might even deny it, as John and Wendy eventually did. In situations that create great anxiety in us, we may courageously resist our social group or community because we feel that it has betrayed its own norms.

We depend on our communities to guide us toward what is morally and socially acceptable. At its best, this community influence can give us the courage to behave morally even though the risks are great. Pearl and Samuel Oliner asked non-Jewish rescuers of Jews during the Holocaust why they had taken such risks to help strangers.[14] The answer often pointed to community norms: We are people who respond compassionately to need; it is expected of us. Notice, however, that teenagers give roughly the same answer in explaining why they follow a fashion. And, sadly, people living under totalitarian regimes also refer to community norms, although they later blame the leaders of their communities if the results are morally questionable. In all of these cases, people fear some form of retaliation if they do not conform.

Today, when character education has again become popular in public schools, we should remember that such education requires a strong community but not necessarily a good one.[15] One responsibility of a good community is to educate its young in critical thinking so that they can raise the kinds of questions that help to keep the community good. It is not enough simply to inculcate values directly or to depend on the unreflective workings of socialization.

Before Foucault got us thinking about the impersonal and pervasive influence of power, some psychologists and sociologists spoke of a *herd instinct*.[16] For some years, invoking the idea of an instinct was a popular way of explaining human behavior, and the herd instinct does seem to capture some of what occurs in groups. However, there is little evidence for such an instinct and quite a lot against it. People do not always stay with the groups into which they are born, and they do not always align themselves even with groups they have chosen. Human beings are social animals, but we are not herd animals. Our own mental capacities and the cultures within which they are developed make us much more complicated.

People are socialized, but we also resist socialization, and it is important for young people to understand this. Sometimes our resistance to a group's press for conformity is a result of moral scruples that were acquired in another group or a larger community. At other times, resistance is as unreflective as the socialization that is rejected. Teenagers may, for example, reject almost everything their teachers offer. This is certainly a powerful form of resistance, but the end result is often exactly what the culture implicitly seeks – to keep a significant number of young people in socially and economically inferior positions.[17] Today we are urged to deny that our society harbors such unworthy motives. We insist that we want all children to learn and to succeed. But when we use coercive methods to prove our good intentions, we are in fact reinforcing a cycle of socialization and resistance that belies our better motives. We would do better to teach students about the effects of socialization and resistance, and invite discussion and reflection. As Diana Meyers has pointed out, reflection is a powerful brake on socialization,[18] but reflection is unlikely to occur unless it is demonstrated, invited, and sustained.

Young people also need to know how the inclination to institutionalize "best" practices often inaugurates a new round of socialization. Much of our public language reveals the continually renewed desire to force people into like-mindedness. This is part of the integrating component of community described by Selznick. We want them to get "with it," "on board," "with the program." In some businesses, employees are simply fired if they oppose the current program. In schools, teachers (who are supposed to have some professional autonomy) are sometimes coerced, given poor evaluations, or even mocked if they do not adopt the latest methods or educational philosophy. Teachers who have opposed – however thoughtfully – small-group work, open education, rote methods, constructivism, assertive discipline, modular scheduling, standardized testing, or the use of technology have been called old-fashioned, uninformed, or even obstructionist.

Selznick points out that attempts to institutionalize new ideas sometimes lead an organization into conflict with its own basic purposes or commitments.[19] Enthusiastic educators might, for example, decide that constructivist teaching is the best form of pedagogy. If, in their zeal, leaders decide to force all teachers to adopt these methods, they risk ignoring the very meaning of constructivism, and they surely risk violating the democratic premises to which most American schools are committed. We see here again how important it is to engage regularly in aims-talk. Why are we doing this new thing? Can we persuade others to try methods that seem promising? Is the new aim, goal, or means compatible with our most basic aims?

The situation may be further complicated by the institutional practice of requiring administrators to be *change agents* rather than facilitators. The coercion that accompanies the institutionalization of a practice is then aggravated by the tendency of leaders to protect their positions, advance the party line, and control the whole process. Indeed, leaders who can do this are widely considered strong leaders. But strong leaders – like strong communities – are not necessarily morally good.

The connection between institutional practices and individual happiness is not always clear. Someone working for a corporation or school may feel a vague discomfort if he or she is not in tune with a newly prescribed direction. A good deal of soul searching may go on, and many people blame themselves for being too slow, fearful, or motivated by personal animosities. Some people give way out of fear and adopt ends or means they have moral reason to reject. Others manage to rationalize practices that should make them deeply unhappy. Can one be really happy working to promote products or practices that are injurious to others? How does one rationalize composing ads for tobacco products, doing research aimed at the production of biological weapons, or experimenting with methods of psychological torture? When people feel that they are forced by circumstances to promote products or activities they find morally abhorrent, they may become deeply unhappy and find themselves vacillating between self-castigation and rage against the world. They may lose entirely that part of happiness derived from self-respect and inner contentment.

Democratic Life

Many people today believe that democratic forms of social life are best, and it can be assumed from this assessment that democratic life contributes something to happiness. It is not clear, however, that

230

people living in liberal democracies are necessarily happier than those who have lived or are living under enlightened monarchies or other benign forms of government. One's private life, so long as it is not actually threatened or controlled too tightly, does not seem to depend greatly on the form of government under which one lives, nor does the inner contentment that may be found in nondemocratic religious affiliation seem to work against happiness. What is it, then, that democracy contributes to happiness?

Defenders of democracy often credit it with three great merits: (1) democracies allow great freedom for individual and collective action; (2) democracies support equality; and (3) democracies identify and best satisfy human needs. The last is especially problematic, and it is sometimes argued that, in fact, some democracies – market democracies – are not very good at satisfying the needs of a significant minority of their populations. Further, they tend to manufacture needs and lead citizens to feel discontent if these artificially created needs are not met. However, I will argue that there is a sense in which democracies are particularly good at the task of meeting needs.

Let's consider first the claim that democracies promote individual and collective freedom. This seems undebatable, but what has freedom to do with happiness? It is clear that some freedom of movement and association is necessary to happiness, but it also seems clear that unlimited freedom can produce fear and anxiety, even anguish.[20] Children who are given freedom without guidance often suffer anxiety, and adults who cannot evaluate the choices before them also become anxious. Thus it is not merely freedom – the absence of constraint in the presence of many possibilities – that contributes to happiness. Indeed, one might plausibly argue that democratic life includes many factors that mitigate against happiness. In particular, the freedom to be more, possess more, and do more may make many people unhappy. It is necessary, then, to examine definitions of freedom and see which are conducive to happiness.

Today there are Muslim societies that pit freedom against virtue. They argue that being virtuous is better than being free. Advocates of freedom retort by insisting that coerced behavior – however consonant it might be with a society's rules – is not virtuous. Conduct worthy of the label *virtuous* must be freely chosen. This is debatable. Even liberal societies often coerce (however gently) good behavior from their young and hope that the virtues thus practiced

231

will be internalized and, eventually, affirmed by rational (free) examination.

The debate made so vivid by worldwide cultural clashes is also familiar in the contest between liberals and communitarians in recent Western philosophy.[21] The essential point of contention is where to start one's social/political thinking – with the right or with the good. Liberals, emphasizing the right – fair rules by which all agree to live – start with the search for rules that will allow each individual maximum freedom; communitarians insist that a vision of the good must precede any discussion of freedom. Ordinary people seeking happiness will likely settle for a compromise (one that favors communitarianism on the theoretical level), looking for a facilitative level of freedom within a worldview that gives some guidance for virtuous living. It is not clear that such worldviews are chosen (as liberals contend); we may deceive ourselves in supposing that we have made choices that were actually forced on us by the impersonal powers of socialization.

The second claim is that democratic life supports equality; that is, democracy recognizes the equal worth of all and makes the good life available to large numbers of people. If we leave aside for the moment the satisfaction of economic needs, we encounter debate about what constitutes the good life. As we have seen throughout the discussion of happiness, there is some disagreement on what should make us happy. We can agree at a rather high level of abstraction that the development of good character plays a significant role in personal happiness, but when we begin to discuss the virtues required for a good character, we may disagree vigorously on both the list of virtues and their description.

The twentieth century was marked by almost continuous debate over the meaning of equality. Recall the remarks of Charles Eliot in Chapter 10. Individuals are demonstrably not equal in terms of genetic predispositions, talents, or interests, and to suppose that they are threatens our democracy. What is required is a sincere and meaningful respect for all positive human capacities. On this, liberals seem to be right in emphasizing freedom to grow according to one's own legitimate inclinations, and conservatives seem to be right in insisting that growth be guided by some commonly accepted norms of conduct. Happy people in a liberal democracy use their freedom to find a satisfying place for themselves without sacrificing the goodwill and approbation of their fellow citizens. Equality construed as equal opportunity to grow, to develop one's own talents, character, personality, and way of life is the concept likely to be most useful in educating for happiness.

The ideals of equality and freedom may come into conflict. Your freedom may interfere with my growth and thus make my opportunities somehow unequal; my growth, then, may require a restriction on your freedom. The debate is often described along liberal–conservative lines. Liberals traditionally have emphasized freedom and have allowed individuals to define their own sense of growth. Conservatives have usually insisted that growth should be defined in terms of certain goods – a virtuous way of life – that should be accepted by all. As we will see, this difference has created an important tension in theories of democratic education.

It seems right to say that an individual's own evaluation of her growth is closely related to her happiness as defined by SWB. People tend to be happy when they feel that their talents are well developed and their needs satisfied. To the degree that democracy supports this development, it contributes to happiness.

We are not finished with equality, growth, or freedom, but let's briefly consider the satisfaction of needs. Today's mature democracies have achieved fairly high levels of prosperity for many of their people. Some nondemocratic nations, however, have also acquired great wealth. The question in connection with happiness is how wealth is distributed and whether another form of government might, through a more equitable distribution, contribute more fully to the satisfaction of needs and thus to happiness. There may be no way at present of answering this question, but it seems reasonable to suggest that democracies should exercise continual vigilance over the ways in which wealth is distributed and needs are satisfied.

If democracy is described, in Dewey's terms, as a mode of associated living,[22] a strong point emerges in its favor. The give-and-take of regular dialogue makes it possible to negotiate between expressed and inferred needs. Members of a democratic society can make their legitimate expressed needs known and expect some form of positive response – if not help, at least noninterference in pursuit of their satisfaction. The society, through its institutions, establishes various inferred needs – for example, schooling, disease prevention, safety regulations – and it tries to persuade citizens to accept these needs as their own. There is constant tension between the desire to impose these needs and the desire of a free people to accept or reject them. The very basis of democratic education is the need of a democratic society to sustain itself in accepting this tension, in finding methods low in coercion, and in encouraging continuous evaluation and negotiation between the two forms of need.

Amy Gutmann has argued persuasively that neither freedom nor virtue can be used to justify democratic education. She writes:

> Shifting the grounds of justification from future freedom to some other substantive end – such as happiness, autonomy, intellectual excellence, salvation, or social welfare – only re-creates the same problem. None of these standards is sufficiently inclusive to solve the problem of justification in the face of dissent by citizens whose conception of the good life and the good society threatens to be undermined by the conception of a good (but necessarily nonneutral) education instituted by some (necessarily exclusive) educational authority.[23]

On these grounds, Gutmann argues that the fundamental justification for a nonneutral democratic education is the maintenance and furtherance of the democratic society itself. But, of course, this does not mean that other aims cannot be included. It means only that no other one aim can serve as the final justification for public education in a democratic society. I've been arguing that happiness should be recognized as an aim of education because it is held by virtually everyone as an aim of life itself. We do not have to argue that everyone embraces the same view of happiness. In a pluralistic, democratic society, setting happiness as an aim of education means at least two things. First, it means that we help students to understand a variety of views on happiness and, through analysis and practice, begin to form a defensible position on their own happiness. Second, it means evaluating everything we do in light of substantial views on happiness; if what we propose to do causes obvious unhappiness (judged from some responsible position), we must either change what we are doing or argue vigorously that, from another perspective, happiness will be served. This vital form of rational dialogue is basic to both education and democracy itself.

Gutmann's analysis is not foolproof. Contrasting views of democracy give rise to different philosophies of education, and these are hotly contested in the name of democracy. It may be useful here to return briefly to the Dewey–Hutchins debate. Both men made their educational recommendations in the name of democracy. Hutchins believed that a common education for all young people would provide the knowledge and commitment to sustain democracy. We know, however, that this uniform curriculum discourages many students and leads to a loss of self-esteem for those whose talents lie elsewhere. In the language I've used earlier, Hutchins puts too much emphasis on inferred needs and not nearly enough on expressed needs. He seems to construe democracy as a fixed form whose traditions can and should be passed along whole to new generations. It is only with this fund of knowledge that citizens can exercise their rights and duties effectively.

Dewey did not deny the need for cultural transmission and common values, but he saw both as dependent on the desire to communicate and the commitment to continued inquiry. What is required for democratic participation, from Dewey's perspective, is not a fund of common factual knowledge but a grasp on the processes and open-minded devotion to continued inquiry and communication.[24] For Dewey, democracy is a mode of associated living that is moral (or social), and it is under continual construction. When we follow Dewey in planning educational programs, we draw on a fund of cultural knowledge to give us guidance in solving present problems and satisfying current conditions. We do not simply pass on an enormous store of information constructed and used in the past.

If we consider happiness as an aim of education, Dewey's approach seems superior. As we saw in Chapter 10, every legitimate human talent can be encouraged in schools. We need not establish a hierarchy of tracks, nor are we forced in the name of equality to push everyone into the "best" academic track. Teachers and curriculum makers must be constantly aware of the tension between expressed and inferred needs, and negotiation between the two becomes a regular part of the educational process.

I would go beyond Dewey in recommending revisions of the school curriculum.[25] Whereas Dewey suggested new rationales for teaching the traditional subjects and new ways to teach them, I would question the whole organization of curriculum and teaching. Where do we address the great existential questions: How should I live? Is there meaning in life? What does it mean to be good? To be happy?

Where do we address the issues traditionally associated with women: What does it mean to make a home? What constitutes good parenting? What do we owe to elderly parents? To other people's children? And where do we address issues that are particularly pressing in our present condition: How can we achieve and maintain peace? What violence and cruelty are we (and I) capable of? How can we restore and preserve our natural environment? What do we owe to nonhuman animals? Can we develop a satisfying spirituality without succumbing to dogma or superstition? What is happiness, and how might one find it?

None of this is to say that traditionalists such as Hutchins, Adler, and Hirsch are completely wrong. There is much beauty and wisdom in the traditions to which they adhere. The question for us – and for any democratic society – is how to make this material available without undue coercion and without ignoring the talents and purposes of students. Democracy must be interpreted in a way that gives support to its own maintenance and to the growth of every individual. It must remain open to the possibility that an even better mode of association might be found. So construed, it contributes to the conditions in which human life may flourish.

Learning to Participate and Serve

I acknowledged at the beginning of this chapter that most of us get the largest part of our happiness from personal relationships and/or occupational life. However, community life and especially a democratic mode of living provide a foundation upon which these primary goods are built and thus make a substantial, if indirect, contribution to happiness.

Active participation in community life may also be a direct source of happiness. We often hear, for example, of retirees who find a new purpose in life through volunteer work. Many privileged young people of college age are strong supporters of volunteer organizations such as Habitat for Humanity, the Peace Corps, and Big Brothers. Some work with religious or ethnic charities, and some devote much of their time to the relief of particular problems such as hunger, homelessness, addiction, and disability. In past generations, women (homemakers) did the greater part of volunteer work, and in some traditional neighborhoods this is still true. Today both female and male professionals may

236

give generous time to pro bono work, exercising their skills in behalf of those who cannot afford to buy their services.[26]

Serving others contributes to the happiness of those who volunteer in at least three ways. First, volunteers may find congenial company and derive happiness from the warmth of relationships with those served and also with other volunteers. Second, those who volunteer are usually people who feel and respond to the needs of others. As we saw earlier, the capacity for unhappiness and a commitment to relieve it are important in achieving personal happiness. People who have this capacity and commitment often have what Reinhold Niebuhr called an *uneasy conscience*. Their happiness depends at least in part on relieving the misery of others.[27] Third, volunteers are often aware that their work sustains the spirit of community and the democratic mode of association. By participating in community life and promoting democracy, they contribute to the maintenance of those foundations of personal happiness.

Schools can promote community participation and service in many ways. Community service is a requirement for graduation in some high schools, and interest in service learning seems to be growing. But these efforts are hampered by the very structure of schools in liberal market societies. When service is required (and sometimes even graded), students and their parents may resent the time taken from "real" subjects. Competing for top grades in real subjects is what school is all about, and one must win the competition to obtain a good position in the next round of competition. One must get a high grade-point average in high school to qualify for one of the best colleges, and one must chalk up a high grade-point average there to get a well-paid job. Then one must outdo fellow workers to secure promotion. Perhaps in retirement one can relax and cooperate with others.

It may seem pessimistic to suggest that schools simply cannot contribute to the happiness derived from cooperative living without changing their basic structure, but the claim is largely accurate. In an earlier chapter, we noted how children suffer when they are told "always do your best in everything" and then receive C's for their efforts. There is something deeply wrong with this system. To make matters worse, when teachers try hard to provide ways in which students can earn good grades through extra effort, they are accused of contributing to grade inflation. As if there were a natural scarcity of A's! How should teachers respond? The best teachers may indeed

237

present grade reports dominated by A's and B's. If a question must be asked, it should concentrate on whether and how students *earned* these grades. If the teacher simply gave them, then the evaluation should be called into question. But if the teacher worked creatively and supportively to help students earn their good grades, the teacher should be credited with fine work.

One way to make service learning and community participation attractive and important would be to give them the same status as, say, algebra and French. What would that mean? It would mean, of course, grading the experience competitively and ensuring that only a few made top grades. The work should be hard. It should be intellectual. Very likely, it would be feared and hated. I have already expressed grave doubts about this way of operating.

An alternative would be for teachers and other school personnel to invite students to participate in the service activities in which they themselves engage. There would be no coercion except, perhaps, for the initial period of exposure. Students might be required to choose some service activity, but they should be allowed to change to a different one, and there should be no grading. Alas – there goes our hope that service might achieve the status of algebra. I don't see how such equality can be established within present school structures.

To avoid ending this section on a glum note, I'll say that service learning should still be promoted. Within the present structure of schooling, it cannot contribute much to happiness, but we can work toward changing that structure.

In this chapter, we have considered ways in which community may contribute to either happiness or misery. Communities socialize their members; from that process there is no escape. However, a good educational system will help students to reflect upon and understand the processes of socialization. What standards should I accept as beneficial for the growth of individuals and the order of society? Which might I reject in the interests of my own growth without hurting others? Which should I reject entirely on moral grounds? Where do I find the strength to resist questionable pressures for conformity?

We then looked at the possible contributions of democracy to happiness. If democracy is viewed as a dynamic arrangement continually under construction, if it is marked by a commitment to inquiry and communication that will produce common values without coercing them, and if it supports the individual growth of its members, it will contribute to happiness. In such a system, freedom is regarded as a capacity to make well-informed decisions in an environment that supports such decision making, and equality is construed as societal support for individual growth defined across the full range of human talents and interests. We noted also that democracy puts a strain on happiness by requiring so much decision making.

Finally, we looked briefly at ways in which participation and service might contribute directly to individual happiness, and we concluded that unless the basic structure of schooling changes, such a contribution will remain largely an ideal, not a reality.

12

Happiness in Schools and Classrooms

In the previous chapters, we've discussed various views of happiness and a wide range of related topics that might be discussed in schools. We have addressed the broad issue of how best to prepare young people for happy lives. But happiness is not best construed as a state earned or promised for future life. Happiness in the present is not incompatible with future happiness, and it may even be instrumental for future happiness. Educators should therefore give attention to the quality of students' present experience.

In this chapter, I will use what we've learned about happiness to make some recommendations for life in classrooms. Then, as suggested earlier, I'll show how we might analyze and evaluate our work using the aim of happiness to guide us.

Happy Classrooms

The satisfaction of needs is a major factor in happiness. But needs may be either expressed or inferred, and individuals do not always know what they need. To complicate matters further, it is not easy to separate needs from mere wants, and the satisfaction of wants also contributes to happiness in the form of pleasure. We could probably discuss most of the forms of happiness within the broad general category of satisfaction of needs, but some are so important in themselves that we should return to them now to see how they are involved in the routines of classroom life.

Schools today pay some attention to the satisfaction of physical needs. Hungry children often get free or reduced-price breakfast and lunch. However, American society still has a long way to go in providing for the physical needs of children. Many need dental work that their families cannot afford. Too many have no medical insurance, and some need eye examinations and corrective glasses. Children who are hungry, in pain, or handicapped by poor vision are unlikely to be happy, and a classroom filled with such children cannot be a happy place.

Even when we feed children, thereby satisfying one important need, we often impose a psychological burden on them. They are publicly recognized as poor, as charity cases. A better alternative would be to supply meals for all our children as a regular part of the school day. Mealtimes should be part of a genuine educational experience, not a break from learning.[1] In many good homes, mealtime is a significant educational experience – an opportunity to learn social graces, to engage in conversation with interested adults, to catch up on what is happening in each one's world, to learn something about nutrition, and to plan for coming events. Many independent schools already incorporate mealtimes into the complete educational day.

Critics might make three objections to my recommendation. First, they might insist that both children and teachers *need* a break from the intensive daily work of instruction. This objection reveals a view of education as hard work, as a grinding duty, from which we all need to escape. But a view of education as a mode of living and learning together, as a way of being in the world, changes the whole picture. Mealtime, from this perspective, is a different setting for continued learning and friendly interpersonal relations. If it must be construed as an escape of sorts, it might be an escape into freer, more informal, and physically satisfying exploration.

The second objection against my plan centers on its obvious expense. Schooling is already very expensive, and a plan that includes feeding children whose parents can well afford their meals seems extravagant. Schools could, however, solicit the help of parents. An account could be sent to every parent, along with a request for contributions, and this solicitation should be part of an ongoing program to convince parents that schooling is a public good, not a consumer good. Many parents, called upon to fill a civic responsibility, would be glad to give a little more than it costs to feed their own children. What would it say about our society if they were not?

The third objection that might be raised is a variation on the all too common insistence on parents' rights. "I don't want the school to feed my children! *I* will decide what they have for lunch, and *I* will give them breakfast." Well, fine. Children should not be forced to eat what the school serves, but if they participate, there should be no differentiation on the basis of who can pay. There might even be "no food" tables at which children could gather at breakfast to talk, perhaps indulging in a juice substitute for the adult coffee day starter. Objections of the parents' rights sort have to be answered with good humor and some imagination. None of the objections raised so far outweighs the advantages of including meals as part of the educational day.

As a society, we must commit ourselves to the satisfaction of other objective needs. It is a moral disgrace that some of our children attend schools with nonfunctioning heating systems, poor lighting, boarded-over windows, filthy restrooms, overcrowded classrooms, and danger-ous stairways.[2] We should be ashamed to allow such conditions, and there can be no counterargument on this one. Further, we should not base our argument for better conditions on the grounds that the chil-dren will learn better in improved surroundings. They probably will learn better, but we should be prompted to provide better conditions by a collective uneasy conscience. Our happiness should be threat-ened by the misery of others, and children should not have to earn decent living and learning conditions.

The distinction between expressed and inferred needs is helpful in analyzing the connection between needs and happiness. Most of the needs met in school are inferred needs – those needs that adults impose on children. Providing for these needs gives us a sense of righteousness, and our conviction that these needs really are needs helps to justify the coercion we exercise so freely on children. I've already suggested that we should be very careful in identifying and pursuing inferred needs, and we should listen respectfully to what children offer as expressed needs.

One feature of happy classrooms is a continually negotiated balance between expressed and inferred needs. Students will do things for teachers whose care is regularly demonstrated, and caring involves responding to the expressed needs of the cared for. Adults will, of course, try to influence these needs – to curb undesirable wants, to shape some wants into real needs, to encourage the conversion of inferred needs to expressed needs. This effort must be made with the greatest sensitivity, always guided and modified by the expressed needs of students. Readers are invited to view classrooms (real and fictional) from this perspective. How is the balance achieved? What does it contribute to happiness? Does it seem to have effects not only on present learning but also on the desire to continue learning?

One expressed need is so universal that it has sometimes (mistakenly) been taken as synonymous with happiness. This is pleasure. Many educators in the past, and even some today, look upon pleasure in the classroom as a sign that little real work is being done. Some years ago, a group of elementary school teachers told me that they were about to give up on a science program that I thought was quite wonderful. The kids were having fun, but the teachers were not sure what their students were learning. Teachers should know a good deal about what students are learning; that is an important part of their job, and these teachers may not have known enough science to help them in making judgments. It may also be, however, that the teachers were bothered by their students' excitement and fun. Science is supposed to be hard work, and these kids seemed to be playing.

Play can contribute directly to learning, especially for elementary school children, and all teachers should be aware of the power of play in learning.[3] Not long ago I read a sad account of middle school children who could not read. These children (not special education students) could not even read their own names. How is this possible? Such children could not have played board games – certainly not Monopoly, where players are constantly challenged by cards that require them to read. Chances are that these children have never played any board games. Opportunities to read, to count and compute, to negotiate with other players, and to have valuable fun have been lost. Every classroom should be well provided with board games and playing cards, and playing with them should count as part of the learning day.

What is learned through this sort of play? There are many biographical accounts of the learning associated with games, but educational researchers still need to study more closely the informal learning associated with games and its effects. Teachers should study these accounts, but they should also watch their own students: observe, reflect, and monitor.

Fun doesn't have to end with elementary school. Teachers should study the recreations associated with their subjects. In mathematics, for example, there are many puzzles, number theoretical tricks, paradoxes, and geometric oddities that can provide fun along with learning. If teachers do not understand what underlies these recreations, students may still have fun, but learning will be limited. The teachers who rejected the challenging elementary science program were in this predicament. They simply did not know enough science. In an important sense, then, worthwhile fun in the classroom is dependent upon teachers' knowledge and artistry.

There is another role for pleasure in education. In discussing the "rhythms of education," Whitehead described stages of learning, emphasizing the first stage, which he called *romance*:

> The stage of romance is the stage of first apprehension. The subject-matter has the vividness of novelty; it holds within itself unexplored connexions with possibilities half-described by glimpses and half-concealed by the wealth of material. . . . Romantic emotion is essentially the excitement consequent on the transition from bare facts to the realisations of the import of their unexplored relationships.[4]

When something gives us pleasure, we are inclined to study it more carefully. It can also happen, of course, that the stage of romance is characterized more by puzzlement and intrigue than by fun. But even then, the process of finding out can be fun because one truly wants to learn, and the end result is a deep form of satisfaction.

It is disheartening to read accounts from the 1960s and early 1970s, during which there was so much enthusiasm for real change in schooling.[5] Critics at that time assailed the mindlessness and boredom that characterized most classrooms. Anne Long wrote:

> I am thoroughly convinced that 95 per cent of all the "academic learning" that goes on in public schools is meaningless blather to the children engaged in it. That the real lessons children learn have to do with the unpleasantness of learning, the lack of joy in books, the grind of doing arithmetic, the drudgery of answering other people's questions instead of one's own, the vast distance between themselves and their teachers, between anything meaningful in their lives and their schooling. As one youngster expressed it to me: "Being in school is like being on a bus; you sit there and watch the world go by, and you can't get off until three-fifteen."[6]

More than thirty years later, school is still boring, and in some ways it is worse today than it was in the 1960s, when reformers were clamoring for change. The effects of standardized testing have aggravated an already dull way of life. Both students and teachers are caught in a deadly serious campaign to amass facts and skills that can be easily tested. Even if scores go up in the next few years (and that is by no means certain), it is not clear how much lasting learning will have taken place.

In addition to pleasure, we agreed with J. S. Mill that the absence of pain contributes to happiness or, at least, that pain makes us unhappy. On reducing pain, we have, arguably, made some progress. Today's readers are rightly appalled by the soul-destroying remarks directed at students (and about students) by teachers even thirty years ago.[7] Teachers have to be, and most want to be, more careful and considerate now, but much abuse remains.[8] Sarcasm and humiliating remarks have no place in the classroom, but they still occur.

As parents and teachers, we sometimes inflict pain on our children and students unintentionally. We are all imperfect beings, and there is no hope of eliminating the pain that accompanies interaction across differences in power. However, we can work at reducing it, and we can analyze all that we do with an eye toward eliminating it where possible. When we are personally at fault, we can admit it and apologize. When the structure of schooling is at fault, we can try to change it.

A simple example may help here. Jules Henry tells the story of a boy, Boris, who was stuck (and on the spot) in trying to reduce the fraction 12/16. He got as far as 6/8 and could go no further. (It would have been interesting to find out what held him back. Did he think that, if you divided once by 2 in a given problem, you are not allowed to do so again? Stranger things have popped up in math classes.) Another child, Peggy, succeeded at the task. Henry remarks that "Boris' failure has made it possible for Peggy to succeed."[9]

Most children do not take such small failures seriously, but these incidents do occasionally cause genuine misery, and there is a way to reduce them. First, we might refuse to engage in *cold calling*, the practice of calling on students who have not volunteered. But, conscientious teachers may object, we want to involve all of our students, and some will never volunteer. Then what? We can ask pairs of students to work on and present a solution. I hit on this strategy late in my career as a math teacher, and I wish I had thought of it earlier. I would ask several pairs of students to work problems at the board while the rest worked at their seats. Then we would hear each pair's explanation. It was all right to be stuck, and I often helped a pair to complete their solution. Because the others were busy and I moved from one group to another, no one paid much attention to my interventions. It is surprising how much easier it is to accept a small failure that is shared (and isn't even regarded as a failure by the teacher), and success does not seem diminished by sharing it with another.

In my university classes, I use the first solution. I tell students at the beginning of a class that I am, to an important degree, at their mercy because I will not call on anyone who has not volunteered. Perhaps, as a result, some relax, daydream, and miss important opportunities to learn, but at least they need not be afraid. I do not want learning to be associated with pain and fear.

Does this solve the problem of saving students who are confused or mistaken from embarrassment? It does not. Students who volunteer may be wrong, confused, or even obnoxious in their comments. Some teachers respond to every student comment with "good" and then call on another student whose answer is also "good." This strategy may avoid inflicting pain, but it does little to advance a student's competence, and the development of intellectual competence is an important aspect of personal happiness. Teachers have to find more honest ways to respond. One might say, "not quite," or "let's explore that a bit," or "the idea is great but you've got X wrong," or "can you ask that a bit more gently?" or "may I ask you a question?" It requires some artistry and some knowledge of each student to find a response that is honest, supportive, and helpful to the whole class. No teacher ever achieves perfection in this crucial work.

The atmosphere of classrooms should reflect the universal desire for happiness. There should be a minimum of pain (and none deliberately inflicted), many opportunities for pleasure, and overt recognition of the connection between the development of desirable dispositions and happiness.

The development of character can be assisted by direct intervention. Not only should teachers refrain from inflicting pain but they should also stop students from giving pain to one another. The method described earlier of immediate intervention, explanation, and showing a better way should be used when infractions occur. Stories can be used also, but they should invite critical thinking, not blind admiration and emulation.

Every student should grow intellectually in the sense that each should learn to use his or her mind well in the affairs of everyday life and in a chosen field of study. Also, since character is an arena in which all should develop well, opportunities for critical thinking on moral/social problems should be extended to everyone. Similarly, self-understanding is so important to happiness that no opportunity for its discussion should be lost.[10] To handle all this well does not require a sacrifice of subject matter. On the contrary, it requires a broadening and deepening of subject matter. Teachers have to make wise judgments on what is really worthwhile and, even then, their selections should usually be offered – not coerced – and student interest should indicate which items are pursued and to what depth.[11]

I have referred several times, in this and earlier chapters, to the criticisms and hopes generated in the 1960s. The ideas offered then were sometimes wild, often wonderful. They were not addressed to the question of how to raise standardized test scores but to the much deeper question of how to keep curiosity alive, foster true learning (Piaget's *developmental learning*), and promote the growth of fully human beings. Paul Goodman summarized the spirit of the times this way:

> Every part of education can be open to need, desire, choice, and trying out. Nothing needs to be compelled or extrinsically motivated by prizes and threats.... What would be saved is the pitiful waste of youthful years – caged, daydreaming, sabotaging, and cheating – and the degrading and insulting misuse of teachers.[12]

I would not go so far as to say that *nothing* needs to be compelled. I urge, rather, that educators ask what needs to be compelled and why. Some things need to be compelled because no spirited being would be bothered with them if they were not compelled. These things clutter the curriculum, as Bruner said, and should be dropped. Other things are instrumentally compelled; that is, we have to master X (which we may dislike) in order to achieve Y (which we want). Usually, this form of compulsion arises naturally in the course of students' activities, but sometimes teachers may have to insist that something be learned. Coercion may have to be used, but it always requires extra work, then, to maintain relations of care and trust. Finally, decent, nonharmful behavior may have to be compelled in the interests of keeping all students safe and helping those who do harmful things to develop better moral selves.

There is another situation in which coercion may be necessary. Consider the case discussed earlier of seventh graders who could not read. School reform advocates are right in insisting that such school failure should not be tolerated, but they are probably wrong in supposing that the establishment of explicit standards and standardized testing will solve the problem. Moreover, the problems of inner-city schools should not dictate a mode of operation for all schools. Indeed, this way of going at the problem seems to be damaging the healthy schools without really helping those mired in failure. If, after several more years of "reform," we find that achievement has improved very little or not at all and both teachers and students are unhappy, then we will have suffered an absolute loss. Something must be done for those who cannot read, but the solution is not standardized tests for everyone.

As Isaiah Berlin reminded us, we sometimes have to sacrifice one great good to attain another. A sacrifice of freedom and creativity in the schools might be worthwhile if it achieved a better basic education for children such as the seventh-grade nonreaders. Concerned parents who fear for their children's future happiness may tolerate – even urge – coercion in the schools if it will help their children learn. It is easy for well-to-do parents to resist, and even mock, the coercive methods (rewards, punishment, rote learning, homework for the sake of discipline) often used in poor schools, but desperate parents will allow the schools to try almost anything that might work.

Instead of using coercive teaching methods, we might do better to separate those who want to learn from those who do not. The late Al Shanker made a recommendation along these lines and received both praise and scathing criticism for it. Critics took him to mean that we should just give up on the multitudes of teenagers who refuse to do their schoolwork and disrupt classes so that others cannot learn. But separating youngsters does not imply giving up on them. It means, first, providing top-notch learning environments for those children and parents who will pledge themselves to facilitative behavior. It means, second, working intelligently with disenchanted students – establishing relations of care and trust, providing relevant curricula, working hard to convince them to join the set of willing learners. This is very hard, important work. Doing it should not detract from the equally important work of educating those who are already eager, or at least willing, to learn. In an important sense, these two educational efforts are two essentially different tasks.

The public schools have been unwilling to recognize these two separate tasks and pursue them on any effective scale. They suspend and expel students but do not convert troubled students, and willing students suffer from neglect. Some cities have tried voucher programs (which have now been declared constitutional), but these programs can serve so few students that they hardly represent a solution. Public schools have the buildings, personnel, and dedicated funds to tackle the problem. It means designating many schools (or parts of schools) as true learning centers, schools to which students and parents must apply and, in their application, agree to an acceptable level of cooperation and industry.[13] There should be *many* of these schools – as many as it takes to accommodate every child wanting an education. No child should be left out because she did not win a lottery, and no child should be excluded because he has a learning difficulty.

The others – those who will not agree to behave – must not be thrown away or left in rotting schools. There must be an intensive effort to invite them to participate in their own education, and that education should be rich and varied, tailored to individuals. It might lead quickly to full-time work, extensive treatment for addiction or mental problems, or further education.

It would take a full volume (and more) to treat the problems alluded to here, but the basic idea is to work conscientiously on each problem, not to attempt their solution through one sweeping mode of reform. We are faced with several problems, not just one, and one solution is not satisfactory for a variety of problems. The quality of present experience matters, and not everyone thrives in a given situation. One might even say that present happiness, in addition to being valued for itself, is instrumental for future happiness. We know that people are often unhappy in schools or classes that are not fitted to their needs and interests.

There are a few strategies that might prove generally useful. One is to separate the willing from the unwilling, as suggested previously. Another is a policy that emphasizes continuity. I recommended in Chapter 9 that students and teachers should stay together for, say, three years instead of the typical one year. This policy might do wonders in terms of establishing relations of care and trust. But it, too, would lose its power if it were mandated. Forcing people to stay together would be counterproductive. The decision to stay together must be made by mutual consent.

Why not try vouchers as a solution? First, without an enormous proliferation of nonpublic schools, voucher plans cannot provide a solution for large numbers of students. Second, the best feature of voucher plans – some choice in the selection of a school – could be handled effectively within the public system. Third, the use of vouchers supports a conception of education as a consumer good instead of a public good. This is enormously dangerous.

I want to say more on this last objection to voucher plans and every form of privatization. In Chapter 11, we saw that a democratic way of life supports – at least indirectly – both individual and collective happiness. The public schools were envisioned as instruments for the maintenance of democracy. It may seem odd at first that a confessed admirer of the radical 1960s would not be enthusiastic about a proliferation of alternative, privately operated schools. What could be more democratic than a variety of choices in schooling? I have already suggested that alternatives – many alternatives – should be welcomed within the public system.

Why not go beyond what the public schools can offer? Why not privatize? I would argue that the public school has long stood between state and parents as an advocate for the child. Parents do not own their children; neither does the state. If parents are allowed to use public funds to send their children to schools run by religious institutions, some children (perhaps many) will be deprived of opportunities promoted by public education. Imagine, for example, what might happen to many girls whose parents choose fundamentalist schools for their education. It is certainly the right of adults to choose fundamentalist religion for themselves but, as Justice William Douglas pointed out in his dissenting opinion in the case that allowed the Amish to keep their children out of high school, some entity or institution must consider the rights of children.[14] The public school at its best is that institution. Parents can direct their children's religious education, but the public school should give children the breadth of knowledge and the critical skills to decide for themselves in their maturity.

Although a thorough examination of the issues is beyond the scope of this book, readers should consider two related decisions that bear on the question of children's rights. We might ask whether the decision to allow private schools was an appropriate one in a liberal democracy. After all, that decision suggests that education is indeed a consumer good. Second, we might ask whether granting the federal government a large role in education was a wise move. Both decisions are often applauded by liberals, but I think both might be questioned on liberal grounds. The first gives too much power to parents, and the second too much to the state.

In a recent Supreme Court Decision (*Zelman v. Simmons-Harris*), a majority of the justices decided that Cleveland's voucher program is constitutional, even though it allows public money to be used in payment of tuition at religious schools. This is a case in which the dissenting opinions are likely to be historically significant. Justices Stephen Breyer, David Souter, and John Paul Stevens expressed fear that the decision would lead ultimately to religious strife. Justice Breyer wrote:

> In a society composed of many different religious creeds, I fear that this present departure from the court's earlier understanding risks creating a form of religiously based conflict potentially harmful to the nation's social fabric.[15]

Such conflict, if it were to become a reality, would certainly damage our democratic way of life and, thus, our collective happiness. Because religious schooling in some of its forms also has the potential to inhibit the full development of individuals, it should not be supported by the public at large.

Evaluating Our Work

If we accept happiness as an aim of education, we will be concerned with both the quality of present experience and the likely contribution of that experience to future happiness. Everything we do will be evaluated in light of this aim and others that have been assessed as compatible with it. As we saw in Chapter 4, there are those who brush aside aims-talk as boring and irrelevant, but this is a great mistake.[16]

Without continual reflection on aims, education becomes merely "what goes on in schools," and our only measure of success becomes how successful we are at what we think we are doing. Today that measure has become almost exclusively standard test scores. Needless to say, these tests do not enhance the quality of present experience either on the days of their administration or in the weeks preceding them. Do they contribute to future happiness? Well, look at the tests. Is mastery of their content in any way necessary to one's adult happiness? If it isn't, we have to ask why this material is in the curriculum at all. If it is – perhaps because it is needed for the accomplishment of a related goal or compatible aim – we must ask whether there is another way of demonstrating that children have learned the material, one through which teachers feel professionally fulfilled. After all, the happiness of teachers is important, too, and happy teachers are more likely to produce happy children. Both ends and means must be justified with respect to aims.

Let's start this discussion with a familiar example, one I addressed briefly in earlier remarks. Poetry is taught in high school English classes. Why? Critics who are impatient with aims-talk may respond that it is now and has always been part of the academic curriculum. This is clearly an unsatisfactory answer. Greek and Latin were once a part of the standard curriculum, but both are rare today. Why were they dropped? If the answer is that no one needs Greek or Latin today and that fact is sufficient reason for dropping them, then the question of who needs poetry may be asked. Engaging in thoughtful aims-talk may lead some educators to suggest abandoning poetry because it has no economic value, but others will argue (as I did earlier) that poetry may well offer some wisdom and promise lifelong pleasure.

If we accept this rationale for including poetry in the curriculum, how should we teach it? Students should get some pleasure from their experience with poetry, and there should be time to discuss the great existential questions it addresses. Some students will never have heard an expression of spiritual longing from an unbeliever and will be deeply moved by the poetry of Thomas Hardy. Some will reject participation in wars after reading the horrors depicted by World War I poets. Some will be drawn to a beautiful place by poetry. Some may want to read the great myths alluded to in poetry. Some will come to love poetry itself and want further experience with it. The possibilities are numerous, but their actualization depends at least in part on how poetry is presented and received. If the aim of teaching poetry is delight and wisdom, then the pedagogical methods chosen should make these ends likely. It means also that, in monitoring the effects of our work, we will look for signs of joy, deep thought, and eagerness to read more and hear more.

Consider another kind of example. Social studies teachers often say that their major goals are process or skill oriented. They want students to be able to use maps effectively, to read charts with understanding, to look for evidence and apply it logically to claims of fact, to gain competence in assessing arguments, and to understand the complex relations among climate, place, and culture. We could add other goals of this type. Does it matter, then, what content is chosen so long as its treatment is likely to advance these goals? The answer to this question depends on what else we are trying to accomplish. If we are concerned with some important world event, we may want to choose content that meets both this concern and our process goals.

As we consider content, we may see that many topics might satisfy our criteria. A wonderful opportunity arises for students to choose content that interests them. It is not necessary for the whole class to march along together on one topic. Because it is difficult for a teacher to manage twenty-five or thirty different topics, she might ask students to choose one of five or six topics for which she is prepared to suggest a rich set of materials. A group of students who have chosen a particular topic might work together, dividing the work further and sharing the results with one another and, finally, with the whole class. Given the goal of mastering processes, the teacher must be sure that the materials provided are rich in both relevance and interest, and she must assess her students' work on their progress toward the stated goals. Notice that this is not an argument for process over or against content. It is an argument for how to proceed if we have chosen process goals.

But even the process goals with which we started must be justified with respect to aims. What aims are they designed to meet? Social studies teachers sometimes try to justify the whole social studies curriculum in terms of citizenship. Some go so far as to say that American history is taught because learning it makes students better citizens. Does it? The claim needs a much more fine-grained argument or some convincing empirical evidence. The second is not available, and we rarely demand the first.

Among the process goals mentioned are two that focus on evidence and argumentation. These can be linked to citizenship, and they can also be connected to happiness through the sort of argument I offered in Chapter 11. They are goals that reflect the needs of citizens in liberal democracies, and when they are achieved, they contribute to the maintenance of such societies.

What about map skills? It would be glib to say that these skills are somehow necessary for citizenship. We can justify some basic map skills on the grounds that they contribute to the competence required in a complex, highly mobile society. For example, children in cities may need to know how to read a subway map. Teenagers learning to drive need to read road maps. Do they also need some familiarity with maps of the world, longitude and latitude, physical features, scales, and other aspects of maps? The temptation is to respond "of course"; such knowledge is part of literacy. That answer is not adequate.

It won't do today to declare that a skill or bit of information is part of literacy and therefore justified as curriculum content. The concept of *literacy* covers too much territory. We all know many things that we've picked up on the way to becoming literate and many more that we continue to accrue because we are literate in the sense that we have the necessary skills of communication. But we don't all know the very same things, and it cannot reasonably be argued that anything I know you should also know. We might be surprised by an adult person's ignorance if he could not locate Europe on a map of the world, but we would not declare him illiterate.

Well, then, should map skills (which we have only loosely described, not defined) be listed with other interesting topics that schools might offer but not insist upon? Some of them no doubt should be among the free gifts we regularly offer to our children, and some might be required of students who have expressed interest in fields where such skills are necessary. However, we can argue more strongly that some map-related topics are essential for all students. Arguing for both history and geography in the curriculum, Dewey put it this way:

> While geography emphasizes the physical side and history the social, these are only emphases in a common topic, namely, the associated life of men. For this associated life, with its experiments, its ways and means, its achievements and failures, does not go on in the sky nor yet in a vacuum. It takes place on earth.[17]

Because the associated life of human beings takes place on earth, Dewey included natural history with geography and history. I have already argued strongly (Chapter 6) that natural history should be part of the curriculum, not only because it provides a foundation for environmental studies but also because love of place contributes so much to human happiness.

History, geography, and natural history offer the promise of self-understanding on the level of groups and whole societies, and self-understanding is crucial to both citizenship and personal happiness. Notice, however, that I would contradict myself if I now said that we have justified history and geography in the curriculum. We've done no such thing. We have justified a careful search through history and geography for topics that may enhance "the associated life of men." Simply being *about* the associated life of men is not sufficient justification for including a topic in the curriculum. Finding the best topics is a huge and fascinating task. Undertaking it means, at least, that when we study the physical features of a place, we look also at the people and other living creatures who call it home, and we study something of what happened there in the past and what might happen in the future to make life better.[18]

I want to say more about map study, lest readers think I regard it as unimportant. Social studies educators must discuss and decide upon exactly what skills and information are necessary. But it has been my experience that children love work with maps. Their eyes shine as they pore over maps. Work with maps is one of those wonderful activities that leads outward into all sorts of other interesting topics – cultural customs, animal and plant life, exploration, travel, climate, mystery, weird words and exotic places, archaeology, catastrophe. Its potential richness is one crucial test of an important subject. Moreover, much of what is learned in connection with maps can be, and should be, learned informally. Maps should be available in every classroom, and students should be encouraged to have fun with them.

As we sort through volumes of material, we sort content into that which must be required, that which provides opportunities for student choice, and that which will be offered freely as gifts to enrich thought and discussion. In the latter two categories, we *invite* student participation; we do not coerce.[19] Then our pedagogical choices must be checked against both aims and the categories of content just mentioned. If the aim governing the choice of a particular topic is to introduce students to something they may enjoy – even find lifelong delight in it – then we do not coerce, make specific assignments, and give tests on it.

Although I have only alluded to it in this volume (Chapters 8 and 11), it would not be farfetched to construct an argument relating world peace to happiness. That would give us another criterion through which to select material from the enormous store of history and geography. It is beyond the scope of this book to engage in a thorough examination of curriculum guided by thoughtful aims-talk, but I hope I have made clear how we might proceed.

In addition to selecting curriculum and pedagogical methods, we should reflect on all the routines of classroom life from the perspective of our stated aims. Should we use seating charts? Why? Must students always raise their hands to speak? Should conscientious teachers assign regular homework? Why? Why? Why?

It seems obvious that we do not need to insist on hand-raising unless several people try to speak at one time. Then we can say, "Whoa! This is exciting, but let's go one at a time." By operating this way, we show that rules are meant to facilitate human interactions. They are not inviolable ends in themselves. Invoking rules when they are needed and explaining why they are needed is part of educating students about socialization. It is not appropriate in a democratic society to simply socialize students, although a good deal of socialization will inevitably occur. Whenever an opportunity arises, we should help students to reflect on and evaluate the process of socialization.

Consider another example. In many schools today, teachers are forced to give homework. A school rule that prescribes a certain amount of homework per night (or week for that matter) is part of the mindlessness decried by Silberman and other critics of schooling in the 1960s and early 1970s.[20] What aim is guiding educators who insist on hefty doses of homework? Surely the aim is not present happiness. Could it be the achievement of future happiness through increased competence? That seems unlikely. Alfie Kohn remarks:

> For some people, the premise here seems to be that we can relax (about the quality of our schools) if kids don't have time to relax. If they have lots of work to do every night, never mind what it is, then they must be learning. With this premise, it seems perfectly acceptable to assign substantial amounts of homework even to first graders. "This is what's demanded to stay competitive in a global market," said one New Jersey principal with a shrug.[21]

This is frightening nonsense. There is little evidence that homework actually increases learning, and for elementary schoolchildren, homework may even impede learning by destroying interest and curiosity. Further, as we have already seen, the connection between a society's test scores and its economic success is tenuous at best. Schools that force homework on young children may be socializing them to obey and to work hard even at tasks they hate, but it is unlikely that they are encouraging learning.

Is there, then, no place for homework? Thoughtful educators deeply involved in aims-talk will almost certainly find defensible uses for homework. Most high school mathematics teachers assign homework because the time in class is too short for the amount of practice required. However, the homework should be clearly connected to goals for learning, and there should be no penalty for getting things wrong. I regularly told students, "This is your opportunity to make mistakes and learn from them," and I never graded homework. When I tell this to preservice teachers today, someone always asks, "Why would students do the homework if it isn't graded?" The answer is that, in fact, students will do homework if they are convinced that it is connected to goals they have chosen (or at least assented to) and the work assigned is reasonable. It is insulting to assume that students will work only for grades. Worse, the assumption and practices resting on it may induce the very condition mistakenly assumed. Students who might have been motivated naturally are now motivated only by grades.

As a math teacher, I believed that homework should be an opportunity to learn – to practice, but also to try things out. There is no expectation that students would (or should) get everything right, and it is often fun to hear the variety of solutions attempted. It is hypocritical to talk about building learning communities and then attach points and grades to everything students do. Moreover, the practice of grading homework suggests that students have already learned the material, and their performance serves as proof that they have been listening. What sort of aim would support such an attitude?

The practice of grading everything and spelling out exactly how many points one can obtain on every requirement is now widespread at the college and university level. I've been disappointed again and again to find such statements on the syllabi of professors who should know better. To give 10 percent or 20 percent for attendance or for participation is bribery. Why should anyone get points for doing something that should be exciting or at least enjoyable?

Another practice to be wary of at the K-12 level is that of coercively involving parents in homework. Some years ago, we made the opposite mistake and shut parents out of the schooling process, insisting that *as experts* teachers should be in charge of children's learning. That was infuriating, and many parents rightly objected. But forcing parents to participate by signing papers to confirm their involvement may do more harm than good. I've looked at some assignments given to second graders and, despite my years of professional experience, I'm often hard put to figure out what the teacher wants. I can well imagine these exercises adding to the tensions of home life instead of bringing parents and children together. If our aim is to increase the happiness latent in parent–child relations, this is probably not the best way to do it. (Picture what happens when, in addition to the original struggle, the assignment gets a poor grade!)

What I am arguing for is an ongoing, serious examination of everything we do in schools. Is the aim worthwhile? Are the goals logically derived from defensible aims? Are our pedagogical methods likely to promote the goals and aims? How do our routines stack up under this sort of evaluation?

It is worthwhile, if discouraging, to reread Silberman's account of what went on the 1960s. There was professional talk of teaching disciplinary structures and probing deeply into a few important concepts:

> But if one looks at what actually goes on in the classroom – the kinds of texts students read and the kind of homework they are assigned, as well as the nature of classroom discussion and the kinds of tests teachers give – he will discover that the great bulk of students' time is still devoted to detail, most of it trivial, much of it factually incorrect, and almost all of it unrelated to any concept, structure, cognitive strategy, or indeed anything other than the lesson plan. It is rare to find anyone – teacher, principal, supervisor, or superintendent – who has asked why he is teaching what he is teaching.[22]

Today, educators cut short the thinking process by answering the "why" question with "Because it's on the standard test." If we ask why "it" is on the test, we are referred to the experts who constructed the test; aims-talk ends in authority.

We may be slipping backward after decades of real reform in schooling. During the early twentieth century, schools were so unfriendly that many children preferred exhausting hours in a sweatshop to the classroom.[23] Gradually, schools have become more humane places. In a recent article (and in Chapter 4), I noted some progress in humanizing schools:

> Many states have abandoned corporal punishment in schools and, even in states that allow it, many districts forbid it. We try harder to keep children in school. We are ashamed of past patterns of racial segregation and are still struggling to overcome its effects. Young women are being encouraged in math and science. Education is being provided for youngsters once labeled "trainable" or not schooled at all. The U.S. sends more students to higher education than any nation in history. Hungry children are being fed breakfast and lunch. In many districts, pre-school education is being provided for three and four year olds. The notion that some kids are slated from the start for manual labor and others for professional work has been rejected. People have even flirted with the idea that education should promote something called "self-actualization."[24]

These are improvements of which we can proud. However, the current standards movement may drive more students away from school, and there are signs that the best classroom practices may be eroding.[25] With recent demands that all students – even those in special education – take the standard tests, we may weaken the progress we've made in the education of children with disabilities. Moreover, some of the improvements are tainted by failure to think through carefully what we are doing. We give children food but make it clear that we are *giving* it to people who cannot afford it. We encourage young women to study math and science but make it seem as though their self-worth depends on their success in these subjects. We sporadically initiate plans for integration but often convey the message that black children cannot do well unless they are schooled with white children. Although we have come far in reducing (but certainly not eliminating) the cruelty of teachers toward students, we have allowed student-to-student cruelty to grow to such an extent that it threatens the well-being of many children. Thus, while we should recognize and applaud significant efforts to humanize our schools, we should persist in analyzing the present situation and evaluating our responses.

Well-intended means do not always match the ends for which they were chosen.

Critics of today's schools often complain that the schools have lost their "academic purpose."[26] However, it is that academic purpose, pursued relentlessly and sometimes cruelly, that drove large numbers of young people out of the schools in an earlier, "more rigorous" era. One purpose of schooling should be to develop the intellect, but that does not mean to stuff the heads of children with material arbitrarily chosen by experts and designed to rank and sort them. It means rather to guide students toward the intelligent use of their intellectual capacities in both personal and public life. It means equipping them with the power to evaluate and direct change, to resist harmful changes and promote those that contribute to human flourishing. Almost any subject matter of genuine interest to students, well taught, can contribute to this end.

Life in the late twentieth century changed dramatically. We can deplore the fact that women are now rarely full-time homemakers whose main duty is the care and guidance of children or we can celebrate the freedom of women to choose their own careers. If we choose to celebrate, we can still recognize the problems that have arisen for children. Children need secure, loving relationships with adult caregivers. They need, and should be able to expect, adult intervention when someone threatens to harm them or when they threaten to harm others. They deserve an enthusiastic introduction to their society's most valued culture, and this should be accomplished without coercion.

In short, the school must do much of the work once charged to families. The best schools should resemble the best homes.[27] What should be meant by *best*? All the things discussed in earlier chapters are relevant to that designation. The best homes provide continuity of caring relations, attend to and continuously evaluate both inferred and expressed needs, protect from harm without deliberately inflicting pain, communicate so as to develop common and individual interests, work together cooperatively, promote joy in genuine learning, guide moral and spiritual development (including the development of an uneasy conscience), contribute to the appreciation of the arts and other great cultural achievements, encourage love of place and protection of the natural world, and educate for both self-understanding and group understanding.

The best homes and schools are happy places. The adults in these happy places recognize that one aim of education (and of life itself) is happiness. They also recognize that happiness serves as both means and end. Happy children, growing in their understanding of what happiness is, will seize their educational opportunities with delight, and they will contribute to the happiness of others. Clearly, if children are to be happy in schools, their teachers should also be happy. Too often we forget this obvious connection. Finally, basically happy people who retain an uneasy social conscience will contribute to a happier world.

Notes

Introduction

1. In the chapters that follow, I will sometimes draw on George Orwell's powerful statement that the "abiding" lesson of his early schooling was that he lived in a world in which it was "not possible" to be good. See "Such, Such Were the Joys" in *The Orwell Reader* (New York: Harcourt, Brace, 1956), p. 5. Even so, Orwell admits that his school days were not entirely unhappy.
2. Neill says plainly: "I hold the aim of life is to find happiness, which means to find interest." See A. S. Neill, *Summerhill* (New York: Hart, 1960), p. 24. I would modify this to claim that happiness is *one* aim of life and that it involves more than finding interest.
3. See Dayle M. Bethel, *Makiguchi the Value Creator* (New York: Weatherhill, 1994).
4. Robin Barrow, *Happiness and Schooling* (New York: St. Martin's Press, 1980).
5. See, for example, Alfie Kohn, *The Schools Our Children Deserve* (Boston: Houghton Mifflin, 1999).

Chapter 1. Happiness

1. William James, *The Varieties of Religious Experience* (New York: Modern Library, 1929), p. 77.
2. See Martha Nussbaum, *The Fragility of Goodness* (Cambridge: Cambridge University Press, 1986); also Amelie Rorty, ed., *Essays on Aristotle's Ethics* (Berkeley: University of California Press, 1980). For a comprehensive study of Greek thought on morality and happiness, see Julia Annas, *The Morality of Happiness* (New York: Oxford University Press, 1993).

263

3. Use of the masculine pronoun here reflects the Greek belief that the highest forms of reason belong to men, not women.

4. For more on this, see the essays in Rorty, *Essays on Aristotle's Ethics*. See also Annas, *Morality of Happiness*.

5. See, for example, his explicit comments in *Democracy and Education* (New York: Macmillan, 1916) and *The Quest for Certainty* (New York: G. P. Putnam's Sons, 1929).

6. Dewey, *Democracy and Education*, p. 256.

7. G. H. Hardy, "A Mathematician's Apology," in *The World of Mathematics*, vol. 4, ed. James R. Newman (New York: Simon & Schuster, 1956), p. 2038. See also Newman's comments introducing Hardy's essay, pp. 2024–2026.

8. "Pleasures of the mind" are defined differently in social science. There the expression refers to ways in which a cast of mind or recollection of past happy associations may make an otherwise neutral occasion pleasurable. See Michael Kubovy, "On the Pleasures of the Mind," in *Well-Being*, ed. Daniel Kahneman, Ed Diener, and Norbert Schwarz (New York: Russell Sage, 1999), pp. 134–154.

9. Sigmund Freud, *The Future of an Illusion*, in *The Freud Reader*, ed. Peter Gay (New York: W. W. Norton, 1989), pp. 685–722.

10. The problems of quietism have been discussed and actively attacked by religious advocates of the social gospel and liberation theology. John Dewey also expressed concern about the attitude of quietism. See Dewey, *A Common Faith* (New Haven, CT: Yale University Press, 1934). A formal concept of quietism was advanced in the seventeenth century by the Spanish priest Miguel de Molinos.

11. See Kahneman, Diener, and Schwarz, eds., *Well-Being*.

12. C. S. Lewis, *Surprised by Joy* (New York: Harcourt Brace Jovanovich, 1955).

13. James, *Varieties of Religious Experience*, p. 47.

14. Saint Augustine, *On Free Choice of the Will*, trans. Anna S. Benjamin and L. H. Hackstaff (New York: Macmillan, 1964).

15. See Abraham H. Maslow, *The Farther Reaches of Human Nature* (New York: Viking Press, 1971).

16. Martin Gardner, *The Whys of a Philosophical Scrivener* (New York: Quill, 1983), p. 331.

17. Paul Tillich, *The Courage to Be* (New Haven, CT: Yale University Press, 1952), p. 47.

18. John Stuart Mill, *On Liberty* and *Utilitarianism* (New York: Bantam Books, 1993), p. 144.

19. Mill, *Utilitarianism*, p. 145.

20. David Hume, *An Enquiry Concerning the Principles of Morals* (Indianapolis: Hackett, 1983), p. 43.

21. See Noddings, *Caring: A Feminine Approach to Ethics and Moral Education* (Berkeley: University of California Press, 1984; 2nd ed., 2003); also Noddings, *Starting at Home: Caring and Social Policy* (Berkeley: University of California Press, 2002).

22. Hume, *Enquiry Concerning Principles of Morals*, pp. 73–74.

23. For a comprehensive summary of research on SWB, see Kahneman, Diener, and Schwarz, *Well-Being*.

24. Robert E. Lane, *The Loss of Happiness in Market Democracies* (New Haven, CT: Yale University Press, 2000), p. 16.

25. Ibid.

26. Ibid., p. 45.

27. Companionship is also identified as a major contributor to happiness by David G. Myers, *The Pursuit of Happiness* (New York: Avon, 1992). See also Myers, *The American Paradox: Spiritual Hunger in an Age of Plenty* (New Haven, CT: Yale University Press, 2000).

28. The quotation appears in Jeffrey Meyers, *Orwell: Wintry Conscience of a Generation* (New York: W. W. Norton, 2000), p. 212.

29. See Ed Diener and Richard E. Lucas, "Personality and Subjective Well-Being," in *Well-Being*, ed. Kahneman, Diener, and Schwarz, pp. 213–229.

30. James, *Varieties of Religious Experience*, p. 87.

31. Ibid., p. 88.

32. Ibid.

33. See again Lane, *The Loss of Happiness* and Myers, *Pursuit of Happiness*.

34. Niall Williams, *As It Is in Heaven* (London: Picador, 1999), pp. 144–145.

35. See the account in Henri Poincaré, "Mathematical Creation," in *The World of Mathematics*, vol. 4, ed. Newman, pp. 2041–2050; also Jacques Hadamard, *The Psychology of Invention in the Mathematical Field* (New York: Dover, 1954); for uses in education, see Nel Noddings and Paul Shore, *Awakening the Inner Eye: Intuition in Education* (New York: Teachers College Press, 1984).

36. See David F. Musto, "Opium, Cocaine, and Marijuana in American History," in *Drugs*, ed. Jeffrey A. Schaler (Amherst, NY: Prometheus Books, 1998), pp. 17–30.

37. Paulo Freire, *Pedagogy of the Oppressed*, trans. Myra Bergman Ramos (New York: Herder & Herder, 1970), p. 111.

38. Theodore Zeldin, *An Intimate History of Humanity* (New York: HarperCollins, 1994), p. 393.

39. Gaston Bachelard, *The Poetics of Space*, trans. Maria Jolas (New York: Orion Press, 1964), p. 4.
40. Ibid., p. 6.
41. Ibid., p. 14.
42. John Elder, *Reading the Mountains of Home* (Cambridge, MA: Harvard University Press, 1998).
43. Edward Casey, *Getting Back into Place* (Bloomington: Indiana University Press, 1993).
44. Bachelard, *Poetics of Space*, p. xxix.
45. Ibid., p. xix.
46. Walt Whitman, "A Song for Occupations," *Poetry and Prose* (New York: Library of America, 1982).
47. See John Mc Phee, *The Pine Barrens* (New York: Farrar, Straus and Giroux, 1968).
48. Hume, *Enquiry Concerning the Principles of Morals*, p. 72.
49. Quoted in Gardner, *Whys of a Philosophical Scrivener*, p. unnumbered.

Chapter 2. Suffering and Unhappiness

1. Viktor E. Frankl, *The Doctor and the Soul* (New York: Vintage Books, 1973), p. 111.
2. See George Orwell, *Nineteen Eighty-Four* (New York: Harcourt, Brace and World, 1949).
3. Frankl, *Doctor and the Soul*, p. xviii.
4. See, for example, B. F. Skinner, *Beyond Freedom and Dignity* (New York: Vintage Books, 1972). Although I believe behaviorists went too far in the other direction (no real freedom), their emphasis on the effects of environment provide a valuable corrective to Frankl's assumption that we are essentially free.
5. See my *Starting at Home: Caring and Social Policy* (Berkeley: University of California Press, 2002).
6. Quoted in Frankl, *Doctor and the Soul*, p. 112.
7. Quoted in William James, *The Varieties of Religious Experience* (New York: Modern Library, 1929), p. 135.
8. Kuno Francke, *A History of German Literature as Determined by Social Forces* (New York: Henry Holt, 1916), p. 531.
9. James, *Varieties of Religious Experience*, p. 137.
10. Ibid.
11. Ibid., p. 160.
12. Friedrich Nietzsche, *The Will to Power*, trans. Walter Kaufmann and R. J. Hollingdale (New York: Vintage Books, 1968), p. 481.

13. Ibid., p. 482.
14. Ibid., p. 483.
15. Among others who have taken this position, two powerful examples are Bertrand Russell and Clarence Darrow.
16. For strong arguments against capital punishment, see Russell Baker, "Cruel and Unusual," *New York Review of Books*, Jan. 20, 2000; Albert Camus, "Reflections on the Guillotine," in *Resistance, Rebellion, and Death* (New York: Alfred A. Knopf, 1969); William McFeely, *Proximity to Death* (New York: W. W. Norton, 1999); George Orwell, *The Orwell Reader* (New York: Harcourt, Brace, 1956); Helen Prejean, *Dead Man Walking* (New York: Vintage Books, 1996).
17. See John Braithwaite and Philip Pettit, *Not Just Deserts: A Republican Theory of Criminal Justice* (Oxford: Clarendon Press, 1990).
18. See James Gilligan, *Violence* (New York: G. P. Putnam's Sons, 1996).
19. See Bernard Williams, *Shame and Necessity* (Berkeley: University of California Press, 1993).
20. See Harold Kushner, *When Bad Things Happen to Good People* (New York: Schocken Books, 1981).
21. Paul Ricoeur, *The Symbolism of Evil* (Boston: Beacon Press, 1969), p. 239.
22. See Anthony Cunningham, *The Heart of the Matter* (Berkeley: University of California Press, 2001).
23. Ibid.
24. Ibid.
25. See William Styron, *Sophie's Choice* (New York: Vintage Books, 1992).
26. The expression is used by Camus in describing capital punishment, "Reflections on the Guillotine," p. 234.
27. Bertrand Russell, for example, says something very like this in *Why I Am Not a Christian* (New York: Simon & Schuster, 1957).
28. See David Ray Griffin, *Evil Revisited* (Albany: State University of New York Press, 1991); John Hick, *Evil and the God of Love* (New York: Macmillan, 1966); Mark Larrimore, ed., *The Problem of Evil* (Oxford: Blackwell, 2001); Nel Noddings, *Women and Evil* (Berkeley: University of California Press, 1989); and Ricoeur, *Symbolism of Evil*.
29. C. S. Lewis, *A Grief Observed* (Toronto: Bantam Books, 1976), p. 50.
30. On the possibility of God's moral fallibility, see Carl Jung, *Answer to Job*, trans. R. F. C. Hull (Princeton, NJ: Princeton University Press, 1973).
31. See Lewis, *The Problem of Pain* (New York: Macmillan, 1962).
32. See Hick, *Evil and the God of Love*.

33. Fyodor Dostoevsky, *The Brothers Karamazov*, trans. Constance Garnett (New York: Modern Library, n.d.). Ivan's argument is reprinted in Larrimore, *The Problem of Evil*, pp. 277–282.

34. For an account of these reasons, see James Turner, *Without God, Without Creed* (Baltimore: Johns Hopkins University Press, 1985); also Nel Noddings, *Educating for Intelligent Belief or Unbelief* (New York: Teachers College Press, 1993).

35. See Paul Tillich, *The Courage to Be* (New Haven, CT: Yale University Press, 1952).

36. For this argument, see David G. Myers, *The American Paradox: Spiritual Hunger in an Age of Plenty* (New Haven, CT: Yale University Press, 2000).

37. See Alan Lightman, *The Diagnosis* (New York: Pantheon Books, 2000).

38. Myers, *American Paradox*, p. 294.

39. Jean Baudrillard, *Fatal Strategies*, trans. Philip Beitchman and W. G. J. Niesluchowski, ed. Jim Fleming (New York: Semiotext(e), 1990).

40. Ibid., p. 156.

41. Ibid., p. 184.

Chapter 3. Needs and Wants

1. The concept of desire is technically important in the analysis of moral motivation, but I am using it here in the everyday sense with which we are all familiar.

2. David Braybrooke, *Meeting Needs* (Princeton, NJ: Princeton University Press, 1987).

3. See Nancy Fraser, *Unruly Practices: Power, Discourse, and Gender in Contemporary Social Theory* (Minneapolis: University of Minnesota Press, 1989).

4. Alison Jaggar, *Feminist Politics and Human Nature* (Totowa, NJ: Rowman & Allanheld, 1983), p. 42.

5. See my argument in *Starting at Home: Caring and Social Policy* (Berkeley: University of California Press, 2002).

6. See Edward O. Wilson, *Biophilia* (Cambridge, MA: Harvard University Press, 1984).

7. Noddings, *Starting at Home*, p. 58.

8. Isaiah Berlin, *Four Essays on Liberty* (Oxford: Oxford University Press, 1969), p. 168.

9. The number of such books has increased greatly with the growth of environmental movements, and almost every discipline now contributes to thought on conservation and the human–nature connection.

10. Berlin, *Four Essays*, pp. 135–136.
11. Joseph A. Schumpeter, *Capitalism, Socialism, and Democracy* (London: Routledge, 1996), p. 392. Orig. 1943.
12. Ibid., p. 395.
13. See Bob Brecher, *Getting What You Want?* (London: Routledge, 1998).
14. See Berlin, *Four Essays*.
15. It seems to me that Brecher, for one, goes too far on this. Few liberal philosophers actually equate autonomy with making choices, especially not with unreflective choices.
16. The term *wanting thing* is applied by Brecher to Hobbes's description of human beings as both determined and moved by wants.
17. See John Stuart Mill, *On Liberty* and *Utilitarianism* (New York: Bantam Books, 1993/1859 and 1871).
18. Martin Buber, "Education," in Buber, *Between Man and Man* (New York: Macmillan, 1965), p. 90.
19. See Alice Miller, *For Your Own Good*, trans. Hildegarde Hannun and Hunter Hannun (New York: Farrar, Straus and Giroux, 1983).
20. See Sigmund Freud, *Civilization and Its Discontents* in *The Freud Reader*, ed. Peter Gay (New York: W. W. Norton, 1989), pp. 722–772.
21. Ibid., p. 763.
22. John Dewey, *Human Nature and Conduct* (New York: Modern Library, 1930), p. 105.
23. Freud, "Formulations on the Two Principles of Mental Functioning," in *Freud Reader*, p. 304.
24. Dewey, *Democracy and Education* (New York: Macmillan, 1916), p. 52, quoting Emerson.
25. John Steinbeck, *The Winter of Our Discontent* (New York: Viking Press, 1961), p. 54.
26. Betty Friedan, *The Feminine Mystique* (New York: W. W. Norton, 1963).
27. See Kent C. Berridge, "Pleasure, Pain, Desire, and Dread: Hidden Core Processes of Emotion," in *Well-Being*, ed. Daniel Kahneman, Ed Diener, and Norbert Schwarz (New York: Russell Sage, 1999), pp. 525–557.

Chapter 4. The Aims of Education

1. William Schubert argues, rightly I think, that there is no settled hierarchy of educational purposes, but he notes that aims, goals, and objectives are widely thought to represent a sequence of

decreasing generality. See Schubert, *Curriculum: Perspective, Paradigm, and Possibility* (New York: Macmillan, 1986).

2. See Schubert, pp. 190–191, on this.

3. See National Education Association, *Cardinal Principles of Secondary Education* (Washington, DC: U.S. Government Printing Office, 1918).

4. Herbert M. Kliebard, *The Struggle for the American Curriculum* (New York: Routledge, 1995), p. 98.

5. See Franklin Bobbitt, *How to Make a Curriculum* (Boston: Houghton Mifflin, 1924).

6. For an excellent analysis of the problems involved in establishing objectives, see Elliot W. Eisner, *The Educational Imagination* (New York: Macmillan, 1979).

7. See Plato, *The Republic*, trans. B. Jowett (Roslyn, NY: Walter Black, 1942), Book II.

8. John Dewey, *Democracy and Education* (New York: Macmillan, 1944/1916), p. 90.

9. Ibid.

10. See *The Republic*, Book III.

11. For an introduction to *Emile*, see William Boyd, ed., *The Emile of Jean Jacques Rousseau: Selections* (New York: Teachers College Press, 1962).

12. For informative analyses of Rousseau's recommendations for Sophie's education, see Jane Roland Martin, *Reclaiming a Conversation* (New Haven, CT: Yale University Press, 1985); also Susan Moller Okin, *Women in Western Political Thought* (Princeton, NJ: Princeton University Press, 1979).

13. Dewey, *Democracy and Education*, p. 100.

14. Alfred North Whitehead, *The Aims of Education* (New York: Free Press, 1967/1929), p. 1.

15. Ibid., pp. 6–7.

16. See National Commission on Excellence in Education, *A Nation at Risk* (Washington, DC: U.S. Government Printing Office, 1983).

17. Ibid., p. 5.

18. See David Berliner and Bruce Biddle, *The Manufactured Crisis: Myths, Fraud, and the Attack on America's Public Schools* (New York: Perseus, 1996); also Gerald Bracey, *Setting the Record Straight: Responses to Misconceptions about Public Education in the United States* (Alexandria, VA: Association for Supervision and Curriculum Development, 1997).

19. Dewey, *The School and Society* (Chicago: University of Chicago Press, 1900), p. 3.

20. See Jeannie Oakes, *Multiplying Inequalities: The Effects of Race, Social Class, and Tracking on Opportunities to Learn Mathematics and Science* (Santa Monica, CA: Rand, 1990); also Oakes, *Keeping Track: How Schools Structure Inequality* (New Haven, CT: Yale University Press, 1995). But for an argument on both the positive and negative effects of tracking, see James E. Rosenbaum, "Track Misperceptions and Frustrated College Plans: An Analysis of the Effects of Tracks and Track Perceptions in the National Longitudinal Survey," *Sociology of Education* 53, 1980: 74–88.

21. See National Council of Teachers of Mathematics, *Principles and Standards for School Mathematics*, Discussion draft (Reston, VA: NCTM, 1998).

22. Ibid., p. 15.

23. Ibid., p. 23.

24. Ibid.

25. For a comprehensive review of the problems involved in meeting this goal, see James Paul, Michael Churton, Hilda Rosselli-Kostoryz, William Morse, Kofi Marfo, Carolyn Lavely, and Daphne Thomas, eds., *Foundations of Special Education* (Pacific Grove, CA: Brooks/Cole, 1997); also Paul, Churton, Morse, Albert Duchnowski, Betty Epanchin, Pamela Osnes, and R. Lee Smith, eds., *Special Education Practice* (Pacific Grove, CA: Brooks/Cole, 1997).

26. For powerful accounts of how difficult it can be for children to escape the label, see Theresa A. Thorkildsen and John G. Nicholls, *Motivation and the Struggle to Learn* (Boston: Allyn & Bacon, 2002).

27. This is a familiar technique used in describing utopias. Two well-known examples are Edward Bellamy, *Looking Backward* (New York: New American Library, 1960/1888), and Samuel Butler, *Erewhon* (London: Penguin, 1985/1872).

Chapter 5. Making a Home

1. Wallace Stegner, *Angle of Repose* (New York: Penguin Books, 1971), pp. 158–159.

2. Ibid., p. 159.

3. On the distinction between residing and wandering, see Edward S. Casey, *Getting Back Into Place* (Bloomington: Indiana University Press, 1993); also Erazim Kohak, "Of Dwelling and Wayfaring: A Quest for Metaphors," in *The Longing for Home*, ed. Leroy S. Rouner (Notre Dame, IN: University of Notre Dame Press, 1996), pp. 30–46; and see Stegner, *Angle of Repose*.

4. Robert Coates, *A Street Is Not a Home* (Buffalo, NY: Prometheus, 1990).
5. See Zoe Oldenbourg, *The Crusades*, trans. Anne Carter (New York: Pantheon Books, 1966); see also Oldenbourg's historical novels on the same period.
6. Larry R. Ford, *The Spaces between Buildings* (Baltimore: Johns Hopkins University Press, 2000), p. 200.
7. See Casey, *Getting Back Into Place*.
8. Plants in such containers are a favorite subject for many photographers. For one charming example, see Linda Garland Page and Eliot Wigginton, eds., *Aunt Arie, A Foxfire Portrait* (New York: E. P. Dutton, 1983).
9. See Nel Noddings, *Starting at Home: Caring and Social Policy* (Berkeley: University of California Press, 2002).
10. Hermann Hesse, *Steppenwolf* (New York: Holt, Rinehart and Winston, 1963), p. 52.
11. See John Kenneth Galbraith, *The Culture of Contentment* (Boston: Houghton Mifflin, 1992).
12. Hesse, *Steppenwolf*, pp. 77–78.
13. Marcel Proust, *Remembrance of Things Past*, Vol. 1, *Swann's Way*, trans. C. K. Scott Moncrieff and Terence Kilmartin (New York: Random House, 1981), pp. 48–51.
14. For one prominent example, see William Pinar, *Autobiography, Politics, and Sexuality* (New York: Peter Lang, 1994).
15. See, for example, Carollyne Sinclaire, *Looking for Home* (Albany: State University of New York Press, 1994).
16. For an analysis of the complexities involved in this work, see Elizabeth Ellsworth, "Why Doesn't This Feel Empowering? Working Through the Repressive Myth of Critical Pedagogy," *Harvard Educational Review* 59(3), 1989: 297–324.
17. See David McCullough, *John Adams* (New York: Simon & Schuster, 2001).
18. See Page and Wigginton, *Aunt Arie*.
19. See Robert Graves, *Goodbye to All That* (London: Folio Society, 1981; orig. 1929).
20. For a brief history of comfort, see Witold Rybczynski, *Home: A Short History of an Idea* (New York: Viking Press, 1986).
21. Casey, *Getting Back Into Place*, p. 120.
22. See Rybczynski, *Home*.
23. Ibid.; see also Laura Shapiro, *Perfection Salad* (New York: Modern Library, 2001).

24. Gaston Bachelard, *The Poetics of Space*, trans. Maria Jolas (New York: Orion Press, 1964), p. 14.

25. See again Rybczynski, *Home*, and Shapiro, *Perfection Salad*.

26. For further examples and an account of how routines figure in intuitive modes, see Nel Noddings and Paul Shore, *Awakening the Inner Eye: Intuition in Education* (New York: Teachers College Press, 1984).

27. James R. Newman, ed., *The World of Mathematics* (New York: Simon & Schuster, 1956), p. 2039.

28. *The New Buckeye Cook Book* (Dayton, OH: Home Publishing, 1891), p. 922.

29. Jerome Bruner, *The Process of Education* (Cambridge, MA: Harvard University Press, 1960), p. 52. Also see Bruner for a description of the spiral curriculum.

30. See Franklin Bobbitt, *How to Make a Curriculum* (Boston: Houghton Mifflin, 1924).

31. See the account in Rybczynski, *Home*.

32. Ibid.

33. See Shapiro, *Perfection Salad*; but for an analysis of the pros and cons of expert knowledge in domestic science, see Patricia Thompson, *Bringing Feminism Home* (Charlottetown, Canada: Home Economics Publishing Collective, 1992).

34. See Irma S. Rombauer and Marion Rombauer Becker, *Joy of Cooking* (Indianapolis: Bobbs-Merrill, 1974; orig. 1931).

35. See Claire Joyes, *Monet's Table* (New York: Simon & Schuster, 1989).

36. Ibid., p. 54.

37. Theodore Zeldin, *An Intimate History of Humanity* (New York: HarperCollins, 1994), p. 437.

38. Ibid., p. 438.

39. Ibid., p. 439.

40. See Bachelard, *Poetics of Space*.

Chapter 6. **Places and Nature**

1. David McCullough, *John Adams* (New York: Simon & Schuster, 2001), p. 31.

2. Ibid., p. 383.

3. Pearl S. Buck, *The Exile* (New York: Triangle, 1936).

4. Wallace Stegner, *Angle of Repose* (New York: Penguin Books, 1971), p. 274.

5. Ibid., p. 277.

6. Brad Leithauser, *"The Selected Poetry of Robinson Jeffers,"* New York *Times Book Review*, Sunday, July 22, 2001, p. 14.

7. Gaston Bachelard, *The Poetics of Space*, trans. Maria Jolas (New York: Orion Press, 1964), p. 93.

8. Ibid., p. 91.

9. Ibid., p. xxix.

10. Ibid., p. xix.

11. See Alfie Kohn, *The Schools Our Children Deserve* (Boston: Houghton Mifflin, 1999).

12. See David Labaree, *How to Succeed in School without Really Learning: The Credentials Race in American Education* (New Haven, CT: Yale University Press, 1997).

13. See Peter Kahn, *The Human Relationship with Nature* (Cambridge, MA: MIT Press, 1999); also Edward O. Wilson, *Biophilia* (Cambridge, MA: Harvard University Press, 1984).

14. See Kahn, *Human Relationship*, for pros and cons on this issue.

15. Alfred North Whitehead, *The Aims of Education* (New York: Free Press, 1967/1929), p. 32.

16. See David Hawkins, "How to Plan for Spontaneity," in *The Open Classroom Reader*, ed. Charles E. Silberman (New York: Vintage Books, 1973), pp. 486–503; also Kohn, *Schools Our Children Deserve*; Charles E. Silberman, *Crisis in the Classroom* (New York: Random House, 1970); Deborah Meier, *The Power of Their Ideas* (Boston: Beacon Press, 1995); and Frances Lothrop Hawkins, *Journey with Children* (Niwot, CO: University Press of Colorado, 1997).

17. Albert Schweitzer, *Out of My Life and Thought*, trans. C. T. Campion (New York: Henry Holt, 1933), p. 272.

18. Robert Paul Smith, *"Where Did You Go?" "Out." "What Did You Do?" "Nothing"* (New York: W. W. Norton, 1957), p. 23.

19. See Gary Paul Nabhan and Stephen Trimble, *The Geography of Childhood: Why Children Need Wild Places* (Boston: Beacon Press, 1994).

20. Rumer Godden, *An Episode of Sparrows* (New York: Viking Press, 1955), p. 55.

21. See Philip W. Jackson, *Untaught Lessons* (New York: Teachers College Press, 1992).

22. William James, *The Varieties of Religious Experience* (New York: Modern Library, 1929/1902), p. 161. See his chapter on the sick soul for many more examples.

23. Wendell Berry, *The Unsettling of America* (San Francisco: Sierra Club, 1977), p. 233.

24. See Michael Pollan, *The Botany of Desire* (New York: Random House, 2001), p. 220.
25. Wendell Berry, *Another Turn of the Crank* (Washington, DC: Counterpoint, 1995), p. xi.
26. See Sara Stein, *Noah's Garden: Restoring the Ecology of Our Own Back Yards* (Boston: Houghton Mifflin, 1993).
27. Adamson, husband of Joy Adamson, who wrote the best-seller *Born Free*, is quoted in Jeffrey Moussaieff Masson and Susan McCarthy, *When Elephants Weep: The Emotional Lives of Animals* (New York: Delacorte Press, 1995), p. xviii.
28. See my *Starting at Home: Caring and Social Policy* (Berkeley: University of California Press, 2002).
29. Older students could read the relevant arguments in Arthur Schopenhauer, *The World as Will and Representation*, trans. E. F. J. Payne (New York: Dover, 1969).
30. Peter Singer, *Animal Liberation*, second edition (New York: New York Review of Books, 1990), p. 6.
31. See Singer, *Animal Liberation*, for horror stories on human treatment of nonhuman animals; also Tom Regan, *The Case for Animal Rights* (Berkeley: University of California Press, 1983).
32. Charles Reich, *The Greening of America* (New York: Random House, 1970), p. 203.
33. Ibid., pp. 342–343.

Chapter 7. **Parenting**

1. See Adrienne Rich, *Of Woman Born* (New York: W. W. Norton, 1976). See also Barbara Ehrenreich and Deirdre English, *Witches, Midwives, and Nurses* (Old Westbury, NY: Feminist Press, 1973).
2. See Lucy Candib, *Medicine and the Family: A Feminist Perspective* (New York: Basic Books, 1995).
3. See Rich, *Of Woman Born*, for a moving account of this story and many more references.
4. Refer to our discussion in Chapter 2. See also Mary Daly, *Beyond God the Father* (Boston: Beacon Press, 1974); Paul Ricoeur, *The Symbolism of Evil* (Boston: Beacon Press, 1969).
5. See John Anthony Phillips, *Eve: The History of an Idea* (San Francisco: Harper & Row, 1984).
6. See, for example, A. N. Wilson, *Against Religion* (London: Chatto & Winders, 1991). Wilson discourages respect for organized religion, urging us to say "boo to a goose." He writes, "The Pope is a very powerful goose. The Ayatollah Khomeini is an even greater goose.

Mrs. Whitehouse is a minor goose. The Reverend Tony Higton and Ian Paisley are noisy little ganders. Boo, boo, boo to them all" (pp. 48–49).

7. See James G. Frazer, *The Golden Bough* (New York: Macmillan, 1951), pp. 415–420.

8. See Geoffrey C. Ward and Ken Burns, *Not for Ourselves Alone: The Story of Elizabeth Cady Stanton and Susan B. Anthony* (New York: Alfred A. Knopf, 1999).

9. See Susan Brownmiller, *Against Our Will* (New York: Simon & Schuster, 1975).

10. See Emilie Buchwald, Pamela R. Fletcher, and Martha Roth, eds., *Transforming a Rape Culture* (Minneapolis: Milkweed Editions, 1993).

11. See my chapter on joy in *Caring: A Feminine Approach to Ethics and Moral Education* (Berkeley: University of California Press, 1984); see also Sara Ruddick, *Maternal Thinking: Towards a Politics of Peace* (Boston: Beacon Press, 1989); Mary O'Brien, *The Politics of Reproduction* (London: Routledge and Kegan Paul, 1981); Joyce Trebilcot and Carolyn Whitbeck, eds., *Mothering: Essays in Feminist Theory* (Totowa, NJ: Rowman & Allenhald, 1984).

12. Madeleine R. Grumet, *Bitter Milk* (Amherst: University of Massachusetts Press, 1988), p. 8.

13. Ibid., p. 11.

14. See Ruddick, *Maternal Thinking*.

15. See my *Starting at Home: Caring and Social Policy* (Berkeley: University of California Press, 2002).

16. See Shulamith Firestone, *The Dialectic of Sex* (New York: Bantam Books, 1972).

17. Firestone, quoted in Rich, *Of Woman Born*, p. 290, n. 30.

18. See my argument (and supporting references) in *Starting at Home*.

19. See Ruddick, *Maternal Thinking*.

20. See Benjamin Spock, *Baby and Child Care* (New York: Pocket Books, 1946); also Spock, *On Parenting* (New York: Pocket Books, 2001).

21. In addition to textbooks, many popular works treat aspects of food production and eating habits. See, for example, *The Cambridge World History of Food*, ed. Kenneth Kiple and Kriemhild Conee Ornelas (Cambridge: Cambridge University Press, 2000); Claire Shaver Haughton, *Green Immigrants* (New York: Harcourt Brace Jovanovich, 1978); Laura Shapiro, *Perfection Salad* (New York: Modern Library, 2001); Reay Tannahill, *Food in History* (New York: Stein and Day, 1973); Theodore Zeldin, *An Intimate History of Humanity*

(New York: HarperCollins, 1994). In addition, of course, there are many cookbooks that provide much more than recipes.

22. See the interesting discussion in Tannahill, *Food in History*.

23. For a fascinating discussion of Johnny Appleseed, see Michael Pollan, *The Botany of Desire* (New York: Random House, 2001).

24. Ibid., p. 21.

25. Ibid., p. 23.

26. Ibid., p. 23.

27. See David McCullough, *John Adams* (New York: Simon & Schuster, 2001), p. 36 and passim.

28. In addition to the works cited by Pollan and Zeldin, see also Carl Kerenyi, *Dionysus: Archetypal Image of Indestructible Life*, trans. Ralph Manheim (Princeton, NJ: Princeton University Press, 1976); David Musto, "Opium, Cocaine, and Marijuana in American History," in *Drugs: Should We Legalize, Decriminalize or Deregulate?* ed. Jeffrey A. Schaler (Amherst, NY: Prometheus Books, 1998), pp. 17–30.

29. See John Dewey, *Experience and Education* (New York: Collier, 1963/Kappa Delta Pi, 1938), p. 36.

30. See Robert Paul Smith, *"Where Did You Go?" "Out." "What Did You Do?" "Nothing"* (New York: W. W. Norton, 1957).

31. For powerful examples of such cases, see Denise Clark Pope, *"Doing School": How We Are Creating a Generation of Stressed Out, Materialistic, and Miseducated Students* (New Haven, CT: Yale University Press, 2001).

32. See an influential series of articles by Diana Baumrind – for example, "Parent Styles and Adolescent Development," in *The Encyclopedia of Adolescence*, ed. R. Lerner, A. C. Peterson, and J. Brooks-Gunn (New York: Garland Press, 1991); also Baumrind, *Child Maltreatment and Optimal Caregiving in Social Contexts* (New York: Garland Press, 1995).

33. See Shirley Brice Heath, *Ways with Words* (Cambridge: Cambridge University Press, 1983).

34. E. D. Hirsch, Jr., *The Schools We Need* (New York: Doubleday, 1996), p. 24. See also Hirsch, *Cultural Literacy: What Every American Needs to Know* (Boston: Houghton Mifflin, 1987).

35. See Philip W. Jackson, *Untaught Lessons* (New York: Teachers College Press, 1992).

Chapter 8. Character and Spirituality

1. See, for example, Thomas Lickona, *Educating for Character* (New York: Bantam Books, 1991); B. Edward McClellan, *Moral Education*

in America (New York: Teachers College Press, 1999); and Alex Molnar, ed., *The Construction of Children's Character* (Chicago: National Society for the Study of Education, 1997).

2. See, for example, Alfie Kohn, "The Trouble with Character Education," in *The Construction of Children's Character*, ed. Molnar, pp. 154–162; also Robert J. Nash, *Answering the "Virtuecrats"* (New York: Teachers College Press, 1997).

3. See Chapter 5, "A Relational Self," in Noddings, *Starting at Home* (Berkeley: University of California Press, 2002).

4. A. S. Neill, *Summerhill* (New York: Hart, 1960), p. 250.

5. See Alice Miller, *For Your Own Good*, trans. Hildegarde Hannun and Hunter Hannun (New York: Farrar, Straus and Giroux, 1983); also Miller, *The Truth Will Set You Free* (New York: Basic Books, 2001).

6. Louis Menand, *The Metaphysical Club* (New York: Farrar, Straus and Giroux, 2001), p. 159.

7. This procedure is very similar to what Martin Hoffman describes as an "induction," but Hoffman does not emphasize the third step – showing a better way. See Hoffman, *Empathy and Moral Development* (Cambridge: Cambridge University Press, 2000).

8. Quoted from a sermon by John Wesley in Sissela Bok, *Lying: Moral Choice in Public and Private Life* (New York: Vintage Books, 1979), p. 34.

9. David Hume, *An Enquiry Concerning the Principles of Morals* (Indianapolis: Hackett, 1983/1751), p. 66.

10. Quoted in Adam Potkay, *The Passion for Happiness: Samuel Johnson and David Hume* (Ithaca, NY: Cornell University Press, 2000), p. 60. Potkay adds, "The only happiness is a shared happiness."

11. Paul Tillich, *The Courage to Be* (New Haven, CT: Yale University Press, 1952), p. 7. This appears in his discussion of Aquinas's analysis.

12. John Dewey also took this position. See Dewey, *Human Nature and Conduct* (New York: Modern Library, 1930).

13. William James, *The Varieties of Religious Experience* (New York: Modern Library, 1929/1902), p. 359.

14. See Jane Roland Martin, *Reclaiming a Conversation* (New Haven, CT: Yale University Press, 1985); also Nel Noddings, *Educating Moral People* (New York: Teachers College Press, 2002).

15. On the role of masculinities in violence, see Jessie Klein and Lynn S. Chancer, "Masculinity Matters: The Omission of Gender from High-Profile School Violence Cases," in *Smoke and Mirrors*, ed. Stephanie Urso Spina (Lanham, MD: Rowman & Littlefield, 2000), pp. 129–162; also James W. Messerschmidt, *Masculinities and Crime* (Lanham, MD: Rowman & Littlefield, 1993).

16. But see some World War I poetry that offers a sharp contrast; for example, Wilfred Owen, "Dulce et Decorum Est," in *Anthem for Doomed Youth*, ed. Lyn Macdonald (London: Folio Society, 2000), p. 200.

17. For an account of women's role in sustaining the military, see Jean Bethke Elshtain, *Women and War* (New York: Basic Books, 1987); for an account of women on both sides of the issue, see Sara Ruddick, *Maternal Thinking: Towards a Politics of Peace* (Boston: Beacon Press, 1989).

18. See Jonathan Glover, *Humanity: A Moral History of the 20th Century* (New Haven, CT: Yale University Press, 2000).

19. See Noddings, *Caring: A Feminine Approach to Ethics and Moral Education* (Berkeley: University of California Press, 1984); also Noddings, *Women and Evil* (Berkeley: University of California Press, 1989); and Noddings, *Educating Moral People* (New York: Teachers College Press, 2002).

20. For a powerful argument on matters that are kept from U.S. citizens, see Donaldo Macedo, *Literacies of Power: What Americans Are Not Allowed to Know* (Boulder, CO: Westview Press, 1994). For instructional purposes, I would like to see Macedo's account balanced with the better side of our society and government.

21. Glover, *Humanity*, p. 414.

22. From Paine's *Age of Reason*, quoted in Michael True, *An Energy Field More Intense Than War* (Syracuse, NY: Syracuse University Press, 1995), p. 14.

23. Ibid., p. 14.

24. See Glover, *Humanity*.

25. See Simon Wiesenthal, *The Sunflower* (New York: Schocken Books, 1976).

26. Brian E. Fogarty, *War, Peace, and the Social Order* (Boulder, CO: Westview Press, 2000), p. 88.

27. In addition to Fogarty, *War, Peace, and the Social Order*, see Herbert C. Kelman and Lee Hamilton, *Crimes of Obedience* (New Haven, CT: Yale University Press, 1989); also Lawrence Le Shan, *The Psychology of War* (Chicago: Noble Press, 1992).

28. Lickona, *Educating for Character*, p. 270.

29. For pedagogical possibilities, see Katherine G. Simon, *Moral Questions in the Classroom* (New Haven, CT: Yale University Press, 2001).

30. A good source for such stories is True, *An Energy Field More Intense Than War*.

31. James Terry White, *Character Lessons in American Biography* (New York: Character Development League, 1909).

32. Quoted from Frances Willard in White, *Character Lessons*, p. 31.

33. Ibid., p. 31.

34. John Knowles, *A Separate Peace* (New York: Macmillan, 1960), p. 46.

35. See Denise Clark Pope, *"Doing School": How We Are Creating a Generation of Stressed Out, Materialistic, and Miseducated Students* (New Haven, CT: Yale University Press, 2001).

36. Martin Buber, *I and Thou*, trans. Walter Kaufman (New York: Charles Scribner's Sons, 1970), p. 57.

37. Jean-Paul Sartre, *Nausea*, trans. Lloyd Alexander (Norfolk, CT: New Directions, 1959/1938), pp. 170–173.

38. James, *The Varieties of Religious Experience*, p. 158.

39. W. G. Sebald, *Austerlitz*, trans. Anthea Bell (New York: Random House, 2001), p. 163.

40. Ibid., p. 93.

41. Ibid., p. 94.

42. Gaston Bachelard, *The Poetics of Space*, trans. Maria Jolas (New York: Orion Press, 1964), p. 67.

43. Carol Ochs, *Women and Spirituality* (Totowa, NJ: Rowman & Allanheld, 1983), p. 6. Her definition is the accepted basic definition. See also Tillich, *Courage to Be*.

44. Ochs, *Women and Spirituality*, p. 13.

45. The expression was used in a letter by John Evelyn to Sir Thomas Browne. Quoted in Edward S. Casey, *Getting Back into Place* (Bloomington: Indiana University Press, 1993), p. 153.

46. This is the famous last line in *Candide*. See *The Portable Voltaire*, ed. Ben Ray Redman (New York: Penguin Books, 1977).

47. From E. B. White's introduction to Katherine S. White, *Onward and Upward in the Garden* (New York: Farrar, Straus and Giroux, 1979), p. xix.

48. Buber, *I and Thou*, p. 62.

49. Anne Morrow Lindbergh, *Gift from the Sea* (New York: Random House, 1955), p. 48.

50. Ibid., p. 52.

51. Ibid., p. 53.

52. Ibid., p. 105.

53. Hannah Arendt, *The Human Condition* (Chicago: University of Chicago Press, 1958), p. 52.

54. See the account in Samuel Oliner and Pearl M. Oliner, *The Altruistic Personality: Rescuers of Jews in Nazi Europe* (New York: Free Press, 1988).

55. Casey, *Getting Back into Place*, p. 19.

Chapter 9. Interpersonal Growth

1. See David G. Myers, *The Pursuit of Happiness* (New York: Avon, 1992); see also David Hume, *An Enquiry Concerning the Principles of Morals* (Indianapolis: Hackett, 1983/1751).

2. See again Myers, *The Pursuit of Happiness;* also Michael Argyle, "Causes and Correlates of Happiness," in *Well-Being*, ed. Daniel Kahneman, Ed Diener, and Norbert Schwarz (New York: Russell Sage Foundation, 1999), pp. 353–373.

3. Hume, *Enquiry Concerning Morals*, p. 71.

4. Myers, *Pursuit of Happiness*, p. 107.

5. Hume, *Enquiry Concerning Morals*, p. 62.

6. Ibid., p. 61.

7. See Ed Diener and Richard E. Lucas, "Personality and Subjective Well-Being," in *Well-Being*, ed. Kahneman, Diener, and Schwarz, pp. 213–229.

8. See E. Diener and M. Diener, "Cross-Cultural Correlates of Life Satisfaction and Self-Esteem," *Journal of Personality and Social Psychology* 68, 1995: 653–663.

9. John Rawls, *A Theory of Justice* (Cambridge, MA: Harvard University Press, 1971), p. 440.

10. Ibid., p. 440.

11. Toni Morrison, *The Bluest Eye* (New York: Plume, 1994/1970), p. 205.

12. Hume, *Enquiry Concerning Morals*, p. 55.

13. See Diener and Lucas, "Personality and Subjective Well-Being."

14. Many recent books help with this task. See, for example: Ruth Charney, *Teaching Children to Care* (Greenfield, MA: Northeast Foundation for Children, 1992); Jonathan Cohen, ed., *Educating Minds and Hearts* (New York: Teachers College Press, 1999); John Nicholls and Theresa Thorkildsen, eds., *"Reasons for Learning"* (New York: Teachers College Press, 1995).

15. Jessie Klein and Lynn S. Chancer, "Masculinity Matters: The Omission of Gender from High-Profile School Violence Cases," in *Smoke and Mirrors*, ed. Stephanie Urso Spina (Lanham, MD: Rowman & Littlefield, 2000), p. 155. For further discussion of this issue, see James W. Messerschmidt, *Masculinities and Crime* (Lanham, MD: Rowman & Littlefield, 1993).

16. On the struggle to get teachers to listen to and discuss problems important to teenagers, see Gregory Michie, *Holler If You Hear Me* (New York: Teachers College Press, 1999).

17. See, again, Klein and Chancer, "Masculinity Matters."

18. See David Flinders and Nel Noddings, *Multiyear Teaching: The Case for Continuity* (Bloomington, IN: Phi Delta Kappa, 2001).

19. For many good suggestions, see John H. Lounsbury and Gordon Vars, *A Curriculum for the Middle School Years* (New York: Harper & Row, 1978).

20. See Theodore Sizer, *Horace's Compromise: The Dilemma of the American High School* (Boston: Houghton Mifflin, 1984).

21. See Deborah Meier, *The Power of Their Ideas: Lessons for America from a Small School in Harlem* (Boston: Beacon Press, 1995).

22. See Myers, *The Pursuit of Happiness*; also Myers, "Close Relationships and Quality of Life," in *Well-Being*, ed. Kahneman, Diener, and Schwarz, pp. 374–391.

23. See Aristotle, *Nicomachean Ethics*, trans. Terence Irwin (Indianapolis: Hackett, 1985).

24. Ibid., p. 212.

25. Ibid., pp. 212–213.

26. Oscar Wilde, *The Picture of Dorian Gray and Other Writings* (New York: Bantam Books, 1982/1890), pp. 129–130.

27. Aristotle, *Nicomachean Ethics*, p. 218.

28. Job 6:14 and 16:2.

29. See Andrew Garrod, Lisa Smulyan, Sally I. Powers, and Robert Kilkenny, *Adolescent Portraits: Identity, Relationships, and Challenges* (Boston: Allyn & Bacon, 2002).

30. Ibid., p. 227.

31. From many possibilities, see Andrew Garrod and Colleen Larimore, eds., *First Person, First Peoples* (Ithaca, NY: Cornell University Press, 1997); also Garrod, Janie Victoria Ward, Tracy Robinson, and Robert Kilkenny, eds., *Souls Looking Back: Life Stories of Growing Up Black* (New York: Routledge, 1999); also Michie, *Holler If You Hear Me*.

32. See David McCullough, *John Adams* (New York: Simon & Schuster, 2001).

33. Lewis Thomas, *Late Night Thoughts on Listening to Mahler's Ninth Symphony* (New York: Viking Press, 1983), p. 142.

34. Anne Morrow Lindbergh, *Gift from the Sea* (New York: Random House, 1955), p. 104.

Chapter 10. **Preparing for Work**

1. John Dewey, *Democracy and Education* (New York: Macmillan, 1916), p. 308.

2. National Commission on Excellence in Education, *A Nation at Risk* (Washington, DC: U.S. Government Printing Office, 1983), p. 5.

3. *The New York Times*, Sunday, August 31, 1997, E-9.
4. On this, see Richard J. Murnane and Frank Levy, *Teaching the New Basic Skills: Principles for Educating Children to Thrive in a Changing Economy* (New York: Free Press, 1996). For an account of how we mislead students with respect to required skills, see Ivar Berg, *Education and Jobs: The Great Training Robbery* (Boston: Beacon Press, 1971).
5. See again Robert E. Lane, *The Loss of Happiness in Market Democracies* (New Haven, CT: Yale University Press, 2000).
6. On this, see Robert E. Lane, *The Market Experience* (Cambridge: Cambridge University Press, 1991).
7. Dropout figures are computed differently in various reports and widely disputed; one should consult a variety of sources. For competing views, see http://nces.ed.gov/pubsearch/pubsinfo.asp?pubid=2002114; Jay Greene, "Graduation Statistics: Caveat Emptor," *Education Week*, Jan. 16, 2002, pp. 52, 37; also www.manhattaninstitute.org/html/cr_baeo.htm
8. See Herbert Kliebard, *The Struggle for the American Curriculum* (New York: Routledge, 1995); Harold S. Wechsler, "Eastern Standard Time: High School–College Collaboration and Admission to College, 1880–1930," in *A Faithful Mirror: Reflections on the College Board and Education in America*, ed. Michael C. Johanek (New York: College Board, 2001), pp. 43–79; and David L. Angus and Jeffrey E. Mirel, *The Failed Promise of the American High School: 1890–1995* (New York: Teachers College Press, 1999).
9. For strong arguments against the increasing standardization of curriculum, see Alfie Kohn, *The Schools Our Children Deserve* (Boston: Houghton Mifflin, 1999); Deborah Meier, *Will Standards Save Public Education?* (Boston: Beacon Press, 2000); and Susan Ohanian, *One Size Fits Few: The Folly of Educational Standards* (Portsmouth, NH: Heinemann, 1999). For a comprehensive analysis of arguments on equality of educational opportunity, see Kenneth Howe, *Understanding Equal Educational Opportunity* (New York: Teachers College Press, 1997).
10. For a discussion of the positive and negative aspects of tracking, see Thomas Loveless, *The Tracking Wars* (Washington, DC: Brookings Institution Press, 1996); Samuel Lucas, *Tracking Inequality* (New York: Teachers College Press, 1999); and James E. Rosenbaum, "Track Misperceptions and Frustrated College Plans: An Analysis of the Effects of Tracks and Track Perceptions in the National Longitudinal Survey," *Sociology of Education* 53, 1980: 74–88.
11. Dewey, *Democracy and Education*, p. 87.

12. In Chapter 1 of *Democracy and Education*, Dewey discusses the human social impulse to communicate and makes that desire the foundation of the search for common values.

13. Dewey, *The Public and Its Problems* (New York: Henry Holt, 1927), p. 184.

14. On Addams, see Jean Bethke Elshtain, *Jane Addams and the Dream of American Democracy* (New York: Basic Books, 2002).

15. Dewey, *Democracy and Education*, p. 8.

16. See the exchange between Dewey and Hutchins in John Dewey, *The Later Works, 1925–1953, Vol. 11: 1935–1937*, ed. Jo Ann Boydston (Carbondale and Edwardsville: Southern Illinois Press, 1991), pp. 391–396, 397–401, 402–407, and 592–597. The exchange originally appeared in *Social Frontier*, 1936 and 1937.

17. For a persuasive argument on the importance of self-evaluation in education, see William Glasser, *The Quality School* (New York: Harper & Row, 1990).

18. For a now classic argument that defines the disciplines and identifies their centrality to liberal education, see Paul H. Hirst, "Liberal Education and the Nature of Knowledge," in *The Philosophy of Education*, ed. R. S. Peters (Oxford: Oxford University Press, 1973), pp. 87–111.

19. The Waldorf Schools, for example, emphasize such a balance.

20. See Howard Gardner, *Frames of Mind* (New York: Basic Books, 1983).

21. See W. Norton Grubb, ed., *Education Through Occupations in American High Schools*, Vols. 1 and 2 (New York: Teachers College Press, 1995). See Grubb, vol. 1: *Approaches to Integrating Academic and Vocational Education*, p. 11.

22. Grubb, ibid., vol. 1, cites a National Education Association committee publication of 1893.

23. The opposing arguments are well described in Angus and Mirel, *Failed Promise of the American High School*; see also Herbert Kliebard, *Schooled to Work: Vocationalism and the American Curriculum 1876–1946* (New York: Teachers College Press, 1999).

24. Eliot is quoted in Kliebard, *Schooled to Work*, p. 43.

25. Ibid.

26. I noted in an earlier chapter that J. S. Mill's conception of liberty and his principle of nonintervention leave children out. Dewey, in contrast, insisted that children must be allowed to make well-informed choices as part of their education in liberal democracy.

27. See Dewey, *Human Nature and Conduct* (New York: Modern Library, 1930).

28. See my argument in *Starting at Home: Caring and Social Policy* (Berkeley: University of California Press, 2002).
29. Kliebard, *Schooled to Work*, p. xv.
30. See Grubb, *Education Through Occupations*.
31. See Mike Rose, *Possible Lives: The Promise of Public Education in America* (Boston: Houghton Mifflin, 1995), pp. 37–43.
32. Dorothy Day, *The Long Loneliness* (San Francisco: Harper & Row, 1952), p. 285.
33. Highly readable accounts can be found in Bud Schultz and Ruth Schultz, *It Did Happen Here* (Berkeley: University of California Press, 1989).
34. This is a popular theme in the literature of education today. See, for example, Holmes Group, *Tomorrow's Teachers* (East Lansing, MI: Author, 1986). For a discussion of the problems that arise (and a distinction between professionalism and professionalization), see my "The Professional Life of Mathematics Teachers," in *Handbook of Research on Mathematics Teaching and Learning*, ed. Douglas A. Grouws (New York: Macmillan, 1992), pp. 197–208.
35. For a discussion of semiprofessions, see Amitai Etzioni, ed., *The Semi-Professions and Their Organization: Teachers, Nurses, and Social Workers* (New York: Free Press, 1969).
36. Steven Levy, "Great Minds, Great Ideas," *Newsweek*, May 27, 2002, 56.
37. See, for example, E. D. Hirsch, Jr., *Cultural Literacy: What Every American Needs to Know* (Boston: Houghton Mifflin, 1987); also Hirsch, *The Schools We Need* (New York: Doubleday, 1996); and Diane Ravitch, *Left Back: A Century of Battles Over School Reform* (New York: Simon & Schuster, 2000).
38. For an account of criticisms of Dewey's supposed anti-intellectualism, see Alan Ryan, *John Dewey and the High Tide of American Liberalism* (New York: W. W. Norton, 1995).

Chapter 11. Community, Democracy, and Service

1. See Robert A. Nisbet, *The Quest for Community* (New York: Oxford University Press, 1953); also Arthur M. Schlesinger, Jr., *The Disuniting of America: Reflections on a Multicultural Society* (New York: W. W. Norton, 1992). On living in an age of perceived meaninglessness, see Paul Tillich, *The Courage to Be* (New Haven, CT: Yale University Press, 1952). For an interesting study of how people try to cope with the loss of meaning and community in the larger society by creating utopian communities, see Rosabeth Moss Kanter,

Commitment and Community: Communes and Utopias in Sociological Perspective (Cambridge, MA: Harvard University Press, 1972).

2. For a good argument in favor of leaving a definition of community vague, see Philip Selznick, *The Moral Commonwealth: Social Theory and the Promise of Community* (Berkeley: University of California Press, 1992), pp. 357–358.

3. Ferdinand Tonnies, *Gemeinschaft und Gesellschaft*, trans. C. P. Loomis (New York: HarperCollins, 1957/1887), p. 248.

4. Bellah and his colleagues make memory the foundation of strong communities. See Robert N. Bellah, Richard Madsen, William M. Sullivan, Ann Swidler, and Steven M. Tipton, *Habits of the Heart* (Berkeley: University of California Press, 1985).

5. Selznick, *Moral Commonwealth*, identifies historicity, identity, mutuality, plurality, autonomy, participation, and integration as "elements" of community.

6. See Tillich, *Courage to Be*.

7. Eric Hoffer, *The True Believer* (New York: Harper & Row, 1951), p. 80.

8. William Galston, "Two Concepts of Liberalism," *Ethics* 105(3), 1995: 529.

9. See Nel Noddings, *Educating for Intelligent Belief or Unbelief* (New York: Teachers College Press, 1993).

10. John Dewey, *The Public and Its Problems* (New York: Henry Holt, 1927), p. 98.

11. See Tillich, *Courage to Be*.

12. See Michel Foucault, *Discipline and Punish: The Birth of the Prison*, trans. Alan Sheridan (New York: Vintage Books, 1979).

13. See Nel Noddings, *Starting at Home: Caring and Social Policy* (Berkeley: University of California Press, 2002), p. 137.

14. See Samuel Oliner and Pearl M. Oliner, *The Altruistic Personality: Rescuers of Jews in Nazi Europe* (New York: Free Press, 1988).

15. See Nel Noddings, *Educating Moral People: A Caring Alternative to Character Education* (New York: Teachers College Press, 2002).

16. In the early part of the twentieth century, instinct was invoked to explain a wide variety of human behaviors. For some of those arguments and the powerful criticisms that challenged them, see Dalbir Bindra and Jane Stewart, eds., *Motivation* (Middlesex, England: Penguin Books, 1971).

17. For a powerful example of resistance that contributes to social class reproduction, see Paul Willis, *Learning to Labour* (Farnborough, England: Saxon House, 1977).

18. See Diana Meyers, *Self, Society, and Personal Choice* (New York: Columbia University Press, 1989).
19. See Selznick, *Moral Commonwealth*, Chapter 9.
20. Jean-Paul Sartre argues that the very recognition of our existential freedom induces anguish. Situational freedom may mitigate this anguish by allowing us to make careful choices or, if we are not prepared to make well-informed choices, our anguish may deepen. See Sartre, *Being and Nothingness*, trans. Hazel E. Barnes (New York: Washington Square Press, 1956).
21. For a sample of this debate, see Alasdair MacIntyre, *After Virtue* (Notre Dame, IN: University of Notre Dame Press, 1981); Michael Sandel, *Liberalism and the Limits of Justice* (Cambridge: Cambridge University Press, 1982); and Charles Taylor, *Sources of the Self* (Cambridge, MA: Harvard University Press, 1989). A good summary of both sides can be found in Shlomo Avineri and Avner de-Shalit, eds., *Communitarianism and Individualism* (Oxford: Oxford University Press, 1992).
22. See John Dewey, *Democracy and Education* (New York: Macmillan, 1916).
23. Amy Gutmann, *Democratic Education* (Princeton, NJ: Princeton University Press, 1987), p. 38.
24. See *Democracy and Education* and *The Public and Its Problems* for Dewey's arguments on this.
25. See Noddings, *The Challenge to Care in Schools* (New York: Teachers College Press, 1992).
26. For impressive accounts of the varieties of volunteer work, see Laurent A. Parks Daloz, Cheryl H. Keen, James P. Keen, and Sharon Daloz Parks, *Common Fire: Lives of Commitment in a Complex World* (Boston: Beacon Press, 1996); Marc Freedman, *The Kindness of Strangers: Adult Mentors, Urban Youth, and the New Voluntarism* (Cambridge: Cambridge University Press, 1999); John W. Gardner, *Self-Renewal* (New York: Harper & Row, 1965); Pearl Oliner and Samuel Oliner, *Toward a Caring Society: Ideas into Action* (Westport, CT: Praeger, 1995); Robert A. Rhoads, *Community Service and Higher Learning: Explorations of the Caring Self* (Albany: State University of New York Press, 1997); and Lisbeth B. Schorr, *Common Purpose: Strengthening Families and Neighborhoods to Rebuild America* (New York: Anchor Books, 1997). On the need for such action, see Bellah et al., *Habits of the Heart*.
27. See Ruth L. Smith, "Happiness and the Uneasy Conscience," in *In Pursuit of Happiness*, ed. Leroy S. Rouner (Notre Dame, IN: University of Notre Dame Press, 1995), pp. 136–146.

Chapter 12. Happiness in Schools and Classrooms

1. See my argument in *The Challenge to Care in Schools* (New York: Teachers College Press, 1992).
2. For a powerful account of how badly we neglect poor children, see Jonathan Kozol, *Savage Inequalities* (New York: Crown, 1991).
3. See, for example, Fraser Brown, ed., *Playwork – Theory and Practice* (Philadelphia: Open University Press, 2002).
4. Alfred North Whitehead, *The Aims of Education* (New York: Free Press, 1967/1929), pp. 17–18.
5. See, for example, Charles E. Silberman, *Crisis in the Classroom: The Remaking of American Education* (New York: Random House, 1970).
6. Anne Long, "The New School – Vancouver," in *Radical School Reform*, ed. Ronald Gross and Beatrice Gross (New York: Simon & Schuster, 1969), p. 296.
7. For samples of such cruel talk, see the essays in Gross and Gross, ibid.
8. See Jean Anyon, *Ghetto Schooling* (New York: Teachers College Press, 1997); also Herve Varenne and Ray McDermott, *Successful Failure* (Boulder, CO: Westview Press, 1999).
9. Jules Henry, "In Suburban Classrooms," in *Radical School Reform*, p. 84.
10. For an impressive account of how often such opportunities are lost, see Katherine G. Simon, *Moral Questions in the Classroom* (New Haven, CT: Yale University Press, 2001).
11. On this, see John Dewey, *Experience and Education* (New York: Collier Books, 1963/1938); also Nel Noddings and Paul Shore, *Awakening the Inner Eye: Intuition in Education* (New York: Teachers College Press, 1984; reissued by Educator's International Press, Troy, NY, 1998).
12. Paul Goodman, "No Processing Whatever," in *Radical School Reform*, ed. Gross and Gross, p. 105; see also Goodman, *Compulsory Miseducation* (New York: Horizon, 1964) and Goodman, *Growing Up Absurd* (New York: Random House, 1960).
13. Securing the cooperation of both students and parents is critical. See Deborah Meier, *The Power of their Ideas: Lessons for America from a Small School in Harlem* (Boston: Beacon Press, 1995); also Meier, *Will Standards Save Public Education?* (Boston: Beacon Press, 2000).
14. *Wisconsin v. Yoder*, 406 U.S. 205 (1971). For a thoughtful discussion of the case, see Stephen Macedo, "Liberal Civic Education and

Religious Fundamentalism: The Case of God v. John Rawls?" *Ethics* 105, 1995: 468–496.

15. See the account in the *New York Times*, "From the Dissent," June 28, 2002, A23.

16. Surprisingly, James Conant confessed a "sense of distasteful weariness" when faced with a discussion of educational aims and philosophy. Similarly, the journalist Martin Mayer dismissed aims-talk as "among the dullest and most fruitless of human pursuits." Quoted in Silberman, *Crisis in the Classroom*, p. 6. So much for Plato, Aristotle, Rousseau, Whitehead, and Dewey!

17. John Dewey, *Democracy and Education* (New York: Macmillan, 1916), p. 211.

18. See Stephen J. Thornton, "From Content to Subject Matter," *The Social Studies*, November/December 2001: 237–242.

19. See William Watson Purkey and John M. Novak, *Inviting School Success* (Belmont, CA: Wadsworth, 1996); also Novak, *Advancing Invitational Thinking* (San Francisco: Caddo Gap Press, 1992).

20. See again Silberman, *Crisis in the Classroom*, and Gross and Gross, eds., *Radical School Reform*.

21. Alfie Kohn, *The Schools Our Children Deserve* (Boston: Houghton Mifflin, 1999), p. 104.

22. Silberman, *Crisis in the Classroom*, pp. 172–173.

23. For a graphic account of this reaction, see David L. Angus and Jeffrey E. Mirel, *The Failed Promise of the American High School: 1890–1995* (New York: Teachers College Press, 1999).

24. Nel Noddings, "Care and Coercion in School Reform," *Journal of Educational Change* 2, 2001: 38.

25. See Linda McNeil, *Contradictions of School Reform* (New York: Routledge, 2000).

26. This accusation is made by (among others) Diane Ravitch, *Left Back: A Century of Battles Over School Reform* (New York: Simon & Schuster, 2000).

27. See Jane Roland Martin, *The Schoolhome: Rethinking Schools for Changing Families* (Cambridge, MA: Harvard University Press, 1992).

Bibliography

Angus, David L. and Mirel, Jeffrey E. *The Failed Promise of the American High School: 1890–1995*. New York: Teachers College Press, 1999.

Annas, Julia. *The Morality of Happiness*. New York: Oxford University Press, 1993.

Anyon, Jean. *Ghetto Schooling*. New York: Teachers College Press, 1997.

Arendt, Hannah. *The Human Condition*. Chicago: University of Chicago Press, 1958.

Aristotle. *Nicomachean Ethics*, trans. Terence Irwin. Indianapolis: Hackett, 1985.

Augustine. *On Free Choice of the Will*, trans. Anna Benjamin and L. H. Hackstaff. New York: Macmillan, 1964.

Avineri, Shlomo and de-Shalit, Avner, eds. *Communitarianism and Individualism*. Oxford: Oxford University Press, 1992.

Bachelard, Gaston. *The Poetics of Space*, trans. Maria Jolas. New York: Orion Press, 1964.

Barrow, Robin. *Happiness and Schooling*. New York: St. Martin's Press, 1980.

Baudrillard, Jean. *Fatal Strategies*, trans. W. G. J. Niesluchowski, ed. Jim Fleming. New York: Semiotext(e), 1990.

Baumrind, Diana. *Child Maltreatment and Optimal Caregiving in Social Contexts*. New York: Garland, 1995.

Bellah, Robert N., Madsen, Richard, Sullivan, William M., Swidler, Ann, and Tipton, Steven M. *Habits of the Heart*. Berkeley: University of California Press, 1985.

Bellamy, Edward. *Looking Backward*. New York: New American Library, 1960. Original work published 1888.

Berg, Ivar. *Education and Jobs: The Great Training Robbery*. Boston: Beacon Press, 1971.

Berlin, Isaiah. *Four Essays on Liberty*. Oxford: Oxford University Press, 1969.

Berliner, David and Biddle, Bruce. *The Manufactured Crisis: Myths, Fraud, and the Attack on America's Public Schools*. New York: Perseus Books, 1996.

Berry, Wendell. *The Unsettling of America*. San Francisco: Sierra Club, 1977. *Another Turn of the Crank*. Washington, DC: Counterpoint, 1995.

Bethel, Dayle M. *Makiguchi the Value Creator*. New York: Weatherhill, 1994.

Bindra, Dalbir and Stewart, Jane, eds. *Motivation*. Middlesex, England: Penguin Books, 1971.

Bobbitt, Franklin. *How to Make a Curriculum*. Boston: Houghton Mifflin, 1924.

Bok, Sissela. *Lying: Moral Choice in Public and Private Life*. New York: Vintage Books, 1979.

Boyd, William, ed. *The Emile of Jean Jacques Rousseau: Selections*. New York: Teachers College Press, 1962.

Bracey, Gerald. *Setting the Record Straight: Responses to Misconceptions About Public Education in the United States*. Alexandria, VA: Association for Supervision and Curriculum Development, 1997.

Braithwaite, John and Pettit, Philip. *Not Just Deserts: A Republican Theory of Criminal Justice*. Oxford: Clarendon Press, 1990.

Braybrooke, David. *Meeting Needs*. Princeton, NJ: Princeton University Press, 1987.

Brecher, Bob. *Getting What You Want?* London: Routledge, 1998.

Brown, Fraser, ed. *Playwork – Theory and Practice*. Philadelphia: Open University Press, 2002.

Brownmiller, Susan. *Against Our Will*. New York: Simon & Schuster, 1975.

Bruner, Jerome. *The Process of Education*. Cambridge, MA: Harvard University Press, 1960.

Buber, Martin. *Between Man and Man*. New York: Macmillan, 1965.
I and Thou, trans. Walter Kaufmann. New York: Charles Scribner's Sons, 1970.

Buchwald, Emilie, Fletcher, Pamela R., and Roth, Martha, eds. *Transforming a Rape Culture*. Minneapolis: Milkweed Editions, 1993.

Buck, Pearl S. *The Exile*. New York: Triangle, 1936.

Butler, Samuel. *Erewhon*. London: Penguin, 1985/1872.

Camus, Albert. *Resistance, Rebellion, and Death*. New York: Alfred A. Knopf, 1969.

Candib, Lucy. *Medicine and the Family: A Feminist Perspective*. New York: Basic Books, 1995.

Casey, Edward S. *Getting Back Into Place*. Bloomington: Indiana University Press, 1993.

Charney, Ruth. *Teaching Children to Care*. Greenfield, MA: Northeast Foundation for Children, 1992.

Coates, Robert C. *A Street Is Not a Home*. Buffalo, NY: Prometheus, 1990.

Cohen, Jonathan, ed. *Educating Minds and Hearts*. New York: Teachers College Press, 1999.

Cunningham, Anthony. *The Heart of the Matter*. Berkeley: University of California Press, 2001.

Bibliography

Daloz, Laurent A. Parks, Keen, Cheryl H., Keen, James P., and Parks, Sharon Daloz. *Common Fire: Lives of Commitment in a Complex World*. Boston: Beacon Press, 1996.

Daly, Mary. *Beyond God the Father*. Boston: Beacon Press, 1974.

Day, Dorothy. *The Long Loneliness*. San Francisco: Harper & Row, 1952.

Dewey, John. *The School and Society*. Chicago: University of Chicago Press, 1900.

Democracy and Education. New York: Macmillan, 1916.

The Public and Its Problems. New York: Henry Holt, 1927.

The Quest for Certainty. New York: G. P. Putnam's Sons, 1929.

Human Nature and Conduct. New York: Modern Library, 1930.

A Common Faith. New Haven, CT: Yale University Press, 1934.

Experience and Education. New York: Collier Books, 1963/1938.

Diener, Ed and Lucas, Richard E. "Personality and Subjective Well-Being," in *Well-Being*, ed. Daniel Kahneman, Ed Diener, and Norbert Schwarz. New York: Russell Sage Foundation, 1999, pp. 213–229.

Dostoevsky, Fyodor, *The Brothers Karamazov*, trans. Constance Garnett. New York: Modern Library, n.d.

Eisner, Elliot. *The Educational Imagination*. New York: Macmillan, 1979.

Elder, John. *Reading the Mountains of Home*. Cambridge, MA: Harvard University Press, 1998.

Ellsworth, Elizabeth. "Why Doesn't This Feel Empowering? Working Through the Repressive Myth of Critical Pedagogy," *Harvard Educational Review* 59(3), 1989: 297–324.

Elshtain, Jean Bethke. *Women and War*. New York: Basic Books, 1987.

Jane Addams and the Dream of American Democracy. New York: Basic Books, 2002.

Etzioni, Amitai. *The Semi-Professions and Their Organization: Teachers, Nurses, and Social Workers*. New York: Free Press, 1969.

Firestone, Shulamith. *The Dialectic of Sex*. New York: Bantam Books, 1972.

Flinders, David and Noddings, Nel. *Multiyear Teaching: The Case for Continuity*. Bloomington, IN: Phi Delta Kappa, 2001.

Fogarty, Brian E. *War, Peace, and the Social Order*. Boulder, CO: Westview Press, 2000.

Ford, Larry R. *The Spaces between Buildings*. Baltimore: Johns Hopkins University Press, 2000.

Foucault, Michel. *Discipline and Punish: The Birth of the Prison*, trans. Alan Sheridan. New York: Vintage, 1979.

Francke, Kuno. *A History of German Literature as Determined by Social Forces*. New York: Henry Holt, 1916.

Frankl, Viktor E. *The Doctor and the Soul*. New York: Vintage Books, 1973.

Fraser, Nancy. *Unruly Practices: Power, Discourse, and Gender in Contemporary Social Theory*. Minneapolis: University of Minnesota Press, 1989.

Frazer, James G. *The Golden Bough*. New York: Macmillan, 1951.

Freedman, Marc. *The Kindness of Strangers: Adult Mentors, Urban Youth, and the New Voluntarism*. Cambridge: Cambridge University Press, 1999.

Freire, Paulo. *Pedagogy of the Oppressed*, trans. Myra Bergman Ramos. New York: Herder and Herder, 1970.

Freud, Sigmund. *The Freud Reader*, ed. Peter Gay. New York: W. W. Norton, 1989.

Friedan, Betty. *The Feminine Mystique*. New York: W. W. Norton, 1963.

Galbraith, John Kenneth. *The Culture of Contentment*. Boston: Houghton Mifflin, 1992.

Galston, William. "Two Concepts of Liberalism," *Ethics* 105(3), 1995: 516–534.

Gardner, Howard. *Frames of Mind*. New York: Basic Books, 1983.

Gardner, John W. *Self-Renewal*. New York: Harper & Row, 1965.

Gardner, Martin. *The Whys of a Philosophical Scrivener*. New York: Quill, 1983.

Garrod, Andrew and Larimore, Colleen, eds. *First Person, First Peoples*. Ithaca, NY: Cornell University Press, 1997.

Garrod, Andrew, Smulyan, Lisa, Powers, Sally I., and Kilkenny, Robert. *Adolescent Portraits: Identity, Relationships, and Challenges*. Boston: Allyn & Bacon, 2002.

Garrod, Andrew, Ward, Janie Victoria, Robinson, Tracy, and Kilkenny, Robert, eds. *Souls Looking Back: Life Stories of Growing Up Black*. New York: Routledge, 1999.

Gilligan, James. *Violence*. New York: G. P. Putnam's Sons, 1996.

Glasser, William. *The Quality School*. New York: Harper & Row, 1990.

Glover, Jonathan. *Humanity: A Moral History of the 20th Century*. New Haven, CT: Yale University Press, 2000.

Godden, Rumer. *An Episode of Sparrows*. New York: Viking Press, 1955.

Goodman, Paul. *Compulsory Mis-education*. New York: Horizon, 1964.

"No Processing Whatever," in *Radical School Reform*, ed. Ronald and Beatrice Gross. New York: Simon & Schuster, 1969, pp. 98–106.

Growing Up Absurd. New York: Random House, 1960.

Graves, Robert. *Goodbye to All That*. London: Folio Society, 1981/1929.

Griffin, David Ray. *Evil Revisited*. Albany: State University of New York Press, 1991.

Gross, Ronald and Gross, Beatrice, eds. *Radical School Reform*. New York: Simon & Schuster, 1969.

Grubb, W. Norton, ed. *Education Through Occupations in American High Schools*, Vols. 1 and 2. New York: Teachers College Press, 1995.

Grumet, Madeleine R. *Bitter Milk*. Amherst: University of Massachusetts Press, 1988.

Gutmann, Amy. *Democratic Education*. Princeton, NJ: Princeton University Press, 1987.

Hadamard, Jacques. *The Psychology of Invention in the Mathematical Field*. New York: Dover, 1954.

Bibliography

Haughton, Claire Shaver. *Green Immigrants*. New York: Harcourt Brace Jovanovich, 1978.

Hawkins, David. "How to Plan for Spontaneity," in *The Open Classroom Reader*, ed. Charles E. Silberman. New York: Vintage Books, 1973, pp. 486–503.

Hawkins, Frances Lothrop. *Journey with Children*. Niwot: University Press of Colorado, 1997.

Heath, Shirley Brice. *Ways with Words*. Cambridge: Cambridge University Press, 1983.

Henry, Jules. "In Suburban Classrooms," in *Radical School Reform*, ed. Ronald Gross and Beatrice Gross, pp. 77–92.

Hesse, Hermann. *Steppenwolf*, trans. Joseph Mileck and Horst Frenz. New York: Holt, Rinehart and Winston, 1963.

Hick, John. *Evil and the God of Love*. New York: Macmillan, 1966.

Hirsch, E. D., Jr. *Cultural Literacy: What Every American Needs to Know*. Boston: Houghton Mifflin, 1987.

The Schools We Need. New York: Doubleday, 1996.

Hoffer, Eric. *The True Believer*. New York: Harper & Row, 1951.

Hoffman, Martin L. *Empathy and Moral Development*. Cambridge: Cambridge University Press, 2000.

Holmes Group. *Tomorrow's Teachers*. East Lansing, MI: Author, 1986.

Howe, Kenneth. *Understanding Equal Educational Opportunity*. New York: Teachers College Press, 1997.

Hume, David. *An Enquiry Concerning the Principles of Morals*. Indianapolis: Hackett, 1983/1751.

Jackson, Philip W. *Untaught Lessons*. New York: Teachers College Press, 1992.

Jaggar, Alison M. *Feminist Politics and Human Nature*. Totowa, NJ: Rowman & Allanheld, 1983.

James, William. *The Varieties of Religious Experience*. New York: Modern Library, 1929/1902.

Joyes, Claire. *Monet's Table*. New York: Simon & Schuster, 1989.

Jung, Carl G. *Answer to Job*, trans. R. F. C. Hull. Princeton, NJ: Princeton University Press, Bollingen Series, 1973.

Kahn, Peter. *The Human Relationship with Nature*. Cambridge, MA: MIT Press, 1999.

Kahneman, Daniel, Diener, Ed, and Schwarz, Norbert, eds. *Well-Being*. New York: Russell Sage Foundation, 1999.

Kanter, Rosabeth Moss. *Commitment and Community: Communes and Utopias in Sociological Perspective*. Cambridge, MA: Harvard University Press, 1972.

Kelman, Herbert C. and Hamilton, V. Lee. *Crimes of Obedience*. New Haven, CT: Yale University Press, 1989.

Kerenyi, Carl. *Dionysus: Archetypal Image of Indestructible Life*, trans. Ralph Manheim. Princeton, NJ: Princeton University Press, 1976.

Klein, Jessie and Chancer, Lynn S. "Masculinity Matters: The Omission of Gender from High-Profile School Violence Cases," in *Smoke and Mirrors*, ed. Stephanie Urso Spina. Lanham, MD: Rowman & Littlefield, 2000, pp. 129–162.

Kliebard, Herbert. *The Struggle for the American Curriculum*. New York: Routledge, 1995.

Schooled to Work: Vocationalism and the American Curriculum 1876–1946. New York: Teachers College Press, 1999.

Knowles, John. *A Separate Peace*. New York: Macmillan, 1960.

Kohak, Erazim. "Of Dwelling and Wayfaring: A Quest for Metaphors," in *The Longing for Home*, ed. Leroy S. Rouner. Notre Dame, IN: University of Notre Dame Press, 1996, pp. 30–46.

Kohn, Alfie. "The Trouble with Character Education," in *The Construction of Children's Character*, ed. Alex Molnar. Chicago: National Society for the Study of Education, 1997, pp. 154–162.

The Schools Our Children Deserve. Boston: Houghton Mifflin, 1999.

Kozol, Jonathan. *Savage Inequalities*. New York: Crown, 1991.

Kushner, Harold. *When Bad Things Happen to Good People*. New York: Schocken Books, 1981.

Labaree, David. *How to Succeed in School without Really Learning: The Credentials Race in American Education*. New Haven, CT: Yale University Press, 1997.

Lane, Robert E. *The Market Experience*. Cambridge: Cambridge University Press, 1991.

The Loss of Happiness in Market Democracies. New Haven, CT: Yale Universitiy Press, 2000.

Larrimore, Mark, ed. *The Problem of Evil*. Oxford: Blackwell, 2001.

Le Shan, Lawrence. *The Psychology of War*. Chicago: Noble Press, 1992.

Levy, Steven. "Great Minds, Great Ideas," *Newsweek*, May 27, 2002: 56–59.

Lewis, C. S. *Surprised by Joy*. New York: Harcourt Brace Jovanovich, 1955.

The Problem of Pain. New York: Macmillan, 1962.

A Grief Observed. Toronto: Bantam, 1976.

Lickona, Thomas. *Educating for Character: How Our Schools Can Teach Respect and Responsibility*. New York: Bantam Books, 1991.

Lightman, Alan. *The Diagnosis*. New York: Pantheon, 2000.

Lindbergh, Anne Morrow. *Gift from the Sea*. New York: Random House, 1955.

Long, Anne. "The New School – Vancouver," in *Radical School Reform*, ed. Ronald Gross and Beatrice Gross, pp. 273–296.

Lounsbury, John H. and Vars, Gordon F. *A Curriculum for the Middle School Years*. New York: Harper & Row, 1978.

Loveless, Thomas. *The Tracking Wars*. Washington, DC: Brookings Institution Press, 1996.

Lucas, Samuel. *Tracking Inequality*. New York: Teachers College Press, 1999.

Macedo, Donaldo. *Literacies of Power: What Americans Are Not Allowed to Know*. Boulder, CO: Westview Press, 1994.

Bibliography

MacIntyre, Alasdair. *After Virtue*. Notre Dame, IN: University of Notre Dame Press, 1981.

Martin, Jane Roland. *Reclaiming a Conversation*. New Haven, CT: Yale University Press, 1985.

    The Schoolhome: Rethinking Schools for Changing Families. Cambridge, MA: Harvard University Press, 1992.

Maslow, Abraham H. *The Farther Reaches of Human Nature*. New York: Viking Press, 1971.

Masson, Jeffrey Moussaieff and McCarthy, Susan. *When Elephants Weep: The Emotional Lives of Animals*. New York: Delacorte Press, 1995.

McClellan, B. Edward. *Moral Education in America*. New York: Teachers College Press, 1999.

McCullough, David. *John Adams*. New York: Simon & Schuster, 2001.

McFeely, William. *Proximity to Death*. New York: W. W. Norton, 1999.

McNeil, Linda. *Contradictions of School Reform*. New York: Routledge, 2000.

McPhee, John. *The Pine Barrens*. New York: Farrar, Straus and Giroux, 1968.

Meier, Deborah. *The Power of Their Ideas: Lessons for America from a Small School in Harlem*. Boston: Beacon Press, 1995.

    Will Standards Save Public Education? Boston: Beacon Press, 2000.

Menand, Louis. *The Metaphysical Club*. New York: Farrar, Straus and Giroux, 2001.

Messerschmidt, James W. *Masculinities and Crime*. Lanham, MD: Rowman & Littlefield, 1993.

Meyers, Diana T. *Self, Society, and Personal Choice*. New York: Columbia University Press, 1989.

Meyers, Jeffrey. *Orwell: Wintry Conscience of a Generation*. New York: W. W. Norton, 2000.

Michie, Gregory. *Holler If You Hear Me*. New York: Teachers College Press, 1999.

Mill, John Stuart. *On Liberty* and *Utilitarianism*. New York: Bantam Books, 1993/1859.

Miller, Alice. *For Your Own Good*, trans. Hildegarde Hannun and Hunter Hannun. New York: Farrar, Straus and Giroux, 1983.

    The Truth Will Set You Free. New York: Basic Books, 2001.

Molnar, Alex, ed. *The Construction of Children's Character*. Chicago: National Society for the Study of Education, 1997.

Morrison, Toni. *The Bluest Eye*. New York: Plume, 1994/1970.

Murnane, Richard J. and Levy, Frank. *Teaching the New Basic Skills: Principles for Educating Children to Thrive in a Changing Economy*. New York: Free Press, 1996.

Musto, David. "Opium, Cocaine, and Marijuana in American History," in *Drugs: Should We Legalize, Decriminalize or Deregulate?* ed. Jeffrey A. Schaler. Amherst, NY: Prometheus Books, 1998, pp. 17–30.

Myers, David G. *The Pursuit of Happiness*. New York: Avon, 1992.

The American Paradox: Spiritual Hunger in an Age of Plenty. New Haven, CT: Yale University Press, 2000.

Nabhan, Gary Paul and Trimble, Stephen. *The Geography of Childhood: Why Children Need Wild Places*. Boston: Beacon Press, 1994.

Nash, Robert J. *Answering the "Virtuecrats."* New York: Teachers College Press, 1997.

National Commission on Excellence in Education. *A Nation at Risk*. Washington, DC: U.S. Government Printing Office, 1983.

National Council of Teachers of Mathematics. *Principles and Standards for School Mathematics*. Discussion draft, October 1998.

Neill, A. S. *Summerhill*. New York: Hart, 1960.

New Buckeye Cook Book. Dayton, OH: Home Publishing, 1891.

Newman, James R., ed. *The World of Mathematics*. New York: Simon & Schuster, 1956.

Nicholls, John G. and Thorkildsen, Theresa A., eds. *"Reasons for Learning."* New York: Teachers College Press, 1995.

Nietzsche, Friedrich. *The Will to Power*, trans. Walter Kaufmann and R. J. Hollingdale. New York: Vintage Books, 1968.

Nisbet, Robert A. *The Quest for Community*. New York: Oxford University Press, 1953.

Noddings, Nel. *Caring: A Feminine Approach to Ethics and Moral Education*. Berkeley: University of California Press, 1984.

Women and Evil. Berkeley: University of California Press, 1989.

The Challenge to Care in Schools. New York: Teachers College Press, 1992.

Educating for Intelligent Belief or Unbelief. New York: Teachers College Press, 1993.

"Care and Coercion in School Reform," *Journal of Educational Change 2*, 2001: 35–43.

Educating Moral People. New York: Teachers College Press, 2002.

Starting at Home. Berkeley: University of California Press, 2002.

Noddings, Nel and Shore, Paul. *Awakening the Inner Eye: Intuition in Education*. New York: Teachers College Press, 1984; reissued by Educator's International Press, Troy, NY, 1998.

Novak, John, M., ed. *Advancing Invitational Thinking*. San Francisco: Caddo Gap Press, 1992.

Nussbaum, Martha. *The Fragility of Goodness*. Cambridge: Cambridge University Press, 1986.

Oakes, Jeannie. *Multiplying Inequalities: The Effects of Race, Social Class, and Tracking on Opportunities to Learn Mathematics and Science*. Santa Monica, CA: Rand, 1990.

Keeping Track: How Schools Structure Inequality. New Haven, CT: Yale University Press, 1995.

O'Brien, Mary M. *The Politics of Reproduction*. Boston: Routledge & Kegan Paul, 1981.

Bibliography

Ochs, Carol. *Women and Spirituality*. Totowa, NJ: Rowman & Allanheld, 1983.

Ohanian, Susan. *One Size Fits Few: The Folly of Educational Standards*. Portsmouth, NH: Heinemann, 1999.

Okin, Susan Moller. *Women in Western Political Thought*. Princeton, NJ: Princeton University Press, 1979.

Oldenbourg, Zoe. *The Crusades*, trans. Anne Carter. New York: Pantheon Books, 1966.

Oliner, Samuel P. and Oliner, Pearl M. *The Altruistic Personality: Rescuers of Jews in Nazi Europe*. New York: Free Press, 1988.

Toward a Caring Society: Ideas into Action. Westport, CT: Praeger, 1995.

Orwell, George. *Nineteen Eighty-Four*. New York: Harcourt, Brace and World, 1949.

The Orwell Reader. New York: Harcourt, Brace, 1956.

Paul, James, Churton, Michael, Rosselli-Kostoryz, Hilda, Morse, William, Marfo, Kofi, Lavely, Carolyn, and Thomas, Daphne, eds. *Foundations of Special Education*. Pacific Grove, CA: Brooks/Cole, 1997.

Peters, Richard S., ed. *The Philosophy of Education*. Oxford: Oxford University Press, 1973.

Phillips, John Anthony. *Eve: The History of an Idea*. San Francisco: Harper & Row, 1984.

Pinar, William. *Autobiography, Politics, and Sexuality*. New York: Peter Lang, 1994.

Plato, *The Republic*, trans. B. Jowett. Roslyn, NY: Walter Black, 1942.

Pollan, Michael. *The Botany of Desire*. New York: Random House, 2001.

Pope, Denise Clark. *"Doing School": How We Are Creating a Generation of Stressed Out, Materialistic, and Miseducated Students*. New Haven, CT: Yale University Press, 2001.

Potkay, Adam. *The Passion for Happiness: Samuel Johnson and David Hume*. Ithaca, NY: Cornell University Press, 2000.

Prejean, Helen. *Dead Man Walking*. New York: Vintage Books, 1996.

Proust, Marcel. *Remembrance of Things Past*, vol. 1, *Swann's Way*, trans. C. K. Scott Moncrieff and Terence Kilmartin. New York: Random House, 1981.

Purkey, William Watson and Novak, John, M. *Inviting School Success*. Belmont, CA: Wadsworth, 1996.

Ravitch, Diane. *Left Back: A Century of Battles Over School Reform*. New York: Simon & Schuster, 2000.

Rawls, John. *A Theory of Justice*. Cambridge, MA: Harvard University Press, 1971.

Redman, Ben Ray, ed. *The Portable Voltaire*. New York: Penguin Books, 1977.

Regan, Tom. *The Case for Animal Rights*. Berkeley: University of California Press, 1983.

Reich, Charles. *The Greening of America*. New York: Random House, 1970.

Rhoads, Robert A. *Community Service and Higher Learning: Explorations of the Caring Self*. Albany: State University of New York Press, 1997.

Rich, Adrienne. *Of Woman Born*. New York: W. W. Norton, 1976.

Ricoeur, Paul. *The Symbolism of Evil*. Boston: Beacon Press, 1969.

Rombauer, Irma S. and Rombauer, Marion Becker. *The Joy of Cooking*. Indianapolis: Bobbs-Merrill, 1974/1931.

Rorty, Amelie, ed. *Essays on Aristotle's Ethics*. Berkeley: University of California Press, 1980.

Rose, Mike. *Possible Lives: The Promise of Public Education in America*. Boston: Houghton Mifflin, 1995.

Rosenbaum, James E. "Track Misperceptions and Frustrated College Plans: An Analysis of the Effects of Tracks and Track Perceptions in the National Longitudinal Survey," *Sociology of Education* 53, 1980: 74–88.

Ruddick, Sara. *Maternal Thinking: Towards a Politics of Peace*. Boston: Beacon Press, 1989.

Russell, Bertrand. *Why I Am Not a Christian, and Other Essays on Religion and Related Subjects*. New York: Simon & Schuster, 1957.

Ryan, Alan. *John Dewey and the High Tide of American Liberalism*. New York: W. W. Norton, 1995.

Rybczynski, Witold. *Home: A Short History of an Idea*. New York: Viking Press, 1986.

Sandel, Michael. *Liberalism and the Limits of Justice*. Cambridge: Cambridge University Press, 1982.

Sartre, Jean-Paul. *Being and Nothingness*, trans. Hazel E. Barnes. New York: Washington Square Press, 1956.

Nausea, trans. Lloyd Alexander. Norfolk, CT: New Directions, 1959/1938.

Schaler, Jeffrey A., ed. *Drugs: Should We Legalize, Decriminalize or Deregulate?* Amherst, NY: Prometheus Books, 1998.

Schlesinger, Arthur M., Jr. *The Disuniting of America: Reflections on a Multicultural Society*. New York: W. W. Norton, 1992.

Schopenhauer, Arthur. *The World as Will and Representation*, trans. E. F. J. Payne. New York: Dover Books, 1969.

Schorr, Lisbeth B. *Common Purpose: Strengthening Families and Neighborhoods to Rebuild America*. New York: Anchor Books, 1997.

Schubert, William H. *Curriculum: Perspective, Paradigm, and Possibility*. New York: Macmillan, 1986.

Schultz, Bud and Schultz, Ruth. *It Did Happen Here*. Berkeley: University of California Press, 1989.

Schumpeter, Joseph A. *Capitalism, Socialism and Democracy*. London: Routledge, 1996/1943.

Schweitzer, Albert. *Out of My Life and Thought*, trans. C. T. Campion. New York: Henry Holt, 1933.

Sebald, W. G. *Austerlitz*, trans. Anthea Bell. New York: Random House, 2001.

Selznick, Philip. *The Moral Commonwealth: Social Theory and the Promise of Community*. Berkeley: University of California Press, 1992.

Bibliography

Shapiro, Laura. *Perfection Salad*. New York: Modern Library, 2001.

Silberman, Charles E. *Crisis in the Classroom: The Remaking of American Education*. New York: Random House, 1970.

Simon, Katherine G. *Moral Questions in the Classroom*. New Haven, CT: Yale University Press, 2001.

Sinclaire, Carollyne. *Looking for Home*. Albany: State University of New York Press, 1994.

Singer, Peter. *Animal Liberation*. New York: New York Review of Books, 1990.

Sizer, Theodore. *Horace's Compromise: The Dilemma of the American High School*. Boston: Houghton Mifflin, 1984.

Skinner, B. F. *Beyond Freedom and Dignity*. New York: Vintage Books, 1972.

Smith, Robert Paul. *"Where Did You Go?" "Out." "What Did You Do?" "Nothing."* New York: W. W. Norton, 1957.

Smith, Ruth L. "Happiness and the Uneasy Conscience," in *In Pursuit of Happiness*, ed. Leroy S. Rouner. Notre Dame, IN: University of Notre Dame Press, 1995, pp. 136–146.

Spock, Benjamin. *Baby and Child Care*. New York: Pocket Books, 1946.

On Parenting. New York: Pocket Books, 2001.

Stegner, Wallace. *Angle of Repose*. New York: Penguin Books, 1971.

Stein, Sara. *Noah's Garden: Restoring the Ecology of Our Own Back Yards*. Boston: Houghton Mifflin, 1993.

Steinbeck, John. *The Winter of Our Discontent*. New York: Viking Press, 1961.

Styron, William. *Sophie's Choice*. New York: Vintage Books, 1992.

Tannahill, Reay. *Food in History*. New York: Stein and Day, 1973.

Taylor, Charles. *Sources of the Self*. Cambridge, MA: Harvard University Press, 1989.

Thomas, Lewis. *Late Night Thoughts on Listening to Mahler's Ninth Symphony*. New York: Viking Press, 1983.

Thompson, Patricia J. *Bringing Feminism Home*. Charlottetown, Canada: Home Economics Publishing Collective, 1992.

Thorkildsen, Theresa A. and Nicholls, John G. *Motivation and the Struggle to Learn*. Boston: Allyn & Bacon, 2002.

Thornton, Stephen J. "From Content to Subject Matter," *The Social Studies*, November/December 2001: 237–242.

Tillich, Paul. *The Courage to Be*. New Haven, CT: Yale University Press, 1952.

Tonnies, Ferdinand. *Gemeinschaft und Gesellschaft*, trans. C. P. Loomis. New York: HarperCollins, 1957/1887.

Trebilcot, Joyce and Whitbeck, Carolyn, eds. *Mothering: Essays in Feminist Theory*. Totowa, NJ: Rowman & Allanheld, 1984.

True, Michael. *An Energy Field More Intense Than War*. Syracuse, NY: Syracuse University Press, 1995.

Turner, James. *Without God, Without Creed*. Baltimore: Johns Hopkins University Press, 1985.

Varenne, Herve and McDermott, Ray. *Successful Failure*. Boulder, CO: Westview Press, 1999.

Ward, Geoffrey C. and Burns, Ken. *Not for Ourselves Alone: The Story of Elizabeth Cady Stanton and Susan B. Anthony*. New York: Alfred A. Knopf, 1999.

Wechsler, Harold S. "Eastern Standard Time: High School–College Collaboration and Admission to College, 1880–1930," in *A Faithful Mirror: Reflections on the College Board and Education in America*, ed. Michael C. Johanek. New York: College Board, 2001, pp. 43–79.

White, James Terry. *Character Lessons in American Biography*. New York: The Character Development League, 1909.

White, Katherine S. *Onward and Upward in the Garden*. New York: Farrar, Straus and Giroux, 1979.

Whitehead, Alfred North. *The Aims of Education*. New York: Free Press, 1967/1929.

Whitman, Walt. *Poetry and Prose*. New York: Library of America, 1982.

Wiesenthal, Simon. *The Sunflower*. New York: Schocken Books, 1976.

Wilde, Oscar. *The Picture of Dorian Gray and Other Writings*. New York: Bantam Books, 1982/1890.

Williams, Bernard. *Shame and Necessity*. Berkeley: University of California Press, 1993.

Williams, Niall. *As It Is in Heaven*. London: Picador, 1999.

Willis, Paul. *Learning to Labour*. Farnborough, England: Saxon House, 1977.

Wilson, A. N. *Against Religion*. London: Chatto & Winders, 1991.

Wilson, Edward O. *Biophilia*. Cambridge, MA: Harvard University Press, 1984.

Zeldin, Theodore. *An Intimate History of Humanity*. New York: HarperCollins, 1994.

Index

Index

Index

Rich, Adrienne, 139, 143, 144
Richards, Ellen, 113
Ricoeur, Paul, 48
Rose, 213
Rousseau, Jean Jacques, 82–83
routines, 108–109
Ruddick, Sara, 143, 145
Rybczynski, Witold, 107

Sartre, Jean Paul, 169
school reform, 244
science education, 125, 243; *see also* nature; natural history
Schubert, William, 269n1
Schumpeter, Joseph, 64
Schweitzer, Albert, 127
Sebald, W. G., 170
self-esteem, 182–183, 203
Selznick, Philip, 221, 229
Semmelweis, Ignaz, 140
Separate Peace, A (Knowles), 166–167
sex and adolescents, 149
shame, 46
Shapiro, Laura, 114
Silberman, Charles, 258
Singer, Peter, 134
Sizer, Theodore, 185
Smith, Robert Paul, 127
socialization, 225–229; reflection as curb on, 229; resistance to, 229
social studies, 253–255; and citizenship, 253; and map skills, 254; and process goals, 253
Socrates, and educational aims, 78–81, 224
solitude, 175–176
Sophie's Choice (Styron), 49
soul-making, 49–53
speciesism, 134
spectacle, 54–55
spirituality, everyday, 168–177; education for, 172

standards, 84, 87, 225–229; and testing, 244, 247, 248, 258
Stanton, Elizabeth Cady, 141
Stegner, Wallace, 97, 120
Stein, Sara, 131
Steinbeck, John, 72
Steppenwolf (Hesse), 101
Styron, William, 49
subjective well being (SWB), 14, 20–22, 34, 38, 233
suffering: animal, 51; glorification of, 41; justification of, 52; and meaning, 39–45; merited, 45–49
Sunflower, The (Wiesenthal), 164

Ten Commandments, 141, 189
theodicies, 50
Thomas, Lewis, 193
Thoreau, Henry, 64
Thornton, Stephen, 289n18
Tillich, Paul, 17, 53, 222
tolerance, 223–224
Tönnies, Ferdinand, 221
tracking, 86–87, 204

ultimate concern, 17
unhappiness, 53–56
utilitarianism, 18

Varieties of Religious Experience (James), 9
violence, 184
virtues, 19, 159–168, 230; ascetic, 19, 63, 161; *see also* honesty; courage; perseverance; loyalty
vocational education, 210, 212–215; literature for, 213
Voltaire, F. M. A., 173
volunteer work, 287n26
vouchers, 250–251

wants, 60–66; conflicts of, 69; and consumption, 62; and